Information Technology Infrastructure and Its Management

Information Technology Infrastructure and Its Management

Prof. Munesh Chandra Trivedi
Institute of Management Studies
Ghaziabad (NCR)

Dr. Ashish N. Jani
S.K. Patel Institute of Management and Computer Studies
Gandhi Nagar, (Gujarat)

Kamaljit I. Lakhtaria
Atmiya Institute of Technology and Science
Rajkot, Gujarat

Amit B. Kalyani
Shri B.S. Gardi College
Rajkot, Gujarat

Khanna Book Publishing Co. (P) Ltd.
Delhi

ISBN: 978-93-80016-31-3

First Edition 2010

Reprint : 2014

Published by:
Khanna Book Publishing Co. (P) Ltd.
1694-95, Nai Sarak, Delhi-110006 (India)
Phone: 011-23283211, 23256658
Mobile: +91-9312459590, 9810362434
Fax: 011-23256658
E-mail: contact@khannaedu.com
Website: www.khannaedu.com

Cover Design & Layout by
Limited Colors, Delhi-92

Printed in India

Dedicated to
Our Parents

Preface

Information Technology Infrastructure and Its Management is a subject that is an integral component of the ubiquitous soft computing paradigm. An in depth understanding and appreciations of the field requires some background knowledge of the Information Technology , Security, Electronic Commerce, IT Management, mathematics and computer programming. This is a difficult task. This book "Information Technology Infrastructure and Its Management" aims to achieve a balanced of these areas. Information Technology Infrastructure and Its Management is the discipline that attempts to provide methods to handle this complexity and enable us to produce reliable real time systems with maximum productivity.

This book is for students who have not had previous training in Information Technology Infrastructure and Its Management, and is suitable for a one-semester course. This book covers syllabus of all India universities. This is also useful for a project based introducing course in Information Technology Infrastructure and Its Management in which both the students and the instructor can follow the chapters in the order given both in the lectures as well as in the project.

Authors

Acknowledgement

At the various stages in the writing of this book, a number of people have given invaluable comments on the manuscript. In this regard, we owe a debt of gratitude to Dr. R.K. Bharadwaj, Director I.M.S. Ghaziabad, Dr. Sanjay M. Shah, Director S. V. Institute of Computer Studies Kadi (Gujarat) and Dr. K.V. Arya, ABV-Indian Institute of Information Technology & Management Gwalior.

We are also grateful to the Dr. S.S. Sarangedevot Director Department of Computer Science & I.T., J.R.N. Rajasthan Vidhyapeeth University, Udaipur for his encouragement at the very outset of this project. An excellent Support in writing this book was received from Dr. B.S. Agarwal, Vadu College of Computer Studies, Vadu (Gujrat).

Authors

Syllabus

ECS-304: INFORMATION TECHNOLOGY INFRASTRUCTURE & ITS MANAGEMENT

UNIT–I

Introduction: Information Technology, Computer Hardware, Computer Software, Network and Internet, Computing Resources,

It Infrastructure: Design Issues, Requirements, IT System Management Process, Service Management Process, Information System Design, IT Infrastructure Library

UNIT–II

Service Delivery Process: Service Delivery Process, Service Level Management, Financial Management, Service Management, Capacity Management, Availability Management

SERVICE SUPPORT PROCESS- Service Support Process, Configuration Management, Incident Management, Problem Management, Change Management, Release Management.

UNIT–III

Storage Management: Backup & Storage, Archive & Retrieve, Disaster Recovery, Space Management, Database & Application Protection, Bare Machine Recovery, Data Retention

UNIT–IV

Security Management: Security, Computer and internet Security, Network security, client\server security trends, Physical Security, Identity Management, Access Management. Intrusion Detection, Security Information Management

UNIT–V

It Ethics-e-busineess and Legal Issues for E-business: Introduction to Cyber Ethics, Intellectual Property, Privacy and Law, Computer Forensics, Ethics and Internet, Cyber Crimes

Emerging Trends in IT- Electronics Commerce, Electronic Data Interchange, Mobile Communication Development, Smart Card, Expert Systems

Contents

CHAPTER 1

Introduction to Information Technology

1.1 INTRODUCTION TO INFORMATION TECHNOLOGY

Information Technology has two components—Information and Technology. Let us begin with the definition of data and information.

Data: Data is the raw material with which we start.

Information: Information is the finished product, i.e. meaningful data.

1.1.1 Definition of Information

Many denitions of information are found in the literature. Four of these denitions are discussed below:

1. It is processed data, which is used to trigger certain actions or gain understanding of what the data implies
2. Intelligent news; that of which one is apprised or told- Oxford Dictionary
3. That which is known/communication of instructive knowledge
4. Information is data that have been put into a meaningful and useful context and communicated to a recipient who uses it to make decisions. Information involves the communication and reception of intelligence or knowledge. It apprises and notices, surprises and stimulates, reduces uncertainty, reveals additional alternatives or helps eliminate irrelevant or poor ones, and influences individuals and stimulates them to action.

Information is a basic resource essential for individuals and organizations in order to survive and succeed in society. Development is closely related to social change, and information has an important role in bringing about both.

1.1.2 The Quality of Information

Accuracy: Information is free from mistakes and errors (human/machine). It conveys an accurate picture to the recipient, which may require a presentation in graphical/tabular form. The information should be free from bias. No altering has been done at lower/higher levels.

Timeliness: Getting information to the recipient within the needed time frame is important attribute of information quality. Yesterdays newspaper today!

Relevancy: Does the information answer specially for the recipient what, why, where, when who and how. The relevancy of information varies from person to person.

Variability: Is the information variable? The recipient can verify various attributes of the information.

1.1.3 Definition of Information Technology

Information Technology means the collection, storage, processing, dissemination and use of Information. It is not conned to hardware and software but acknowledges the importance of man and the goals he sets for his technology, the values employed in making these choices, the assessment criteria used to decide whether he is controlling the technology and is being enriched by it. (source: Information Technology Serving Society - USA, 1979)

The scientific, technological and engineering disciplines and the management techniques used in information handling and processing; their applications; computers and their interaction with men and machines and associated social, economic and cultural matters.

1.2 IT INFRASTRUCTURE HIERARCHY

The successful application of information technology can be viewed as a hierarchy of component building blocks as illustrated in Figure 1.1. Most successful large application deployments consists of two independent components: the programs, servers and workstations forming the core information technology component that implements the intended system functions, and an enabling communications component that ties the various pieces of the application together. The information technology component consists of the hardware and software, coupled with an overriding requirement for appropriate education and relevant experience. It is really this "soft" component that ultimately

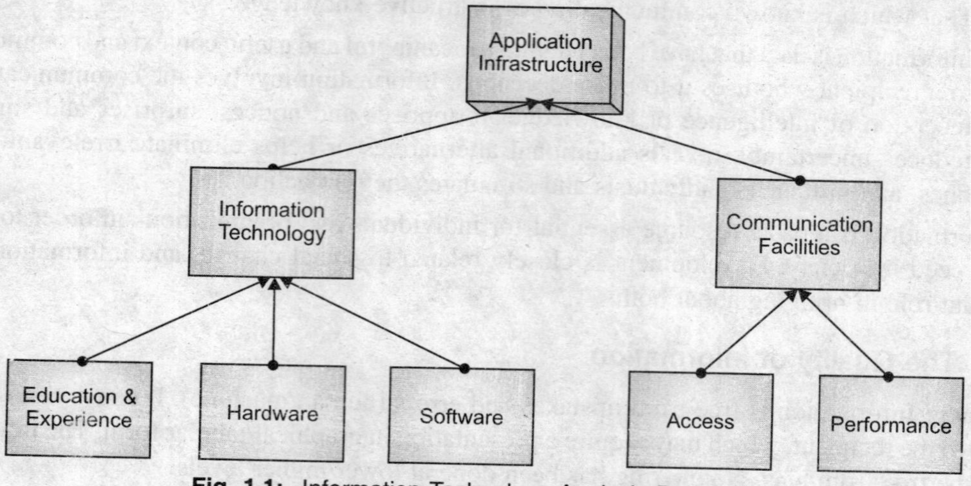

Fig. 1.1: Information Technology Analysis Breakdown

determines the degree of success of a particular application. In many cases, IT applications are introduced to modernize operations and administrative procedures. That is, they automate current procedures in accordance with existing polices without having to redesign the underlying concepts.

1.3 INFORMATION TECHNOLOGY IN INDIA

Recent years have seen a complete revolution in how information is gathered, archived and used in both business and government around the world. Throughout much of the world, the workplace has been transformed from one based on paper documents, fraught with errors and delays, to one based on information technology (IT). While IT can bring vast improvements in accuracy and timeliness, IT, by itself, does not change the basic problems of personnel competence or administrative inertia.

While information technology can be used to great advantage even in isolation, its real strength lies in the ability to interconnect different systems for the purpose of sharing and exchanging information. At the present time there are no ministries within the Government that exchange information online or in real time. To date, the impact of the information revolution on Maldives has been modest relative to its potential. However, with a small scattered population, an economy based to a great extent on fishing and tourism, and isolation from outside countries the potential benefits from greater IT use, as well as the challenges to it, are significant.

1. Super Computers

India wanted to import Cray X super computer for use in weather forecast, which US did not permit. India thus set out to produce a supercomputer. C-DAC has since then developed many models of PARAM, which is a cluster of Spark processors working in parallel to achieve top speed of 100 gigaops. It has been sold to four organizations in Germany, Russia and Canada.

2. Information Technology and Manufacturing

Two streams of applications of IT to manufacturing can be identified -

The Direct Application: The computers or a network of computers monitors and controls the hardware in a manufacturing plant such as machine tools, inspection machines, and robots and automated guided vehicles, which physically transform or transport or assemble components.

The Indirect Application: Computer Aided Design (CAD), production, planning and control, inventory control, marketing, sales and other Factory Management Systems (FMS) used for management of production. Business software such as Material Requirements Planning Manufacturing Resources Planning Optimized Production Technology Spreadsheets Word Processing Packages Database Management Packages are available for indirect applications.

3. Industrial Robots

The number of robots in an industry has become synonymous with high productivity. There is also a widespread use of robots in hazardous environment such as toxic, chemical industries, assembly of explosives, deep-sea, underground, high altitude and mountainous terrains, cold climates and nuclear reactors.

4. Satellite Communications and VSAT

Domestic satellite communication in India commenced in 1977 when we became a member of Intelsat (International Telecommunications Satellite Organization). Commercial services began in 1979 on capacity leased from Intelsat. With INSAT series of satellites launched, the service truly expanded.

INSAT-1D : 1990,
INSAT-2A : 1992,
INSAT-2B : 1993,
INSAT-2E : 1997,
INSAT- 3B : March 2000

VSAT (Very Small Aperture Terminal- earth stations with antennas less than two meters) came on Indian scene in 1988 when NICNET was established. The master earth center is at Delhi with a capacity of 650 VSATs covering all districts of India. RABMN (Remote Area Business Message network) is another VSAT network started in 1991, which has main station in Sikandrabad (U.P.). It has capacity of 1000 VSATs. These networks became commercially available through VSNL (Videsh Sanchar Nigam Ltd.), Dot (Department of Electronics) and MTNL (Mahanagar Telephone Nigam Ltd.)

ERNET (Educational and Research Network) in India was being used exclusively by educational institutions. Recently, it has been opened to people outside the education eld. Internet access in India is available through VSNL. The main node is at Bombay which is connected to US through satellite link and to Europe through a submarine cable. Delhi, Calcutta and Madras have remote Internet nodes which are connected to Bombay node via Dot inter city links.

1.4 NETWORKING

Definition

- The two or more computers are connected together by a medium and they are sharing resources. The shared resources can be files, printers, hard drives or CPU number crunching power.

OR

- Interconnected collection of autonomous (independent) computer peripheral devices is computer networking.

OR

- A computer network is a collection of computers and peripheral devices connected by communication links that allows the network components to work together.

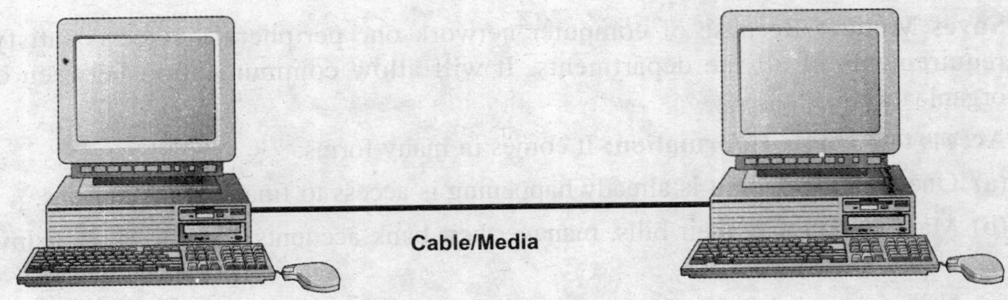

Fig. 1.2

A network can consist of two computers connected together on a desk or it can consist of many Local Area Networks (LANs) connected together to form a Wide Area Network (WAN) across a continent.

1.5 GOALS (USES) OF COMPUTER NETWORK

1. **Resource Sharing:** It allows department to shared hardware. Companies often want peripheral devices that are affordable only if they are shared by computer components. So, all programs, equipment and especially data available to anyone on the network without regard to the physical location of the resource and the user.
2. **High Reliability:** A second goal is high reliability having alternative sources of supply. For example, all files could be replicated on two or three machines so if one of them is unavailable the other copies could be used.
3. **Information Sharing:** It allows information to be shared.
4. **Saves money:** Small computers have a much better price and performance ration than large ones.
5. **Scalability:** The ability to increase the performance gradually as the workload grows just by adding more processors with centralized mainframes. When the system is full, it must be replaced by a larger one, usually at great expense and even greater disruption to the users with the client server model. New client and new servers can be added as needed.
6. **Communication Medium:** A Computer network can provide a powerful communication medium among widely separated employees. Using a network it is easy for two or more people who live far apart to write a report together. When one worker makes a change to an online document the others can see the change immediately instead of waiting several days for a letter.

1.6 ADVANTAGES OF COMPUTER NETWORK

There are lots many advantages given below:

1. **Resource Sharing:** It allows department to shared hardware. Companies often want peripheral devices that are affordable only if they are shared by computer components.

2. **Saves Money:** Because of computer network one peripheral device is satisfying the requirements of all the departments. It will allow communication between different organizations.
3. **Access to Remote Information:** It comes in many forms:
   (a) One area in which it is already happening is access to financial institutions.
   (b) Many people pay their bills, manage their bank accounts and handle their investment electronically.
   (c) Home shopping is also becoming popular with the ability to check the online catalogs of thousands of companies.
4. **Person-to-Person Communication:** Electronic mail (E-mail) is already widely used by millions of people and will soon routinely contain audio and video as well as text. This technology also makes it possible to have virtual meetings called videoconference.
5. **Interactive Entertainment:** Like hide and seek in a virtual dungeon, photographic quality moving images.
6. **Marketing and Sales:** It comes in different forms:
   (a) Computer networks are used extensively in both marketing and sales organizations.
   (b) Marketing professionals use them to collect, exchange and analyze data relating to customer needs and product development cycles.
   (c) Sales application include tele-shopping which uses order entry computers or telephones connected to an order processing network and online reservation services for hotels, airlines and so on.
7. **Financial Services:** Toady it comes in many forms:
   (a) Todays financial services are totally dependent on computer networks.
   (b) Application include credit history searches, foreign exchange and investment services and electronic funds transfer (EFT) like ATM (Automated Teller Machine) and APD (Automatic Paycheck Deposit) which allows a user to transfer money without going into a bank.
8. **Manufacturing:** It also comes in many forms:
   (a) Computer Networks are used today in many aspects of manufacturing including manufacturing process itself.
   (b) Two applications that use network to provide essential services are Computer Assisted Design (CAD) and Computer Assisted Manufacturing (CAM). Both of which allow multiple users to work on a project simultaneously.
9. **Information Services:** It includes bulletin boards and data banks. It allows information to be shared. A WWW (World Wide Web) site offering the technical specifications for a new product is an information service.
10. **Electronic Data Interchange:** It allows business information to be transferred without using paper.

1.7 DISADVANTAGES OF COMPUTER NETWORK

There are also many disadvantages given below:

(a) For a network to be useful sensitive data must be **protected** from **unauthorized access**.

(b) As the network is accessible from many points, it can be easily affected (susceptible) to **computer viruses**.

(c) The financial **cost** of local area networking is still high in comparison with many other alternate. If one plan to use a network to share a laser printer the user might find it cheaper to purchase another laser printer than to purchase todays networking hardware and software.

(d) Networking **software** requires **memory space** in each of the computers used on the networks. This reduces the memory spaces available for the users programs.

(e) Networking adds another level of **complexity** to the computer operation. User may have difficulty in learning the network communication.

(f) Some **control** on the part of the user is lost. You may have to share a printer with other users. One may face a situation like entire network suddenly locking up because one user has made a mistake.

(g) Many current application programs will not run in a **network environment**. The program may require too much memory or have other technical constraints.

1.8 DATA COMMUNICATION NETWORK CRITERIA

The major criteria that a Data Communication Network must meet are:

(I) Performance

(II) Consistency

(III) Reliability,

(IV) Recovery and

(V) Security

1.8.1 Performance

Performance is the defined as the rate of transferring error free data. It is measured by the Response Time and transit time. Response Time is the elapsed time between the end of an inquiry and the beginning of a response. Request a file transfer and start the file transfer. Transit time is the amount of time required for message to travel from one device to other device. Factors that affect Response Time are:

(a) *Number of Users:* More users on a network - slower the network will run

(b) *Transmission Speed:* speed that data will be transmitted measured in bits per second (bps)

(c) *Media Type:* Type of physical connection used to connect nodes together

(d) *Hardware Type:* Slow computers such as XT or fast such as Pentiums

(e) *Software Program:* How well is the network operating system (NOS) written

1.8.2 Consistency

Consistency is the predictability of response time and accuracy of data.

(a) Users prefer to have consistent response times; they develop a feel for normal operating conditions. For example: if the "normal" response time is 3 sec. for printing to a Network Printer and a response time of over 30 sec happens, we know that there is a problem in the system!

(b) Accuracy of Data determines if the network is reliable! If a system loses data, then the users will not have confidence in the information and will often not use the system.

1.8.3 Reliability

Reliability is the measure of how often a network is useable. MTBF (Mean Time between Failures) is a measure of the average time a component is expected to operate between failures nrmally provided by the manufacturer. A network failure can be: hardware, data carrying medium and Network Operating System

1.8.4 Recovery

Recovery is the Network's ability to return to a prescribed level of operation after a network failure. This level is where the amount of lost data is nonexistent or at a minimum. Recovery is based on having Back-up Files.

1.8.5 Security

Security is the protection of Hardware, Software and Data from unauthorized access. Restricted physical access to computers, password protection, limiting user privileges and data encryption are common security methods. Anti-Virus monitoring programs to defend against computer viruses are a security measure.

1.8.6 Applications

In the day-to-day life we are using the following general applications of a data communication network:

(i) Electronic Mail (e-mail or Email) replaces snail mail. E-mail is the forwarding of electronic files to an electronic post office for the recipient to pick up.

(ii) Scheduling Programs allow people across the network to schedule appointments directly by calling up their fellow worker's schedule and selecting a time!

(iii) Videotext is the capability of having a 2-way transmission of picture and sound. Games like Doom, Hearts, distance education lectures, etc...

(iv) Groupware is the latest network application; it allows user groups to share documents, schedules databases, etc... Ex. Lotus Notes.

(v) Teleconferencing allows people in different regions to "attend" meetings using telephone lines.

(vi) Telecommuting allows employees to perform office work at home by "Remote Access" to the network.

(vii) Automated Banking Machines allow banking transactions to be performed everywhere: at grocery stores, Drive-in machines etc...

(viii) Information Service Providers: provide connections to the Internet and other information services. Examples are CompuServe, Genie, Prodigy, America On-Line (AOL), etc...

(ix) Electronic Bulletin Boards (BBS - Bulletin Board Services) are dialup connections (use a modem and phone lines) that offer a range of services for a fee.

1.9 DIFFERENT TYPES OF NETWORKS:

Networks are classified depending on its size, its ownership, the distance it covers (the geographical area covered) by network and its physical architecture.

There are basically three types of categories:

(a) Local Area Network (LAN)

(b) Metropolitan Area Network (MAN)

(c) Wide Area Network (WAN)

1.9.1 Local Area Network (LAN)

- Local Area Networks (LAN) are privately owned networks within a single building or campus of up to a few kilometers in size.
- They are widely used to connect personal computers and workstations in company office and factories to share resource and exchange information.
- The resources to be shared can include hardware, software or data.
- Depending on the needs of an organization and the type of technology used, a LAN can be as simple as two computers and a printer in someone s home office or it can extend throughout a company and include voice, sound and video peripherals.
- A common example of a LAN, found in many business environment links a work group of task related computers, for example, engineering workstations or accounting computers.
- One of the computers may be given a large capacity disk drive and become a server to the other clients.
- Software can be stored on this central server and used as needed by the whole group.
- LANs are distinguished from other kind of networks by three characteristics:

  (i) Their size

(ii) Their transmission technology and

(iii) Their topology.

- Only one type of transmission medium is used by a given LAN.
- The most common LAN topologies are bus, ring and star.
- LANs had data rates in the 4 to 16 Mbps (Megabits per second) range. Today, speeds are increasing normally 10/100 to 1000 Mbps.
- Broadcast networks can be more divided into static and dynamic depending on how the channel is allocated.
- Dynamic allocation channel are centralized and decentralized.
- In the centralized channel allocation method there is a single entity for transmission.
- In the decentralized channel allocation method there is no central entity; each machine must decide for itself whether or not to transmit.

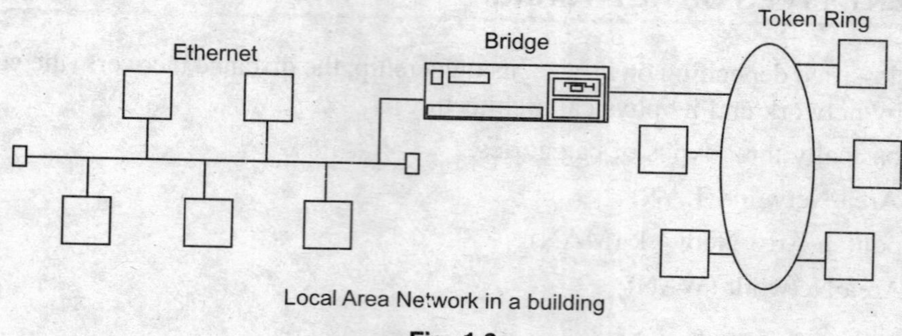

Fig. 1.3

Advantages of LAN

- Improves productivity due to faster work
- Provides easy maintenance
- New systems can be installed and configured easily

Disadvantages of LAN

- Limited number of systems can only be connected
- Cannot cover large area
- Network performance degrades as number of users exceeds

1.9.2 Metropolitan Area Network (MAN)

- A MAN is basically a bigger version of a LAN.
- It covers the area inside a town or a city and supports data and voice transmission.
- It is designed for customers who need a high speed connectivity like Internet, and have endpoints spread over a city or part of city.

- A good example of a MAN is the part of the telephone company network that can provide a high speed DSL line to the customer.
- It may be a single network such as a cable television network but today can also be used for high speed data connection to the internet or it may be a means of connecting a number of LANs into a larger network so that resource my be shared LAN to LAN as well as device to device.

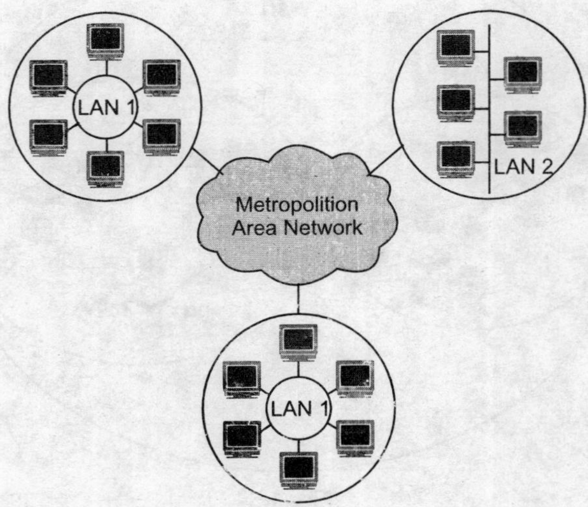

Fig. 1.4

- For example, a company can use a MAN to connect the LANs in all of its offices throughout a city.
- A MAN may be wholly owned and operated by a private company or it may be a service provided by a public company such as a local telephone company.
- Many telephone companies provide a popular MAN service called Switched Multi megabit Data Services (SMDS).

1.9.3 Wide Area Network (WAN)

- A WAN usually interconnects multiple LANs and MANs.
- A WAN spans a large geographical area often a country or continent or even the whole world.
- It provides long distance transmission of data, image, audio and video information.
- They transfer data at lower speed
- Connectivity and resources especially the transmission media are managed by third party carrier like telephone or Cable Company.
- Two types of WAN are (I) Enterprise WAN (II) Global WAN.

- Enterprise WAN connects widely separated computer resources of an organization. An enterprise WAN connect private and commercial network services but is dedicated to particular organization.
- Global WAN interconnects network of several organization.

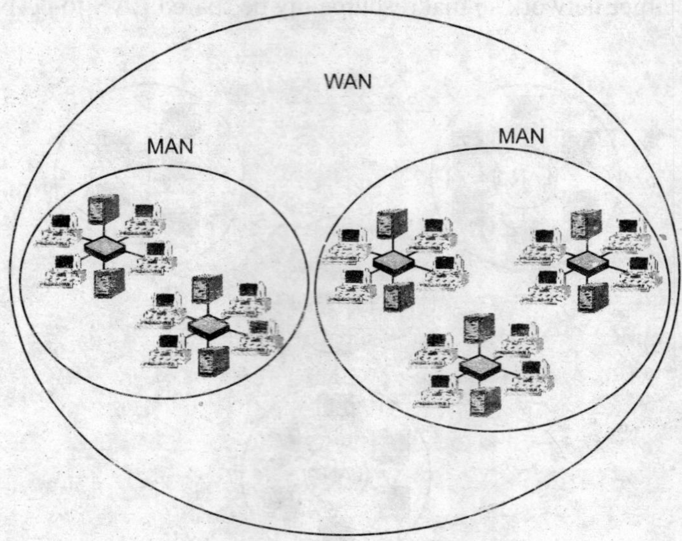

Fig. 1.5

1.10 NETWORK CATEGORIES (NETWORK MODEL)

Device can share the resources and software capabilities on a network. Services offered on a network include file, print, message, application, and database services. Each device on a network can request or provide a service.

Computer networks generally fall within one of these two network types:

1. Server-Centric Networks
2. Peer-to-Peer Networks

1.10.1 Server-Centric Networks

A server-based network consists of a group of user-oriented PCs, called *clients,* which request and receive network services from specialized computers called *servers*. Servers are generally higher-performance systems; optimized to provide network services to other PCs. (Some common server types include file servers, mail servers, print servers, fax servers, and application servers.)

On a server-centric network, one or more servers process the requests centrally. The server provides services for the other computers on a network, as it is a terminal with high processing power. The terminal that accesses the resources available on a server is known as a client.

Multiple client devices are connected to a single server. As the clients have relatively low or no processing capabilities of there own, so the clients do not play any role in processing the requests. They only send the request to the server for processing.

A server-centric network is a highly reliable network set-up for ensuring the security and reliability of data. As the data is stored and accessed from a central location so chances of unauthorized access are less because only the server needs to be monitored and managed. Whereas complete loss of data may occur, in case a failure occurs at the server end.

File server is a server that stores files on the network for users. A user at a client machine can save a file to a hard drive located on the file server. If the user wants to access the file later, can access the file from the client machine through a network connection to the file server. Maintaining a central location for file storage on the server makes it easier to provide a backup copy of important files and implement a fault-tolerance system. A server also manages access to network printing resources, thus enabling several client machines to use the same printer (See Figure)

An example of a client/server system is Microsoft Exchange Server. Your PC is responsible for constructing and displaying email messages, to name a couple of the possible tasks. The Exchange server is responsible for delivering outgoing email and for receiving email intended for you. In short, the client/server model is a network in which the role of the client is to issue requests and the role of the server is to service requests.

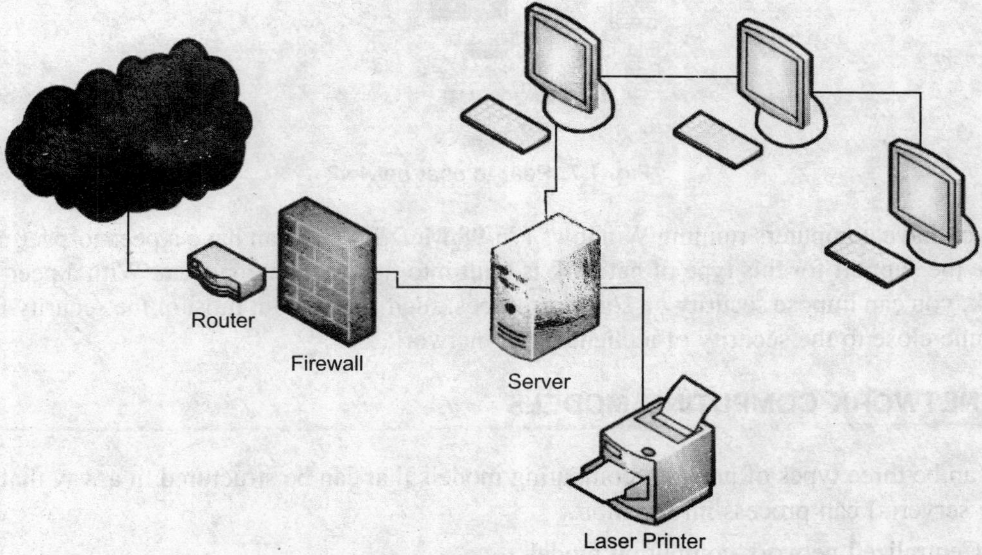

Fig. 1.6: Server centric network

1.10.2 Peer-to-Peer Network

A peer-to-peer network is a group of user oriented PCs that basically operate as equals. Each PC is called a Peer. The peers share resources, such as files and printers, but no specialized servers exist. Each peer is responsible for its own security, and, in a sense, each peer is both a client, because it requests services from the other peers, and a server, because it offers services to the other peers. Small networks usually group of 10 machines may work well in this configuration.

A peer-to-peer network sometimes is called a workgroup. Peer-to-peer networks are ideal for small organizations where security is not of concern. Peer-to-peer networks also provide a decentralized alternative for situations in which server administration would be too large or complex a task.

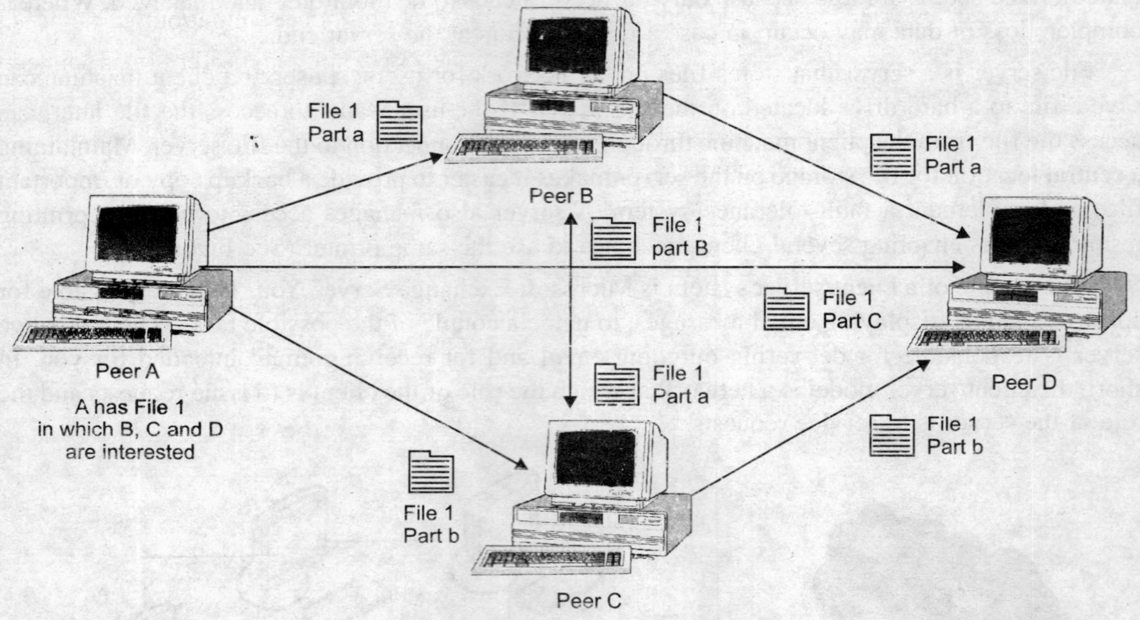

Fig. 1.7: Pear to pear network

If you have computers running Windows (95/98/Me/XP), you can have a peer-to-peer network because the support for this type of network is built into the operating system. With a peer-to-peer network, you can impose security on some resources, such as files, but most of the security features dont come close to the security of a client/server network.

1.11 NETWORK COMPUTING MODELS

There can be three types of network computing models that can be structured in a way that clients and the server(s) can process information.

1. Centralized network computing model
2. Distributed network computing model
3. Collaborative network computing model

1.11.1 Centralized Network Computing Model

In the centralized network-computing model, the clients computers utilize the resources of high capacity servers, to process the information. In this model the clients are also refereed to as dumb terminals with very low or no processing capability. The clients connect only to the server and not to each others.

In summary, the centralized computing model involves the following:

- All processing takes place in the central server computer.
- Terminals are connected to the central computer and function only as input/output devices.
- Networks may be employed to interconnect two or more server computers. Terminals connect only to the mainframe, never to each other.

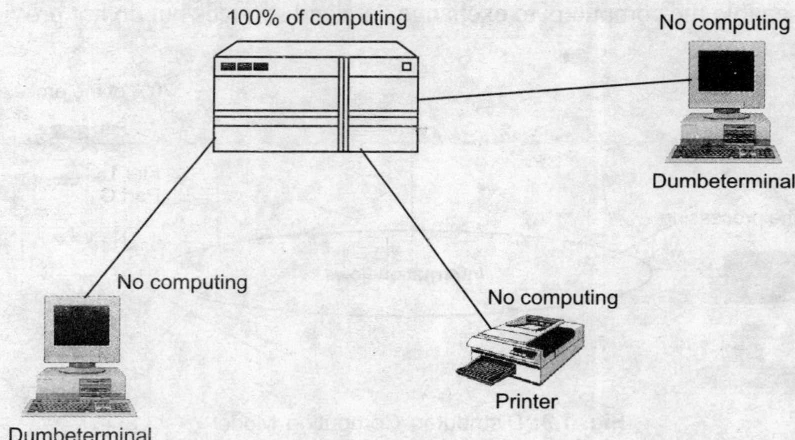

Fig. 1.8: Centralized computing model

Advantages

Centralized data management: Data is stored on the server in the case of a centralized network-computing model. This leads to an increase in the reliability of data as all data related modifications are stored centrally.

High Security: A network security can be monitored and implemented centrally from the server.

Cost effectiveness: The overall cost of setting up a centralized network is highly reduced as even through high-end investment is required for establishing a high capacity and secure server, but the clients require very low investment.

Limitation

Low Performance, Low Speed: In centralized network server performs all processes simultaneously. This may increase network traffic, which consequently reduces the speed and performance of network.

Central Server Failure: The server is the central place for storing and manipulating data for the entire client computers, thus failure of the server leads to the trouble in the functioning of the entire network.

1.11.2 Distributed Network Computing Model

The distributed computing model permits all network computers to take part in processing from their respective ends, separately. This does not help the other network computers in processing but it does allow sharing of data and services. In this model, a processing intensive task is distributed among multiple devices after being broken down into a subset of tasks.

In summary, distributed computing involves the following:

- Multiple computers are capable of operating alone.
- Tasks are completed locally on various computers.
- Networks enable the computers to exchange data and services but do not provide processing assistance.

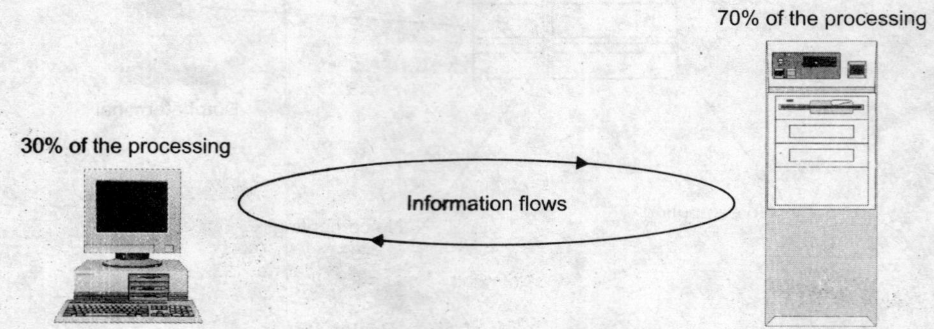

Fig. 1.9: Distributed Computing Model

Advantages

Faster Data Access: as the distributed network model allows a device to store the information locally, so data can be accessed faster as compared to the centralized network model.

High reliability: In this, the network does not entirely depend on a single device, so no single point failure exists.

Customized network setup: this model offers flexibility of different computers acting as a client and servers. As the roles of the server and the client are interchangeable, so it allows the optimized use of resources.

1.11.3 Collaborative Network Computing Model

The collaborative network-computing model is an advanced distributed computing model. Separately from sharing data, resources, and other services, devices also share processing capabilities in this model. Thus we can say that processes can run on two or more computers.

In a collaborative computing environment, one computer might make use of processing power by running a program on other computers on the network. Or, processes might be designed so that they can run on two or more computers.

In summary, collaborative computing involves the following:

- Multiple computers cooperate to perform a task
- A network that enables the computers to switch over data and services
- Software designed to take advantage of the collaborative environment.

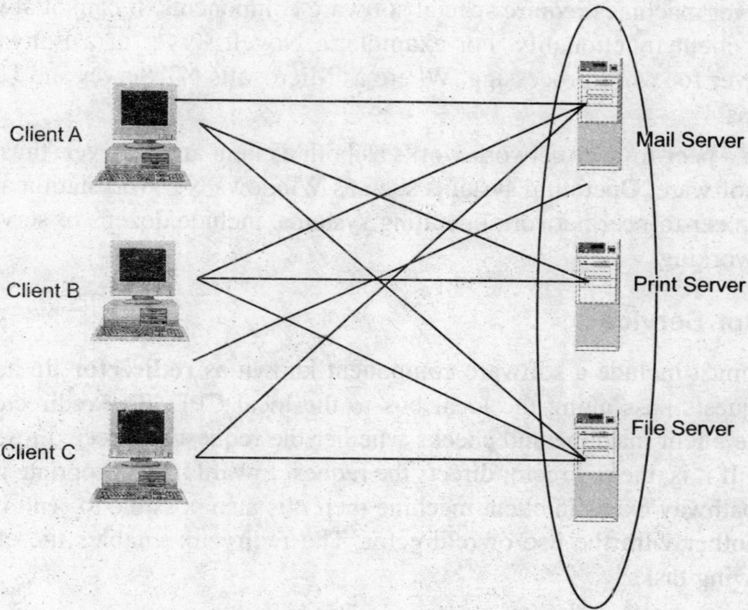

Fig. 1.10: Collaborative computing model

The main benefit of collaborative network is it share the task of processing the request, this leads to a reduction in the processing time and increase the overall network performance.

1.12 NETWORK SERVICES

When we connect computers, network services are the fundamental cause. Services are what a company wants to have performed or provided. Based on the services a company purchases a specific program and operating system and wants to utilize it.

1.12.1 Basic Connectivity Services

Computers in network must include special system software that enables them to function in a networking environment. The first network operating systems were add-on packages that supplied the networking software for existing operating systems such as MS-DOS or OS/2. But now a day networking components comes built in, such as Windows 95 and Windows NT, operating system.

An analogy might help you differentiate fully integrated systems from add-ons. A box can hold goods, but it is not specifically designed to go anywhere. You can place a set of logs on the ground to act as rollers for the box, thus providing a mechanism for transporting or moving the box. This is similar to how old network systems used to work. Newer operating systems are like trucks. A truck is designed from the ground up with a chassis that supports a box to move goods. The box and the mechanism for transportation (the chassis) are integrated from the beginning; they are designed to operate with each other.

Client and server machines require special software components. It cannot always possible for server to provide client functionality. For example, a Novell server or a Banyan server, a user cannot use the server for word-processing. Where as Microsofts NT Server and UNIX servers can run client programs.

A computer in a peer-to-peer network works as both a client and a server; thus, it requires both client and server software. Operating systems such as Windows NT Workstation and Windows 95, both of which are peer-to-peer network operating systems, include dozens of services and utilities that facilitate networking.

1.12.2 Redirector Service

A network client must include a software component known as **redirector**. In a usual individual computer, I/O requests pass along the local bus to the local CPU. The redirector intercepts I/O requests within the client machine and checks whether the request is directed toward a service on another computer. If it is, the redirector directs the request toward the appropriate network entity. If the transmission pathway exists in client machine then it is also possible to send information from one computer to other with the use of redirector. The redirector enables the client machine to perform the following tasks:

- Log on to a network
- Access shared resources
- Access and participate in distributed applications

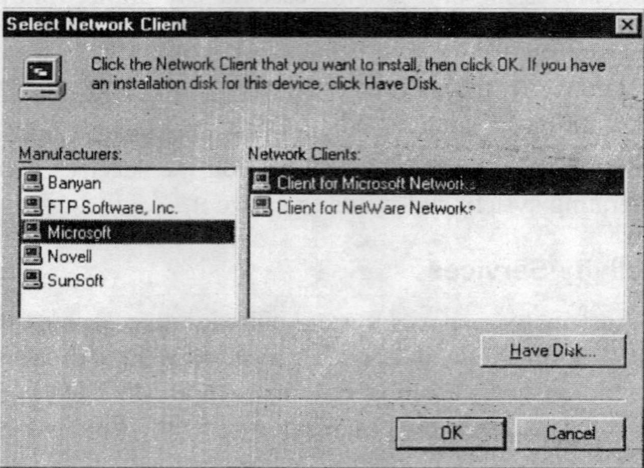

Fig. 1.11: The dialog box on a win95 machine that shows a redirector is being installed.

Redirector is also known as **requester** in some operating system. The workstation service acts as a redirector on Windows NT systems. In the field, people often refer to a redirector as a *client*. To connect a Windows 95 machine to a Windows NT machine, for example, it often is said, "Install the Microsoft Client for Microsoft Networks." If you want this Windows 95 machine to connect to a Novell server, you might say, "Install a Novell Client on the Windows 95 machine".

Server Service

A network server machine must have a component that accepts I/O requests from clients on the network and that fulfills those requests by routing the requested data back across the network to the client machine. In Windows NT, the server service performs the role of satisfying client requests.

1.12.3 File Services (Server)

- The most important point of networking of computers is the file services capability.
- It allows networked computers to share files with each other.
- It includes all network functions dealing with the storage, retrieval, or movement of data files.
- It facilitates users to read, write, and manage files and data.
- This includes moving files between computers and archiving files and data.
- It is an important part of client/server and peer-to-peer networks.
- Computers providing files services are referred to as file servers (see Figure).
- There are two types of server available: **Dedicated and non-dedicated.**
- **Dedicated servers** are originating (establishing) in client/server machine.

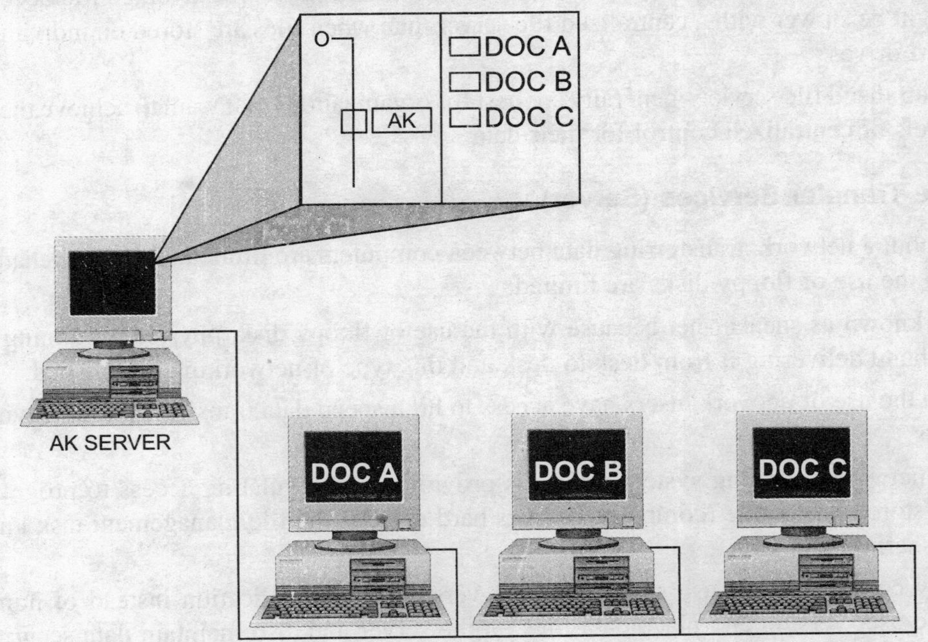

Fig. 1.12: A file server stores files for users on other network machines

- Its duty is to accomplish requests to network clients.
- **Non-dedicated servers** do double duty.
- They allow a user to go onto the machine acting as a file server and request the use of files from other machines; at the same time, they give files to users who request them from other computers on the network (see Figure).
- Non-dedicated file servers often are found in peer-to peer networks.
- An example of a non-dedicated server is a Windows 95 machine that accesses files from other computers on the network and that provides access to its hard drive for other computers.
- Dedicated file servers have the following benefits:
  - — Files are stored in a specific place where they can be reliably archived.
  - — Central file servers can be managed more efficiently because there is a single point of storage.
  - — Central file servers can contain expensive high-performance hardware that expedites file services and makes file servers more reliable.

The cost of specialized file server technology is shared by a large number of users. Centralized networks are more scalable. The following drawbacks, however, should be considered with regard to centralized file services:

(a) When all data is stored on a single server, a single point of failure exists. If the server fails, all data becomes unavailable.

(b) Because all clients contend for file services from a single source, average file-access times might be slower with a centralized file server than when files are stored on individual local hard drives.

(c) Centralized file services generally are best for organizations that want to achieve the highest levels of centralized control for their data.

1.12.4 File Transfer Services (Server)

- Without a network, transferring data between computers are limited and can exchange files with the use of floppy disks are limited.
- It is known as sneaker-net because with the use of floppy disk, physically running around and hand delivering it from desk to desk and this type of networking established.
- With the use of network, users have access to high speed data transfer without leaving their desks.
- The network operating system (NOS) is providing and regulating access to programs and data stored on the file (computer) servers hard drive is the file management task known as file sharing.
- Many companies can use single network version of an application instead of number of single user version and place data files on the server and also maintain data security, data control and backup.

- There are main three types of file storage are available.
  (a) Online storage (b) Offline storage
  (c) Nearline storage
- In the **online file storage**, data is stored on hard disks that are accessible on demand.
- In the **offline file storage**, removable media like tape or and optical disk are used to store data, after written data on the storage medium it can be removed from the server and can be shelved and can be used when needed.
- In the **Nearline file storage**, it is also known as jukebox (one kind of machine), it is used to manage large numbers of tapes or optical disks automatically. Without human intervention, when the data needed proper tape or disk is retrieved and mounted by the jukebox. It is the very useful storage because large amounts of data can be access within a short delay and at a much lower cost comparing to store data on hard drives.
- The other file transfer services are data migration, file archiving and file update synchronization.

1.12.5 Print Services (Server)

- Print service is the second most important incentive for installing a LAN after file services.
- Advantages of print server:
  (a) Many users can share the same printers
  (b) Printers can be located anywhere in the network.
  (c) Queue based network printing is more efficient than direct printing.

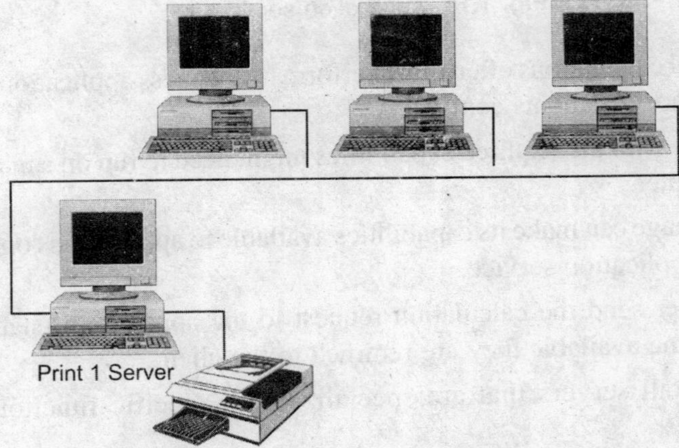

Fig. 1.13: Printer service

- Because files and printers are so basic and so important to most networks, file and print services are very basic components of most network operating systems, and a single machine commonly acts (or is able to act) as both a file server and a print server.

1.12.6 Application Services (Server)

- It is a server that actually runs an application or a part of an application for the client.
- This server permits applications to leverage (control) the computing power and specialized capabilities of other computers on a network.
- A file server simply holds data (in the form of a file) that then is retrieved and processed at the client; an application server performs all or part of the processing on the server end.
- An application server might search through a large database to provide a requested record for a client. Or, an application server might be part of a client/server application, in which both the client and the server perform some of the processing.

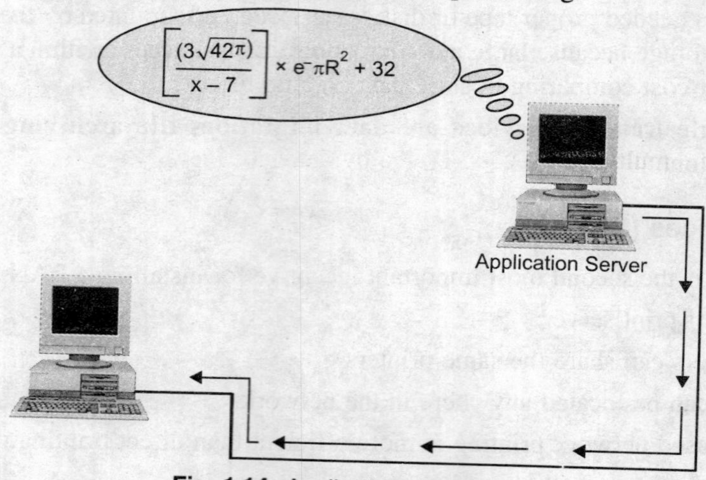

Fig. 1.14: Application service

- Complex statistical calculations often must perform by business applications, which is beyond the scope of the most of clients computers.
- Statistical software with the required capabilities might need to run on a mainframe computer or on a minicomputer.
- The statistical package can make its capabilities available to applications on clients computers by providing an application service.
- The client computer send the calculation request to the application (statistics) server and when results become available they are returned to the client.
- Organizations install servers that are specialized for specific functions are known an application services.
- Application server examples are database server, messaging/communication servers, groupware servers and directory servers.
- An application server makes a network more scalable.
- If new application needs more services then additional application servers can be added

means if more power is necessary for an application, only the application server needs to be upgraded.

1.12.7 Database Services

- Database servers are the most familiar type of application servers.
- Because database services facilitate applications to be designed in separate client and server components, such applications known as client/server databases.
- Using a client/server database, the client and server applications are designed in such a way that they can take advantage of the special capabilities of client and database are as below:
  (a) The client application manages data input from the user like screen displays, reporting of output and data retrieval request send to the database server.
  (b) The database server manages the data handling: adds, delete and modifies records in the database, queries the database, generates the results and send output to the client. At the same time multiple requests service by database server.

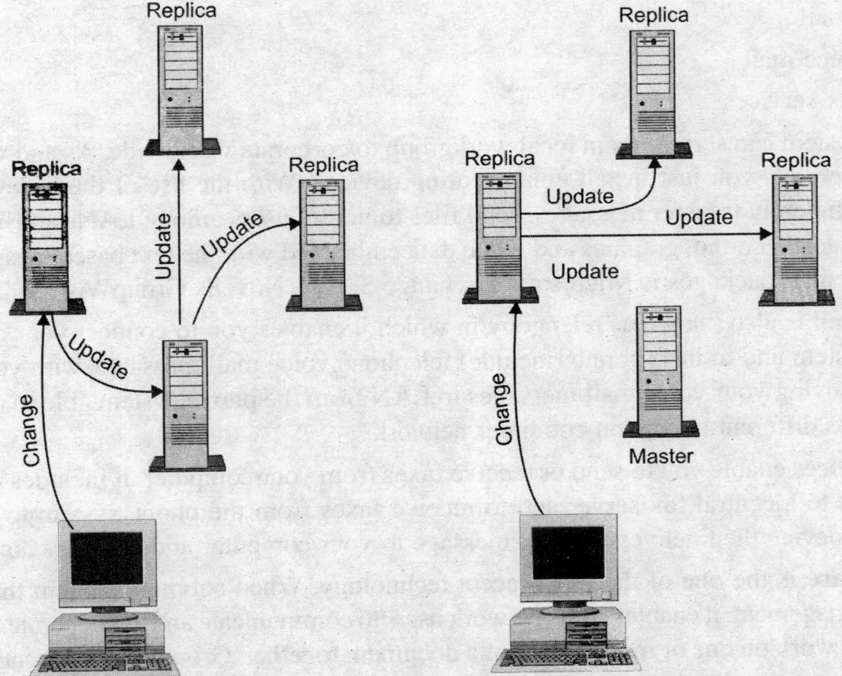

Fig. 1.15: Master driven and locally driven database replications

- A modern database server can perform the following functions:
  (a) It provides database security.
  (b) It optimize the performance of database operations

(c) It distributes data among multiple database servers.

(d) Service large numbers of clients by reducing the time

- Microsoft SQL Server and Oracle are two examples of applications that run at the server but are able to perform tasks request by clients.
- These applications were designed in such a way that both require a server as a backend component and a client as a front-end component.
- There are two strategies for replicating databases are following:
- **Master-driven updates:** A single master server receives all updates and updates all replicas.
- **Locally driven updates:** Any local server can receive an update and is responsible for distributing the change to other replicas.

1.12.8 Communication Services

- A messaging /communication service transfers information from one place to another.
- It broken down into three categories:

1. Email
2. Voice mail
3. Fax services

Email system can service from local workgroup to corporate worldwide. As and when we need to you this service, you just install email routing devices. With the use of these devices you can easily and efficiently transfer messages, send files to no. Of users among LANs and WANs. It also supports to transfer sound, graphics and video data embedded with the text based messages (email). Example of email packages is Microsofts Exchange Server, Novells GroupWise and Lotus Notes.

Voice Mail is also known as telephony in which it enables you to connect your computer to a telephone system and to incorporate (include) telephone voice mail messages with your computer. It involves moving your voice mail messages to LAN from the phone system able to distribute this information to different clients on computer network.

Fax Services enable you to send or receive faxes from your computer. It includes the capability to send faxes to a central fax server and to receive faxes from the phone system to a central fax device. That device then delivers the fax message to your computer and it occurs automatically.

Groupware is the one of the most recent technology. When solving problem through shared document management, it enables some network users to communicate and to cooperate. Its capability is many users work on one or more copies of a document together. Groupware applications example is interactive conferencing, screen sharing and bulletin boards. Microsofts Exchange Server, Novells GroupWise and Lotus Notes are example of applications with groupware features.

1.12.9 Directory Services

- It is also known as x.500 standard.
- It provides location information for different entities on the network.

- Their main function is to act as an information booth, directing resource requests on the network to the location of the resource.
- When client is requested to use a printer or file servers or to find a server or even a specific application, the directory service tells the client where the resource is on the network and available or not.
- Novell NetWare 4.11, Banyan VINES, Microsoft Exchange Server and Windows NT 5.0 are the example of computer system that uses directory services.

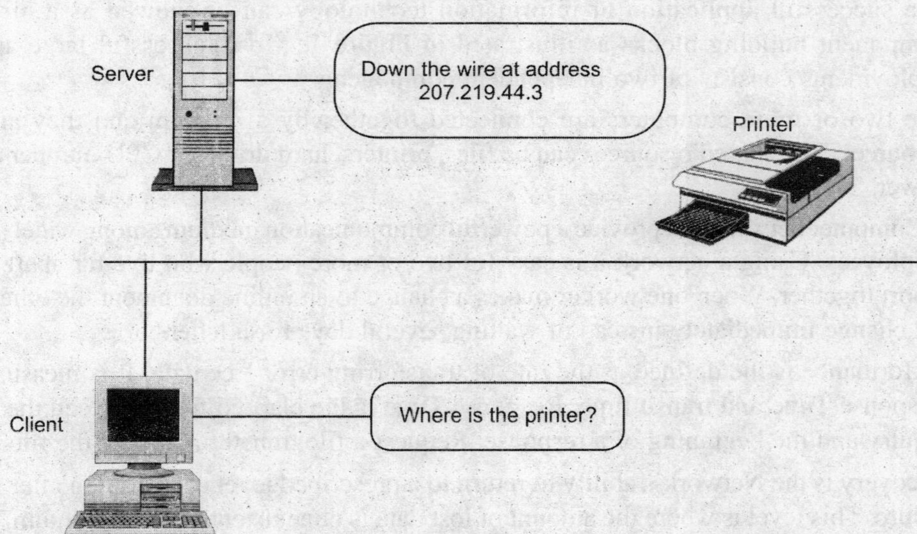

Fig. 1.16: Directory Service

1.12.10 Security Services

- It is the most important service on a network.
- When users share resource and data on a network, they should be able to control who can access the data or resource and what the user can do with it.
- For example, a file showing the financial records of a company. If this file is on a file server, it is important to be able to control that has access to the file. Also who is able to read and change the file?
- One other example is shared printer in which who can use the expensive color laser printer or when a person can use this printer.
- This service is deal with a user account database or something like the directory services.
- This database of users often contains a list of names and passwords. So when a user wants to access the network, s/he must log on to the network.
- Example of security services is Win-NT server.

1.13 SUMMARY

- Information is a basic resource essential for individuals and organizations in order to survive and succeed in society. Development is closely related to social change, and information has an important role in bringing about both.
- Information Technology means the collection, storage, processing, dissemination and use of Information.
- The successful application of information technology can be viewed as a hierarchy of component building blocks as illustrated in Figure 1. Most successful large application deployments consists of two independent components:
- The two or more computers are connected together by a medium and they are sharing resources. The shared resources can be files, printers, hard drives or CPU number crunching power.
- A Computer network can provide a powerful communication medium among widely separated employees. Using a network it is easy for two or more people who live far apart to write a report together. When one worker makes a change to an online document the others can see the change immediately instead of waiting several days for a letter.
- Performance is the defined as the rate of transferring error free data. It is measured by the Response Time and transit time. Response Time is the elapsed time between the end of an inquiry and the beginning of a response. Request a file transfer and start the file transfer.
- Recovery is the Network's ability to return to a prescribed level of operation after a network failure. This level is where the amount of lost data is nonexistent or at a minimum. Recovery is based on having Back-up Files.
- A server-based network consists of a group of user-oriented PCs, called *clients,* which request and receive network services from specialized computers called *servers*. Servers are generally higher-performance systems.
- A peer-to-peer network is a group of user oriented PCs that basically operate as equals. Each PC is called a Peer. The peers share resources, such as files and printers, but no specialized servers exist.
- The collaborative network-computing model is an advanced distributed computing model. Separately from sharing data, resources, and other services, devices also share processing capabilities in this model.

1.14 REVIEW QUESTIONS

1. Discuss the network model and differentiate server centric network with peer to peer network.
2. Explain the different network computing model.
3. Discuss the various types of network services.
4. Explain the IT infrastructure hierarchy.

CHAPTER 2

Internet

2.1 INTRODUCTION

- By the turn of the century, information, including access to the Internet, will be the basis for personal, economic, and political advancement.
- Internet name is comes from Interconnected Network.
- The popular name for the Internet is the **Information Superhighway**.
- Whether you want to find the latest financial news, browse through library catalogs, exchange information with colleagues, or join in a lively political debate, the Internet is the tool that will take you beyond telephones, faxes, and isolated computers to a burgeoning networked information frontier.
- The Internet supplements the traditional tools you use to gather information, Data Graphics, News and correspond with other people. Used skillfully, the Internet shrinks the world and brings information, expertise, and knowledge on nearly every subject imaginable straight to your computer.

2.2 WHAT IS THE INTERNET?

- The Internet links are computer networks all over the world so that users can share resources and communicate with each other.
- Some computers, have direct access to all the facilities on the Internet such as the universities and other computers, e.g. privately-owned ones, have indirect links through a commercial service provider, who offers some or all of the Internet facilities.
- In order to be connected to Internet, you must go through service suppliers. Many options are offered with monthly rates. Depending on the option chosen, access time may vary.
- The Internet is what we call a **Metanetwork**, that is, a network of networks that spans the

globe. It's impossible to give an exact count of the number of networks or users that comprise the Internet, but it is easily in the thousands and millions respectively.

- The Internet employs a set of standardized protocols which allow for the sharing of resources among different kinds of computers that communicate with each other on the network. These standards, sometimes referred to as the Internet Protocol Suite, are the rules that developers adhere to when creating new functions for the Internet.
- The Internet is also what we call a distributed system; there is no central archives. Technically, no one runs the Internet. Rather, the Internet is made up of thousands of smaller networks. The Internet thrives and develops as its many users find new ways to create, display and retrieve the information that constitutes the Internet.

2.3 HISTORY AND DEVELOPMENT OF THE INTERNET

- In its infancy, the Internet was originally conceived by the **Department of Defense** as a way to protect government communications systems in the event of a military strike.
- The original network, dubbed **ARPANet** (for the Advanced Research Projects Agency that developed it) evolved into a communications channel among contractors, military personnel, and university researchers who were contributing to ARPA projects.
- The network employed a set of standard protocols to create an effective way for these people to ***communicate and share data with each other***.
- ARPAnet's popularity continued to spread among researchers, and in the 1980's the National Science Foundation, whose NSFNet, linked several high speed computers, took charge of the what had come to be known as the Internet.
- By the late 1980's, thousands of cooperating networks were participating in the Internet. In 1991, the U.S. High Performance Computing Act established the NREN (National Research and Education Network). NREN's goal was to develop and maintain high-speed networks for research and education, and to investigate commercial uses for the Internet. The rest, as they say, is history in the making.
- The Internet has been improved through the developments of such services as Gopher and the World Wide Web.
- Even though the Internet is predominantly thought of as a research oriented network, it continues to grow as an informational, creative, and commercial resource every day and all over the world.

2.4 WHO PAYS FOR THE INTERNET?

- There is no clear answer to this question because the Internet is not one "thing", it's many things. No one central agency exists that charges individual Internet users.
- Rather, individuals and institutions who use the Internet pay a local or regional Internet service provider for their share of services. And in turn, those smaller Internet service providers might purchase services from an even larger network.

- So basically, everyone who uses the Internet in some way pays for part of it.

2.5 WHAT MAKES THE INTERNET WORK?

- The unique thing about the Internet is that it allows many different computers to connect and talk to each other. This is possible because of a **set of standards**, **known as Protocols**, that govern the transmission of data over the network:
- TCP/IP (Transmission Control Protocol/Internet Protocol)

2.6 THE CLIENT/SERVER MODEL

- The most popular Internet tools operate as client/server systems. You're running a program called a **Web client**.
- This piece of software displays documents for you and carries out your requests. If it becomes necessary to connect to another type of service—say, to set up a Telnet session, or to download a file—your Web client will take care of this, too. Your Web client **connects** (or "talks") to a Web server to ask for information on your behalf.

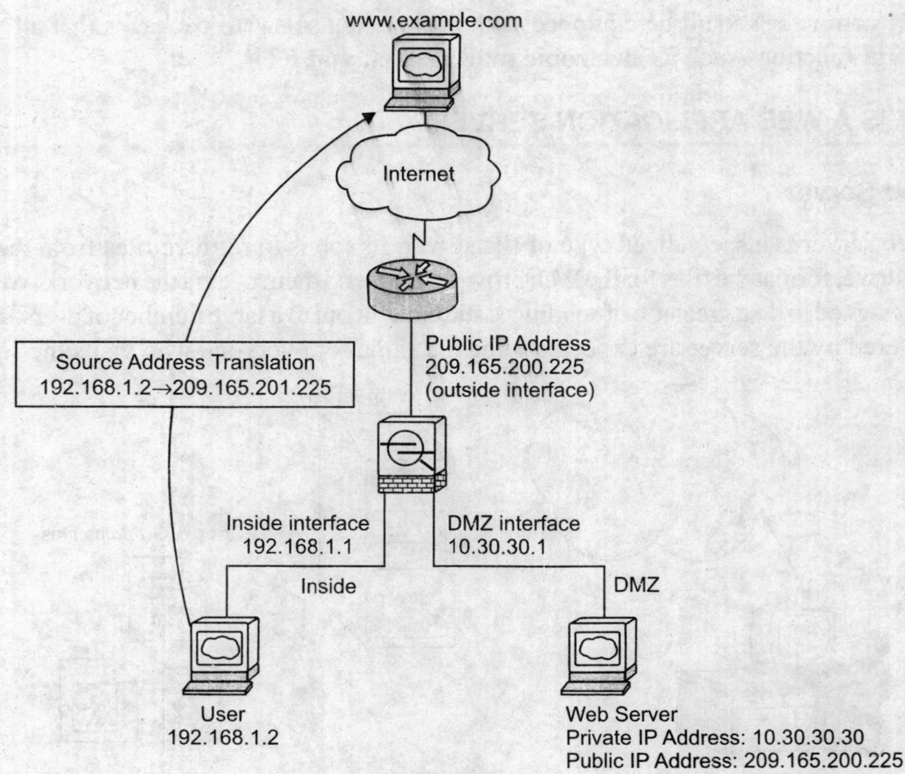

Fig. 2.1

- The **Web server** is a computer running another type of Web software which provides data, or "serves up" an information resource to your Web client.
- All of the basic Internet tools—including Telnet, FTP, Gopher, and the World Wide Web—are based upon the cooperation of a client and one or more servers.
- In each case, you interact with the client program and it manages the details of how data is presented to you or the way in which you can look for resources.
- In turn, the client interacts with one or more servers where the information resides.
- The server receives a request, processes it, and sends a result, without having to know the details of your computer system, because the client software on your computer system is handling those details.
- The advantage of the client/server model lies in distributing the work so that each tool can focus or specialize on particular tasks—the server serves information to many users while the client software for each user handles the individual user's interface and other details of the requests and results.

2.7 THE USE OF LOCAL CLIENTS

- Every computer should be equipped with basic client software packages that allow you to perform functions such as **electronic mail, Telnet, and FTP**.

2.8 WHAT IS A WEB APPLICATION SERVER?

2.8.1 Web Server

- A web server is a specialized type of file server. Its job is to retrieve files from the server's hard drive, format the files for the Web browser, and send them out via the network. Web servers are designed to do a great job of sending static content out to a large number of users. The pages delivered by the server are expected to be the same for everyone who visits the server.

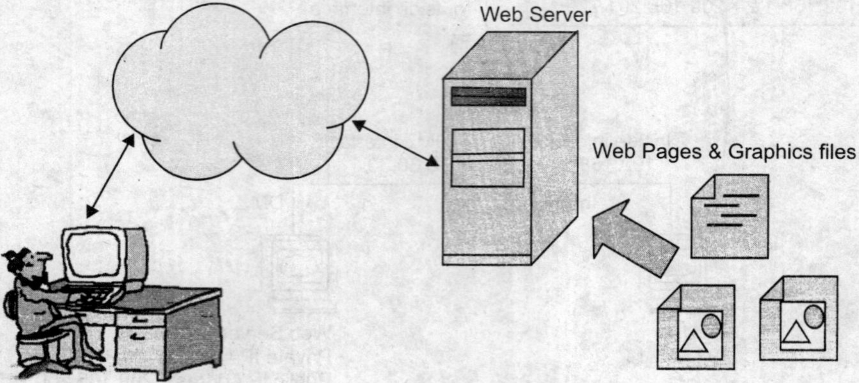

Fig. 2.2

- The function of a typical Web server is shown below. The user requests a web page. The Web Server finds the web page file in a local directory and sends it back out to the user. When graphic files are requested, the same thing happens. The Web Server finds the requested graphic files and sends them back to the user.
- The Web Server standards were originally designed to publish static documents on the Internet. There was a limited capability for accessing dynamic content, but this was never intended to support high volume, highly interactive Web applications.
- Then, as the Internet and Web browsers became popular in the mid-1990's, organizations saw an opportunity to provide web pages that contained dynamic content like stock prices, weather information, inventory levels, and shipping status for a package. Web browsers became such a pervasive way to access information that users and organizations desired to access a wide variety of information and applications through their Web browser. So, Web servers had to be extended to allow software application development and access to databases.

2.8.2 Web Application Server

- Web application servers are designed specifically to extend web servers to support dynamic content. The application server software "hooks in" to the web server software and automatically intercepts any user requests for dynamic content. The web server still sends out static web pages and graphic files—Just like before. But now, the application server can create dynamic content by mixing data with templates, running programs, or by accessing databases.

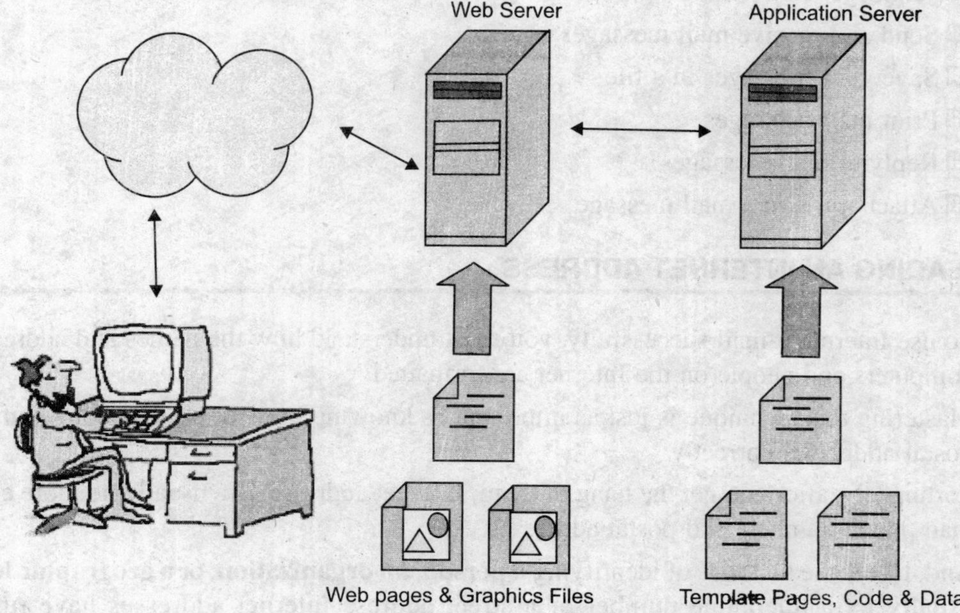

Fig. 2.3

2.9 ELECTRONIC MAIL ON THE INTERNET

- Electronic mail, or e-mail, is probably the most popular and widely used Internet function.
- E-mail, email, or just mail, is a fast and efficient way to communicate with friends or colleagues.
- You can communicate with **one person at a time or thousands**; you can receive and send **files and other information**.
- You can even subscribe to electronic **journals and newsletters**.
- You can send an e-mail message to a person in the same building or on the other side of the world.

2.9.1 How does E-mail Work?

- E-mail is an asynchronous form of communication, meaning that the person whom you want to read your message doesn't have to be available at the precise moment you send your message. This is a great convenience for both you and the recipient.
- On the other hand, the telephone, which is a synchronous communication medium, requires that both you and your listener be on the line at the same time in order for you to communicate (unless you leave a voice message).
- It will be impossible to discuss all the details of the many e-mail packages available to Internet users.
- Fortunately, however, most of these programs share basic functionality which allow you to:
  - Send and receive mail messages
  - Save your messages in a file
  - Print mail messages
  - Reply to mail messages
  - Attach a file to a mail message

2.10 READING AN INTERNET ADDRESS

- To use Internet e-mail successfully, you must understand how the names and addresses for computers **and** people on the Internet are formatted.
- Mastering this technique is just as important as knowing how to use telephone numbers or postal addresses correctly.
- Fortunately, after you get the hang of them, Internet addresses are usually no more complex than phone numbers and postal addresses.
- And, like those methods of identifying **a person, an organization**, or a **geographic location** usually by a telephone number or a street address Internet addresses have rules and conventions for use.

Sample Internet Address: principal@vsc.edu.in

The Internet address has three parts:

1. a user name [principal in the example above]
2. an "at" sign (@)
3. the address of the user's mail server [vsc.edu.in edu in the example above]

- Sometimes it's useful to read an Internet address (like custcare@aucegypt.edu) or a domain name from right to left because it helps you determine information about the source of the address.
- An address like 201B6DQF@asu.edu doesn't tell me much about the person who's sending me a message, but I can deduce that the sender is affiliated with an educational institution because of the suffix edu.
- The right-most segment of domain names usually adhere to the naming conventions listed below:

EDU	Educational sites
COM	Commercial sites
GOV	Government sites
NET	Network administrative organizations
MIL	Military sites
ORG	Non-profit organizations

2.11 INTRODUCTION TO THE WORLD WIDE WEB

- The World Wide Web (also referred to as WWW or **W3**) is the fastest growing area of the Internet. World Wide Web has raised excitement about the Internet to new heights. What makes the World Wide Web appealing and innovative is its use of hypertext as a way of linking documents to each other.
- A highlighted word or phrase in one document acts as a pointer to another document that amplifies or relates to the first document. When looking at a WWW document, the reader doesn't have to follow every pointer, or link (also called a hypertext link), only those that look interesting or useful. In this way, the user tailors the experience to suit his or her needs or interests.
- The other very appealing aspect of the World Wide Web is the use of graphics and sound capabilities. Documents on the WWW include text, but they may also include still images, video, and audio for a very exciting presentation. People who create WWW documents often include a photograph of themselves along with detailed professional information and personal interests. (This is often called a person's home page.)

2.11.1 What makes the WWW work?

- WWW is another example of client/server computing. Each time a link is followed, the client is requesting a document (or graphic or sound file) from a server (also called a Web server) that's part of the World Wide Web that "serves" up the document.
- The server uses a protocol called **HTTP** or **HyperText Transport Protocol**. The standard for creating hypertext documents for the WWW is **HyperText Markup Language** or **HTML**. HTML essentially codes plain text documents so they can be viewed on the Web.

2.11.2 Uniform Resource Locators or URLs

- A Uniform Resource Locator, or URL is the address of a document you'll find on the WWW. Your WWW browser interprets the information in the URL in order to connect to the proper Internet server and to retrieve your desired document.
- Each time you click on a hyperlink in a WWW document, you're actually instructing your browser to find the URL that's embedded within the hyperlink.
- The elements in a URL:Protocol://server's address/filename

  Hypertext protocol: http://www.aucegypt.edu

  File Transfer Protocol: ftp://ftp.dartmouth.edu

  Telnet Protocol: telnet://pac.carl.org

2.11.3 WWW Clients or "Browsers"

- The program you use to access the WWW is known as a browser because it "browses" the WWW and requests these hypertext documents.
- Browsers can be graphical, like **Internet Explorer, Mozilla Firefox, Netscape** and **Orra**, allowing you to see and hear the graphics and audio; text-only browsers (i.e., those with no sound or graphics capability) are also available.
- All of these programs understand http and other Internet protocols such as FTP, gopher, mail, and news, making the WWW a kind of "one stop shopping" for Internet users.

2.11.4 Chatting

- Internet Relay Chat (IRC), the other method for Internet conversation, is less common than talk because someone must set up the Chat before others can join in.
- Chat sessions allow many users to join in the same free-form conversation, usually centered around a discussion topic.
- When users see a topic that interests them, they type a command to join and then type another command to choose a nickname. Nicknames allow people in the session to find you on IRC Networks or Channels.
- Chat Applications are as follows :

  - Yahoo Chat

- Rediff Bol
- Google Talk
- Mebo

2.11.5 A look at search engines

- The World Wide Web is "indexed" through the use of search engines,
- These search engines comb through the Web documents, identifying text that is the basis for keyword searching. Each search engine works in a different way. Some engines scan for information in the title or header of the document; others look at the bold "headings" on the page for their information.
- The fact that search engines gather information differently means that each will probably yield different results. Therefore, it's wise to try more than one search engine when doing Web searching.
- The list below lists several search engines and how each one gathers information, plus resources that evaluate the search engines.
- Most of users are made search on search engine for their requirements, but day by day search engine provide specialized search facility like
- **Web search :** For searching web pages
- **Image search :** For searching image
- **Book search :** For Book Searching
- **Blog search :** For searching Blogs online

Selected Search Engines

- **www.Google.com**
- **www.Yahoo.com**
- **www.Altavista.com**
- **www.MSN.com**
- **www.Ask.com**

2.12 BOOKMARKING WEB SITES

What is a bookmark?

- A bookmark is a way of saving your favorite Web pages so that you can find them again later.
- When book marking your favorite Web pages you will also be able to put them into categories that will make finding them among all your other bookmarks really easy.
- They are called **Bookmarks in Netscape** & they are called **Favorites in Internet Explorer**. Even though they have different names, they are the same thing.

The Best Way To Find Your Favorite Things

- Maybe you've been surfing the Web looking at all the great personal Web sites out there when you come across one you really feel you like and you want to visit again. The problem is that you don't remember how you got there. Bookmark it!

Adding A Bookmark In Netscape 6

1. Click on "**Bookmarks**" at the top of your browser.
2. Click on "**Add Current Page**".

Managing Bookmarks in Netscape 6

1. Click on "**Bookmarks**" at the top of your browser.
2. Click on "**Manage Bookmarks...**".
3. Click on bookmark you want to move and drag it to the folder you want to add it to.
4. To add a new folder click on "File", then click on "New", then click on "New Folder".

Adding To Favorites in Internet Explorer 6.0

1. Click on "**Favorites**".
2. Click on "**Add to Favorites...**".
3. When box pops up click on the folder that you want to add the bookmark to and then click "OK", or just click on "OK" without clicking on a folder to add to your general favorites category.

Organizing Favorites in Internet Explorer 6.0

1. Click on "**Favorites**".
2. Click on "**Organize Favorites.**".
3. When box pops up click on the bookmark you want to move and drag it to the folder you want to add it to.
4. Create a new folder by clicking on "Create Folder".
5. Rename folders by clicking on the folder you want to rename and clicking on "Rename Folder".

2.13 SAVING WEB PAGES

- With Internet Web browser like Internet Explorer User can save an exact copy of a web page on to your local hard disk.
- User not only preserves all elements of the web page - images, links, frames, Java, style sheets, etc. - but the way, you can archive important web based content, even online transaction receipts with a minimum of hassle.

Four easy ways to save

1. Press the **Save** button located in the toolbar
2. Click on the link **Save Web Page** located in the Secure IE Toolbox
3. Use the keyboard shortcut **CTRL+S**
4. Or select **File-Save**
   - A User can save not only web page But Copy Content with Copy command
   - As well User can individually Copy or Save Image, Graphics as well as Photos from webpage.

Download

- To download is to receive data from a remote or central system, such as a webserver, FTP server, mail server, or other similar systems.
- A download is any file that is offered for downloading or that has been downloaded. The word's primary usage comes in the form of a verb.
- That is, "download" is used to mean "receive and save" instead of simply "receive".

Upload

- The opposite operation, to upload, is to send data from a local system to a remote system, FTP server, or website.
- For example, "Uploading a Photo to Orkut" means sending a Photo to the website.

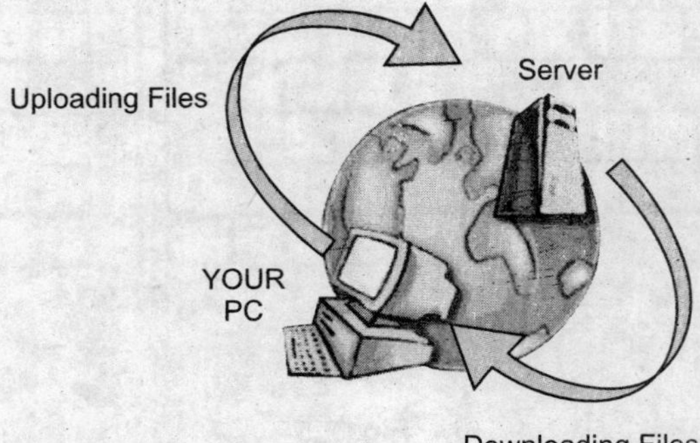

Fig. 2.4

2.14 COMPUTER HARDWARE

The term computer hardware refers to the physical components of a computer, namely Keyboard, Monitor, Mouse, and Printer, including the digital circuitry. Computer hardware is an integral part embedded in all modern day automobiles, microwave ovens, electrocardiograph machines, compact disc players, and other devices. The hardware of a computer is not changed frequently, in contrast with software and data. The present computers are much advanced in terms of processing speed and have an efficient memory structure.

2.14.1 Personal Computers

A personal computer, very commonly known as the PC or the home computer, refers to a microcomputer whose price, size, and capabilities make it suitable for personal usage. They are normally single-microprocessors, single user systems designed for general-purpose applications. They have sufficiently large amount of internal memory to store programs and documents. A computer, indeed, is a machine that can perform a number of tasks for us. It can accept and store data, process it and produces the output. For performing these functions, computer systems consist of Input devices, a Central Processing Unit (CPU) and Output Devices.

2.14.2 Input Devices

The foremost task of a computer is to accept data. An input device is used to accomplish this task. An input device is used to enter the data and instructions into the computer. Advancement in the computer technology has resulted in a variety of input devices being available in the market. Keyboard and mouse are the most commonly used input devices.

Keyboard: Keyboard is the most popular input device that allows users to type alphabets, numbers, and operators, and also to control the cursor on the screen. A simple keyboard layout is given below:

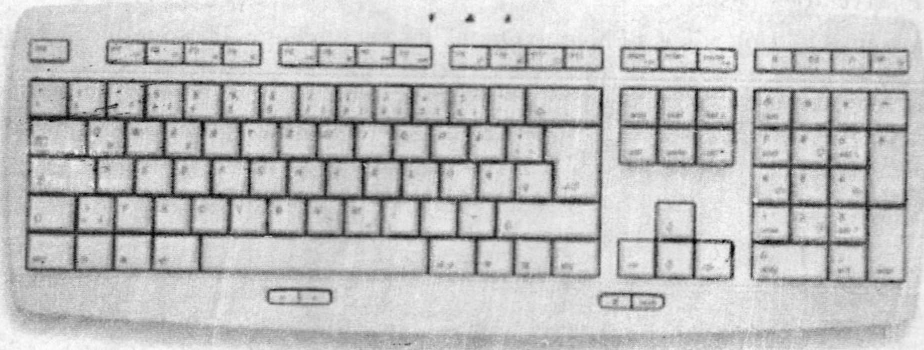

Fig. 2.5

Mouse: Mouse is a pointing device that allows user to point to a specific position on the screen. It has two or three buttons on top for selecting/executing different operations. Pressing buttons of mouse is known as clicking of mouse. The mouse is placed on flat surface and moved around to move its controlling arrow on screen. The arrow showing the position of mouse on screen is known as mouse pointer. Left button of mouse is used execute the operation associated with it. Right button/Middle buttons are associated with special operations in different situations.

Joy Stick: It is a device used to control cursor on screen. Normally it is used in Games and specially designed simulation software.

Light Pen: It is a device used for drawing pictures and for directly controlling screen operations.

Microphone: It is a device used to accept audio inputs from the user.

Scanner: It is a device used to capture digital images of printed documents, graphics or other printed media.

Touch Screens: It is a display device, which is touch-sensitive and allows user to interact with the computer system by touching an area on The screen.

Bar Code: Reader It is used to accept barcode inputs. A barcode is a series of vertical bars representing numbers and alphabets printed on product labels. One must have noticed all standard items like perfumes, greeting cards, books, cassettes available in the market have similar lines known as bar codes. These can be read with the help of bar code readers. Web Camera It is an easy to connect low resolution digital camera normally employed for transfer of images on the web-based conferencing.

Digital Camera: It is a high-resolution camera, which captures images and stores them in digital format. It has provision to connect to the computer using special computer communication cables (such as USB cables).

2.14.3 Output Devices

It is a device used to provide the processed data from the computer to the user. Monitor (VDU/Screen) and printer are the most commonly used output devices.

Monitor: A Monitor is an output device, very similar to the television screen. It displays the information as it is typed and also displays the processed result or the output. It is available in many forms cathode ray picture tube based display, liquid crystal based display (LCD), plasma panel display, and touch panel display.

Printer: It is an output device to produce paper copy (hard copy) for a document, pictures etc. The job of a printer is to put on paper what is seen on the monitor. Printers vary mainly in cost, quality, speed and noise levels. Eg: Dot Matrix Printer

Inkjet Printer
Deskjet Printer
Bubblejet Printer
Laser Printer

2.14.4 Storage Devices

Storing data is an important part of a computer system. The main concern of all computer designers is to create fast and efficient storage devices. As is commonly known, the primary memory inside the computer (Random Access Memory or RAM) is volatile i.e. whatever is stored in RAM is lost as soon as the computer is switched off. So if there is a need to save data from getting lost, it can be put on a storage device like floppy disk, hard disks and CD-ROMS before switching off the Computer.

Floppy Disk

It is a smaller capacity removable storage device. It is made up of thin and flexible plastic material. This thin plastic film is coated with a magnetic material known as iron oxide for recording data and is protected by a hard outer cover. It is very useful in transferring data from one computer to another.

Although technology has not changed substantially, floppy disks have certainly changed considerably in order to meet the very demanding needs of the marketplace. From an 8-inch size they have evolved to a much smaller size with larger capacities. Today's standard 3.5-inch diskettes hold a formatted capacity of about 1.44 megabytes. The evolution of the personal computer acted as a catalyst primary for designers to reduce the size and cost of floppies. Very quickly the floppy became the standard method of exchanging data between personal computers. It also became the popular method of storing moderate amounts of information outside of the computer's hard drive. Diskettes are small, inexpensive, readily available, easy to store, and have a good shelf life if stored properly.

Types of storage Devices

Floopy Disk

CD Rom

DVD ROM

USB Pen Drive

2.15 COMPUTER SOFTWARE

Computer software is a general term used to describe the role that computer programs, procedures and documentation play in a computer system. Computer software is often regarded as anything but hardware, meaning that the "hard" are the parts that are tangible while the "soft" part is the intangible objects inside the computer.

Various types of computer software are used to simplify the operations and applications of computer programs. Computer software enables the computer system to perform in accordance with the given tasks. Computer software involves all types of software related applications. Electronic media content is also explained by the computer software.

2.15.1 Classification of Computer Software

Different types of computer software are available in the global computer market. Programming software, system software and application software are the three main types of computer software used in computer networking. System software is the most commonly used variety of computer software. System software offers a protective shield to all software applications. It also provides support to the physical components of computers. System software coordinates all external devices of computer system like printer, keyboard, displays etc.

Programmers use the programming software to develop the programming languages necessary to run computer software. Compliers, interpreters, linkers and text editors are some of the basic tools used in programming software.

Application software is used for commercial purpose. The application software is widely used in educational, business and medical fields. Computer games are the most popular forms of application software. Industrial automation, databases, business software and medical software prove to be of great help in the respective fields. Educational software is widely used in educational institutes across the globe.

2.15.2 Functioning of Computer Software

Computer software works through computer programming. The whole process runs like a chain reaction. Transfer of commands initiates the chain. Machine code generated by computer software ends the entire process.

Overview of Softwares

Software encompasses an extremely wide array of products and technologies developed using different techniques like programming languages, scripting languages or even microcode or a FPGA state. The types of software include web pages developed by technologies like HTML, PHP, Perl, JSP, ASP.NET, XML, and desktop applications like Open Office, Microsoft Word developed by technologies like C, C++, Java, or C#. Software usually runs on an underlying software operating systems such as the Linux or Microsoft Windows. Software also includes video games and the logic systems of modern consumer devices such as automobiles, televisions, and toasters.

2.15.3 Software Relationship with Computer Hardware

Computer software is so called to distinguish it from computer hardware, which encompasses the physical interconnections and devices required to store and execute (or run) the software. At the lowest level, software consists of a machine language specific to an individual processor. A machine language consists of groups of binary values signifying processor instructions that change the state of the computer from its preceding state. Software is an ordered sequence of instructions for changing the state of the computer hardware in a particular sequence. It is usually written in high-level programming languages that are easier and more efficient for humans to use (closer to natural language) than machine language. High-level languages are compiled or interpreted into machine language object code. Software may also be written in an assembly language, essentially, a mnemonic

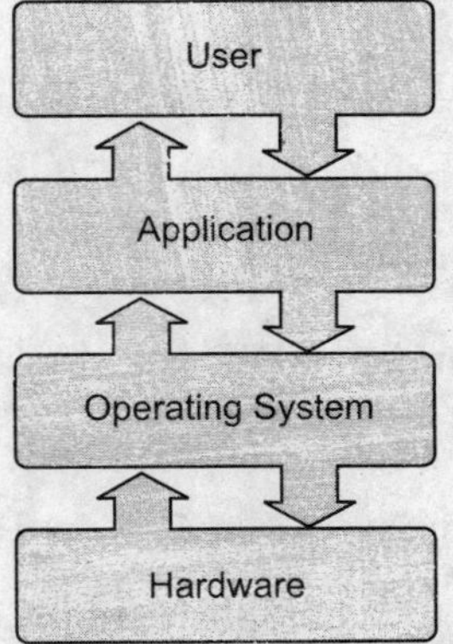

Fig. 2.6: Software Hardware Relationship

representation of a machine language using a natural language alphabet. Assembly language must be assembled into object code via an assembler.

2.16 TYPES OF SOFTWARE

Practical computer systems divide software systems into three major classes:

- System software
- Programming software
- Application software.

2.16.1 System Software

System software helps run the computer hardware and computer system. It includes combination of the following:

- Device drivers
- Operating systems
- Servers
- Utilities
- Windowing systems

The purpose of systems software is to unburden the applications programmer from the details of the particular computer complex being used, including such accessory devices as communications, printers, readers, displays and keyboards, and also to partition the computer's resources such as memory and processor time in a safe and stable manner.

2.16.2 Programming Software

Programming software usually provides tools to assist a programmer in writing computer programs, and software using different programming languages in a more convenient way. The tools include:

- Compilers
- Debuggers
- Interpreters
- Linkers
- Text editors

An Integrated development environment (IDE) is a single application that attempts to manage all these functions.

2.16.3 Application software

Application software allows end users to accomplish one or more specific (not directly computer development related) tasks. Typical applications include:

- Industrial automation
- Business software
- Computer games
- Telecommunications (i.e., the internet and everything that flows on it)
- Databases
- Educational software
- Medical software
- Military software

Application software exists for and has impacted a wide variety of topics.

2.17 HISTORY OF COMPUTING TECHNOLOGY

Let us brief look at the history of computing technology which dates back to 500 BC.

- 500 BC: Wire and bead abacus invented in Egypt.
- 1642: First Numerical calculating Machine was built by Blaise Pascal in Paris based on a design by Hero of Alexandria 2AD.
- 1833: Charles Babbage designed the Analytical machine that follows instructions from punched cards. It is often considered to be the first general-purpose computer.
- 1946: Electronic Numerical Integrator and Calculator ENIAC were built which had 18,000 vacuum tubes, used 180,000 watts of power and weighed 80 tons. It could do 5,000 additions and 360 multiplications per second. It used Punch card input and output. Programming by wiring up plug boards. It is commonly accepted that ENIAC was the first successful high-speed digital computer.
- 1948: Transistor is invented, 1958: First Integrated Circuit is fabricated
- 1964: Integrated circuit fabricated.
- 1970: VLSI the entire assemblies became available as computer "chips". MS-DOS, Unix, Operating Systems, Network, Distributed Operating Systems all came into existence around this time.
- 1971: Intel 4004, a team headed by Marcial Ho, developed first Microprocessor. The development of this chip meant that computers could become small enough and cheap enough to be owned by individuals rather than only by large companies.

2.18 SUMMARY

- The Internet links are computer networks all over the world so that users can share resources and communicate with each other.
- A web server is a specialized type of file server. Its job is to retrieve files from the server's hard drive, format the files for the Web browser, and send them out via the network. Web

servers are designed to do a great job of sending static content out to a large number of users. The pages delivered by the server are expected to be the same for everyone who visits the server.

- Web application servers are designed specifically to extend web servers to support dynamic content. The application server software "hooks in" to the web server software and automatically intercepts any user requests for dynamic content.
- E-mail is an asynchronous form of communication, meaning that the person whom you want to read your message doesn't have to be available at the precise moment you send your message. This is a great convenience for both you and the recipient.
- A bookmark is a way of saving your favorite Web pages so that you can find them again later.
- When book marking your favorite Web pages you will also be able to put them into categories that will make finding them among all your other bookmarks really easy.
- They are called **Bookmarks in Netscape** & they are called **Favorites in Internet Explorer**. Even though they have different names, they are the same thing.
- The term computer hardware refers to the physical components of a computer, namely Keyboard, Monitor, Mouse, and Printer, including the digital circuitry. Computer hardware is an integral part embedded in all modern day automobiles, microwave ovens, electrocardiograph machines, compact disc players, and other devices. The hardware of a computer is not changed frequently, in contrast with software and data.
- Computer software is a general term used to describe the role that computer programs, procedures and documentation play in a computer system. Computer software is often regarded as anything but hardware, meaning that the "hard" are the parts that are tangible while the "soft" part is the intangible objects inside the computer.
- The purpose of systems software is to unburden the applications programmer from the details of the particular computer complex being used, including such accessory devices as communications, printers, readers, displays and keyboards, and also to partition the computer's resources such as memory and processor time in a safe and stable manner.
- Application software allows end users to accomplish one or more specific (not directly computer development related) tasks.

2.19 REVIEW QUESTIONS

1. Discuss the history and development of internet.
2. Explain the client server model of internet.
3. Write short notes on
   (i) Web server (ii) Web application server
   (iii) E-mail (iv) URL
4. Explain the concept of bookmarking on web sites.

CHAPTER 3

Service Support Process

3.1 SERVICE SUPPORT PROCESS

Service support is about responding to change. The needs of users change. Configurations change. Unexpected events occur. The specific details of these changes will vary, but how systems managers' respond should not. A set of well-defined processes is at the core of service-oriented systems management. Those processes — incident management, problem management, configuration management, change management, and release management — are discussed in detail later in this chapter. In this section, the focus is on the shared attributes and interdependencies of these processes.

3.1.1 Interdependent Service Support Processes

Service support processes have different specific goals depending on the area of service delivery they address. For example, in incident management, something has disrupted the normal flow of operations, and the goal is to restore normal services as soon as possible. Problem management, in contrast, takes a more holistic approach and attempts to prevent incidents by detecting patterns in incidents and identifying root causes. Even with their different goals, service support processes are highly interdependent.

In some cases, those root causes could be the result of improperly configured devices, in which case, configuration management processes must be examined. Were they applied properly? Is there a deficiency in the process that allowed a flawed configuration to enter production service? Perhaps the correct configuration specifications had been defined but they were not properly installed; in that case, the release management procedures require review.

It is clear from these simple examples that information relevant to one process can be vital to the proper implementation of other processes. It is also clear that errors in one set of procedures can have ripple effects that cause other processes to be activated. For both of these reasons, automated configuration management services can improve service support.

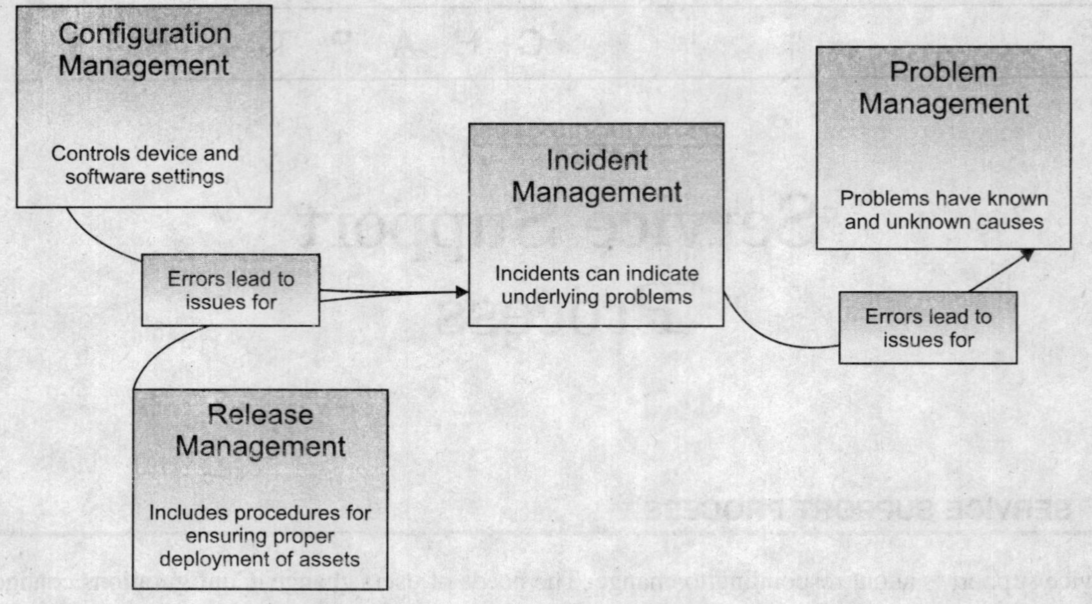

Fig. 3.1: Service support processes components relationships

3.2 AUTOMATED CONFIGURATION MANAGEMENT

The objective of automated configuration management is twofold. First, it is to obtain and maintain information about the state of devices and applications deployed throughout the IT infrastructure. The second objective is to support multiple IT operations, especially service support.

Automated configuration management is a mechanism that supports all parts of service support, not just traditional configuration management. This mechanism should not be confused with early configuration management tools that provided limited information and provide little support for related service support operations.

To meet these objectives, automated configuration management applications use several modules, including:

- Agents for collecting configuration and other status information
  - — Centralized data repository
  - — Process flow support
  - — Information retrieval

Together, these modules provide the core services of automated configuration management.

3.2.1 Data Collection Procedures

Data is gathered from devices using agents, or applications that collect information locally and transmit it to a central repository. These agents should be relatively lightweight and autonomous; once installed and configured, they should require little systems manager intervention.

The configuration processes entail setting a number of characteristics, including:

- Data collection policies
- Frequency of data collection
- Data transmission information
- Authentication mechanism

The data collection policies define what information is gathered and how frequently it is transmitted. The information gathered can include local security policy settings, storage utilization, significant system events, and other audit-related details.

The frequency of data collection will determine how often the agent sends information to the central repository. There is a tradeoff with this setting. Devices that frequently update the central repository are less likely to have outdated data, but the data collection process places additional demands that can adversely impact the performance of other applications.

When depending on agents, it is important for the central repository to accept data only from authenticated agents. Distributed applications such as these are vulnerable to spoofing — that is, an attacker or an attacker's program pretending to be the real agent. An attacker, for example, might want to cover his or her tracks by sending false information about failed login attempts or the amount of disk space in use. By using cryptographic techniques, such as digitally signing all transmissions, the repository can significantly reduce the chance of attacks.

3.2.2 Centralized Data Repository

A centralized data repository for configuration management is one that supports multiple functions related to service delivery, including managing configurations, which, in turn, support both service delivery and security enforcement. Although the basic role of the repository is to answer queries about the state of devices, it must be designed to support queries from multiple domains. For example, from an incident management perspective, the database might be queried about the software installed on a particular device and the dependencies between those applications. This is useful in cases in which a newly installed application is not working properly but works correctly on other similarly configured clients. In such a case, one of the first questions to answer is—What are the differences between clients with a working installation of the application and clients without?

In the case of problem management, support personnel may discover that a particular version of a browser add-in causes parts of an application interface to fail. They may also find that rolling back to an earlier version of the add-in resolves the problem. In this case, the configuration database could be used to determine all devices that have both the problematic plug and need to run the thin-client application. After the correct plug-in has been deployed, the database can be queried to verify installation (assuming agents have updated the repository). These are relatively simple examples; other more complex issues may require multi-step procedures.

3.2.3 Process Flow Support

Configuring IT devices often entails dependencies between components. Mechanisms for supporting process flow can help control procedures that must be aware of those dependencies.

Consider requirements for rolling out a Web-based application that uses Java-based technologies in clients' browsers. In addition to updating client browsers with the latest security patches, the release requires that the JRE is installed to a particular revision level. Once the browser is patched and the JRE installed, a plug-in must be installed within the browser as well. Each of these steps must be done in sequence and if one step fails, the succeeding steps should not occur. The results of the installation must be verifiable.

A process flow engine within a configuration management system could meet these requirements if it supports:

- Ordered deployment of modules
- Tests for success of each step
- Conditional processing — for example, if the browser does not contain a particular patch, it is installed; otherwise, it is not
- Detail logs of each step

Logged information about the deployment process should be available by querying the CMDB.

3.2.4 Information Retrieval

Information retrieval sounds trivial — you simply want to display data that is stored in a database. What is not trivial is precisely specifying what data it is that you want displayed. At one end of the information retrieval spectrum, there are query languages used by database developers and the occasional power user. Even for relatively simple queries, this is not a reasonable tool for most users. Consider the following query: a systems manager wants to list all resource associations, the associated resource type, the name of the resource, and a brief description, sorted by resource type.

3.3 CONFIGURATION MANAGEMENT

Configuration management is the process of controlling changes to device configurations in an IT environment. There are five basic operations in configuration management:

- Planning
- Identification
- Control
- Status accounting
- Verification and audit

Together, these operations provide the means to control the establishment and maintenance of device configurations.

3.3.1 Planning

Planning within configuration management is similar to other IT operations; that is, the focus is on setting an overall strategy, defining the policies and procedures necessary to implement that strategy, and identifying configuration items that should be tracked within the CMDB. The configuration management strategy defines the scope and objectives of the configuration management process. For example, the scope of a typical plan includes all managed devices within an organization; the objectives include maintaining the availability and integrity of devices, ensuring efficient use of resources, and minimizing maintenance and training costs.

The planning process also defines roles and responsibilities. A single device may be maintained by several roles. A server, for example, may be the responsibility of a systems manager who is responsible for the OS and access controls, a network administrator who is responsible for configuring network hardware and protocols, and an application administrator who maintains services provided by the server. The CMDB is used across service support operations, but its function and maintenance fall under the scope of configuration management planning.

Configuration management planning is not a one-time event. These plans are typically subject to change as business and organizational requirements change. Although the planning process focuses on the overall configuration management process, the identification process addresses the details of the operation.

3.3.2 Identification

Any entity tracked by configuration management is known as a configuration item (CI). Several characteristics of configuration items are recorded:

- Name and description
- Owner of item
- Relationships to other items
- Versions
- Unique identifiers

It is important to identify CIs to the level of independent change. For example, if laptops are treated as a single unit and hard drives are not moved among laptops, there is no need to track the hard drives independently of the laptop. However, optical drives used for backups and moved among servers should be managed as distinct devices.

3.3.3 Control

The control process ensures that all configuration items are properly identified, their information is recorded in the CMDB, and any changes are done in accordance with change management procedures. (Change control is discussed in detail later.)

3.3.4 Status Accounting

Status accounting is the process of recording state changes to a configuration item. The most common states are:

- On order

- Received, pending testing
- Under test
- Installed to production
- Under repair
- Disposed

All state changes should be recorded so that the CMDB always has an accurate representation of the IT infrastructure. This information is also useful for problem management, especially for detecting devices with high incidents of repair or long repair periods.

3.3.5 Verification and Audit

During verification and audit, the contents of the CMDB are compared with the physical configuration items to ensure that information about them is correctly recorded. Documentation about changes to configuration items should also be verified during audits.

Configuration management is an ongoing operation. Some processes, such as planning and verification, occur at regular intervals. The other processes are continuous.

Configuration management (CM) is a field of management that focuses on establishing and maintaining consistency of a system's or product's performance and its functional and physical attributes with its requirements, design, and operational information throughout its life. For information assurance, CM can be defined as the management of security features and assurances through control of changes made to hardware, software, firmware, documentation, test, test fixtures, and test documentation throughout the life cycle of an information system.

3.4 SOFTWARE CONFIGURATION MANAGEMENT

The traditional software configuration management (SCM) process is looked upon as the best solution to handling changes in software projects. It identifies the functional and physical attributes of software at various points in time, and performs systematic control of changes to the identified attributes for the purpose of maintaining software integrity and traceability throughout the software development life cycle.

The SCM process further defines the need to trace changes, and the ability to verify that the final delivered software has all of the planned enhancements that are supposed to be included in the release. It identifies four procedures that must be defined for each software project to ensure that a sound SCM process is implemented. They are:

1. Configuration identification
2. Configuration control
3. Configuration status accounting
4. Configuration audits

These terms and definitions change from standard to standard, but are essentially the same.

- Configuration identification is the process of identifying the attributes that define every aspect of a configuration item. A configuration item is a product (hardware and/or software) that has an end-user purpose. These attributes are recorded in configuration documentation and baselined. Baselining an attribute forces formal configuration change control processes to be effected in the event that these attributes are changed.
- Configuration change control is a set of processes and approval stages required to change a configuration item's attributes and to re-baseline them.
- Configuration status accounting is the ability to record and report on the configuration baselines associated with each configuration item at any moment of time.
- Configuration audits are broken into functional and physical configuration audits. They occur either at delivery or at the moment of effecting the change. A functional configuration audit ensures that functional and performance attributes of a configuration item are achieved, while a physical configuration audit ensures that a configuration item is installed in accordance with the requirements of its detailed design documentation.

Configuration management is widely used by many military organizations to manage the technical aspects of any complex systems, such as weapon systems, vehicles, and information systems. The discipline combines the capability aspects that these systems provide an organization with the issues of management of change to these systems over time.

Outside of the military, CM is equally appropriate to a wide range of fields and industry and commercial sectors.

3.4.1 Computer Hardware Configuration Management

Computer hardware configuration management is the process of creating and maintaining an up-to-date record of all the components of the infrastructure, including related documentation. Its purpose is to show what makes up the infrastructure and illustrate the physical locations and links between each item, which are known as configuration items.

Computer hardware configuration goes beyond the recording of computer hardware for the purpose of asset management, although it can be used to maintain asset information. The extra value provided is the rich source of support information that it provides to all interested parties. This information is typically stored together in a configuration management database (CMDB).

The scope of configuration management is assumed to include, at a minimum, all configuration items used in the provision of live, operational services.

Computer hardware configuration management provides direct control over information technology (IT) assets and improves the ability of the service provider to deliver quality IT services in an economical and effective manner. Configuration management should work closely with change management.

All components of the IT infrastructure should be registered in the CMDB. The responsibilities of configuration management with regard to the CMDB are:

- identification

- control
- status accounting
- verification

The scope of configuration management is assumed to include:

- physical client and server hardware products and versions
- operating system software products and versions
- application development software products and versions
- technical architecture product sets and versions as they are defined and introduced
- live documentation
- networking products and versions
- live application products and versions
- definitions of packages of software releases
- definitions of hardware base configurations
- configuration item standards and definitions

The benefits of computer hardware configuration management are:

- helps to minimize the impact of changes
- provides accurate information on CIs
- improves security by controlling the versions of CIs in use
- facilitates adherence to legal obligations
- helps in financial and expenditure planning

3.4.2 Software Configuration Management

Software configuration management (SCM) is the task of tracking and controlling changes in the software. Configuration management practices include revision control and the establishment of baselines.

SCM concerns itself with answering the question "Somebody did something, how can one reproduce it?" Often the problem involves not reproducing "it" identically, but with controlled, incremental changes. Answering the question thus becomes a matter of comparing different results and of analysing their differences. Traditional configuration management typically focused on controlled creation of relatively simple products. Now, implementers of SCM face the challenge of dealing with relatively minor increments under their own control, in the context of the complex system being developed.

Purposes

The goals of SCM are

- **Configuration identification:** Identifying configurations, configuration items and baselines.

- **Configuration control:** Implementing a controlled change process. This is usually achieved by setting up a change control board whose primary function is to approve or reject all change requests that are sent against any baseline.
- **Configuration status accounting:** Recording and reporting all the necessary information on the status of the development process.
- **Configuration auditing:** Ensuring that configurations contain all their intended parts and are sound with respect to their specifying documents, including requirements, architectural specifications and user manuals.
- **Build management:** Managing the process and tools used for builds.
- **Process management:** Ensuring adherence to the organization's development process.
- **Environment management:** Managing the software and hardware that host our system.
- **Teamwork:** Facilitate team interactions related to the process.
- **Defect tracking:** Making sure every defect has traceability back to the source.

3.5 NETWORK CONFIGURATION MANAGEMENT (NCM)

Network configuration management (NCM) is the process of organizing and maintaining information about all the components of a computer network. When a network needs repair, modification, expansion or upgrading, the administrator refers to the network configuration management database to determine the best course of action. This database contains the locations and network addresses of all hardware devices, as well as information about the programs, versions and updates installed in network computers.

Network configuration management tools can be vendor-neutral or vendor-specific. Vendor-neutral tools, by far the more common, are designed for networks containing hardware and programs from multiple suppliers. Vendor-specific tools usually work only with the products of a single company, and can offer enhanced performance in networks where that vendor dominates.

Advantages of network configuration management include:

- Streamlining the processes of maintenance, repair, expansion and upgrading.
- Minimizing configuration errors.
- Minimizing downtime.
- Optimizing network security.
- Ensuring that changes made to a device or system do not adversely affect other devices or systems.
- Rolling back changes to a previous configuration if results are unsatisfactory.
- Archiving the details of all network configuration changes

3.6 INCIDENT MANAGEMENT

Definition of Incident Management: Incident Management (IM) is the way that the Service Desk puts out the 'daily fires'. An 'Incident' is any event which is not part of the standard operation of the service and which causes, or may cause, an interruption or a reduction of the quality of the service.

The objective of Incident Management is to restore normal operations as quickly as possible with the least possible impact on either the business or the user, at a cost-effective price.

Inputs for Incident Management mostly come from users, but can have other sources as well like management Information or Detection Systems. The outputs of the process are RFC's (Requests for Changes), resolved and closed Incidents, management information and communication to the customer.

3.6.1 Incidents, Problems and known Errors

Incidents may match with existing 'Known Problems' (without a known root cause) or 'Known Errors' (with a root cause) under the control of Problem Management and registered in the Known Error Database (KeDB). Where existing work-arounds have been developed, it is suggested that accessing these will allow the Service Desk to provide a quick first-line fix. Where an incident is not the result of a Known Problem or Known Error, it may either be an isolated or individual occurrence or may (once the initial issue has been addressed) require that Problem Management become involved, possibly resulting in a new problem record being raised.

3.6.2 Incidents and Changes

Incidents are the result of failures or errors in the IT infrastructure. The cause of Incidents may be apparent and the cause may be addressed without the need for further investigation, resulting in a repair, a Work-around or a request for change (RFC) to remove the error.

Where an incident is considered to be serious in nature, or multiple occurrences of similar incidents are observed, a problem record might be created as a result (it's possible that the Problem will not be recorded until several incidents have occurred). The management of a problem varies from the process of managing an incident and is typically performed by different staff and therefore is controlled by the Problem Management process. When a problem has been properly identified and a work-around is known, the problem becomes a 'known problem'. When its 'root cause' has been identified, it becomes a 'known error'. Finally, a request for change (RFC) may be raised to modify the system by resolving the known error. The Change Management process covers this process.

A request for new additional service is not regarded as an incident, but as a Request for Change (RFC).

Activities of the Incident Management process:

- Incident detection and recording
- Classification and initial support
- Investigation and diagnosis
- Resolution and recovery
- Incident closure

- Incident ownership, monitoring, tracking and communication

These elements provide a baseline for management review.

Incident management software able to addresses both of those challenges. Regardless of the incident that has occurred, the ability to have a quick response time and internal transparency for every step in the incident management process, including feedback ensures customer satisfaction, while simultaneously allowing your organization to reduce contact center costs.

- **Tracking Customer Contact:** When your customer calls with a problem, having to repeat that problem to multiple customer service representatives is not good incident management. Incident management software allows you to capture important information from each customer interaction so that your customer service representatives are informed each time an incident arises.
- **Desktop Workspaces:** Intuitive, customizable desktops workspaces are a key component of RightNow's incident management software. When your customer service representatives can instinctively grab essential information on the fly, their ability to provide swift resolutions with a personalized touch is greatly increased.
- **Reporting:** To improve a process, you first need the ability to measure it. In an incident management system, this means receiving reporting for items such as response time, initial contact resolutions, and answer usefulness. RightNow's incident management software provides those capabilities, allowing you to examine performance and find areas for improvement in your incident management process.
- **Feedback:** After an incident has been resolved, don't guess as to whether your customer was satisfied with the service your organization provided; get feedback. With post-incident feedback surveys, you can learn how your customers feel and either reward your customer relations team or find opportunities to improve your incident management system.

The Difference Between Incident Management And Problem M0anagement

Incidents and Service Requests are formally managed through a staged process to conclusion. This process is referred to as the "Incident Management Lifecycle". The objective of the Incident Management Lifecycle is to restore the service as quickly as possible to meet Service Level Agreements. The process is primarily aimed at the user level.

Problem Management deals with resolving the underlying cause of one or more Incidents. The focus of Problem Management is to resolve the root cause of errors and to find permanent solutions. Although every effort will be made to resolve the problem as quickly as possible this process is focused on the resolution of the problem rather than the speed of the resolution. This process deals at the enterprise level.

3.7 PROBLEM MANAGEMENT

3.7.1 Problem Definition

A problem is defined as:

- A deviation from "Expected Service Delivery", or

- A "Standards and Procedures" violation.

When these conditions occur, then they must be reported as a problem

The Problem Management System has been established to capture and report on encountered problems. It employs the APRIORI Problem Management System product from Answer Systems, Inc. as a front-end and problem repository.

The Problem Management System is used to record problem events, assign them to a resolve, and track problems until they are successfully resolved. If problems are of a high priority, or outstanding beyond an acceptable period of time, then the problem Management System will escalate the problem in priority. When this occurs, the next level in problem support is activated and additional manpower is applied to resolving the problem.

3.7.2 Definition of Problem Management System

The Technology Operations Problem Management System will:

- Record,
- Resolve,
- Escalate,
- Track, and
- Report

on any situation that is a deviation from the Service Delivery expectation.

Problems occur with procedures, hardware, operating systems, the environment, and software applications.

Problem Management is the process of detecting and reporting problems that impact services supplied by Technology Operations. A **problem** is any unplanned deviation from standards or an expected service delivery.

Problems include:

- Hardware mainframe through data network;
- Software systems, sub-systems, applications, and utilities;
- Communications applications, devices, and lines;
- Data Network applications, and devices;
- Human errors;
- Procedures; and
- Environmental failures (i.e., Heating, Ventilation, Air Conditioning, Power, Water, Raised Floor, etc.).

Intervention may be required to determine, eliminate, or circumvent problems as they are identified.

3.7.3 Problem Management Objectives

Mission Statement

Provide critical information on problems to Lehman Brothers Management and Technical personnel, so that appropriate business decisions can be made through these

- Recording of all encountered problems,
- Resolution of all reported problems in the most efficient manner,
- Escalation of unresolved problems in accordance with critically and duration,
- Communication of problem information to senior management,
- Addressing of reoccurring problems,
- Generation and distribution of problem reports, as required.

The **Mission** of the Problem Management System is to employ standard procedures for reporting and resolving problems. The goal of this process is to reduce the impact of failures on service expectations to an acceptable level.

Problem Reporting is used to inform Management and Technical personnel of problems that affect service expectations. Problems are assigned to resolvers through the Technology Operations department and/or the Global Systems Help Desk. Escalation's designed to raise the priority of a problem, are incorporated into the Problem Management Process so that appropriate resolution actions can be taken and the outage's duration reduced.

The Problem Management Process will record, assign, escalate, track, resolve and report on any situation that is a deviation from expected service deliveries or standards.

Post Mortem procedures are utilized to review resolved problems that have impacted multiple users, or are of a high priority. The goal of the Post Mortem process is to implement improved problem recovery and resolution procedures, as deemed necessary.

3.7.4 Objectives of Problem Management

- **Ensure** all encountered problems are reported,
- **Prioritize** problems as to their criticality and business impact,
- **Log** problems to Problem Record in Problem Repository,
- **Resolve** a majority of reported problems at Global Systems Help Desk,
- **Assign** problems to resolvers that cannot be resolved by Global Systems Help Desk,
- **Track** and manage problems (from origination through resolution),
- **Escalate** problem resolution in accordance with criticality and duration,
- **Close** problems when resolved,
- Conduct **Post Mortems** on resolved problems,
- Recommend updates to supportive **documentation**,
- Produce and distribute Problem **Reports**.

These objectives are met through:

- The use of the **APRIORI** Problem Management System,
- Personnel assigned to the **Global Systems Help Desk**,
- **Internal Resolvers** assigned to the departments of Technical Operations, and
- **External Resolvers** assigned to problems under the management of Internal Resolvers.

3.7.5 Scope

The Problem Management Process begins with the recognition of a problem and ends when a problem is closed. In both cases, the problem reporter must be included; initially as the reporter or a problem and finally as the approver of the problem's resolution.

In some cases, the Systems Manager, or On-Line Manager, must also approve the resolution to ensure that the closed problem does not impact other areas beyond the reporters domain (i.e., problems that affect multiple users, but are reported by only one user, etc...). This "checks-and-balances" procedure is accomplished via periodic problem review meetings and the distribution of problem reports.

3.8 SMC DISCIPLINE INTERFACES

The Systems Management and Controls (SMC) disciplines interfacing with the Problem Management System are:

Batch Management: Provide problem reports for Batch Jobs and their recovery/restart procedures.

Capacity Management: Provides problem reports on abends due to capacity shortages, such as DASD Space and Region Sizes. May also be used to isolate the need for additional hardware and/or the reconfiguration of existing resources.

Performance Management: Provides problem reports for performance related weaknesses, such as transaction response times, Batch Job turnaround times, etc.

Change Management: Provides problem reports for failures that occur due to a weakness in the Change Management process, such as version and release information, benchmark, testing, etc.

Recovery Management: Provides problem reporting when errors in the recovery process occur, such as recovery planning for critical assets, sizing requirements for recovery facilities, and failed recovery/restart procedures.

Service Level Management: Provides problem reports when service level delivery to clients is below expected limits, as determined via Service Level Reporting.

Inventory Management: Provides problem reporting for items not included in the Inventory, or wrongly reported in the Inventory System (i.e., Acquisition, Redeployment, Termination, or Surplus).

Configuration Management: Provides problem reports on failures related to the Configuration as depicted in Configuration Diagrams showing: hardware, software, communications, power, water, facilities, etc.

3.8.1 Process Overview

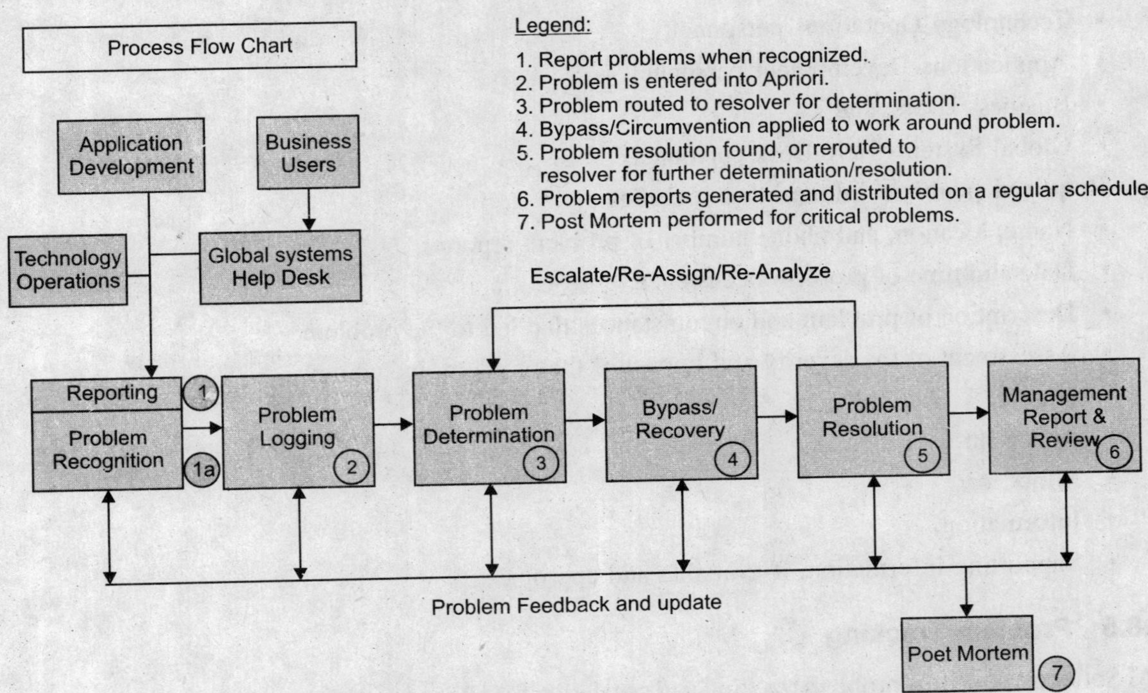

Fig. 3.2: Proposed Problem Management Process Flow

Problem Management System procedures are described below.

3.8.2 Problem Definition

A problem is categorized as:

- A deviation from "Expected Service Delivery", or
- A "Standards and Procedures" violation.

When these conditions are recognized, then they must be reported as a problem.

3.8.3 Problem Recognition

The detection and identification of problems, or potential problems, through monitoring, trend analysis, or observation. The recognition of a problem can come from any point in the system; when identified, problems must be entered into the Problem Management System and routed to a problem resolver.

3.8.4 Problem Reporting and Logging

Problem entry is performed via the program product from Answer Systems. This is a Problem Repository data base and is equipped with front-end displays used to enter, access, research, assign, track, and resolve problems.

Problem reporters include:

- Technology Operations personnel,
- Applications Development personnel,
- Business Users, and
- Global Systems Help Desk personnel.

Required problem information includes

- Name, location, and phone number of problem reporter,
- Date and time of problem occurrence,
- Description of problem and circumstances that led to the problem,
- Assessment of the severity and impact of the problem, including:
- Urgent,
- Important,
- Minor, or
- Information.
- Supporting information, if available and appropriate.

3.8.5 Problem Tracking

PM Sofiware performs problem tracking and escalation for all reported problems. Problem reporting will be performed on a periodic basis. Problem turnaround to resolution is dependent upon severity. Urgent problems will be addressed immediately (within 1/2 hour), while less urgent problems may take longer to address.

The resolver, or Help Desk, must contact the problem reporter to gain their acceptance of the problem solution before problem closure procedures can be performed. Systems Managers may also be informed of problem solutions and their approval sought for some types of problems. This guarantees that problem reporters are satisfied with resolutions and that problems are truly repaired.

3.8.6 Problem Determination

Problems are identified through searches of past problems contained in the database, or through analysis efforts performed by the resolve. The intent of problem determination is to identify the source of the problem at a level sufficient enough to enable corrective action(s) to be performed.

Once the problem is assigned to the resolve, they are responsible for defining the problem's "root cause" and for developing a solution to the problem. Restore/ Recovery and Bypass/ Circumvention procedures should also be supplied by the resolver whenever possible. This information is added to the free-form text section of the Apriori problem record and made available to future problem searches by reporters/resolvers.

3.8.7 Problem Resolution

Problems are assigned to resolvers responsible for supporting the area impacted by the problem. If a problem has to be reassigned, or escalated, it is coordinated through the Global Systems Help Desk. If external resolvers are needed, an internal resolver must be responsible for monitoring and coordinating the actions of the external resolver. All problem determination, work-around, and resolution information must be entered into the free-form text section of the problem record.

Problem solutions that require change control activity will be processed through Change Management before verification of problem solutions can be accomplished. Solutions that do not require change control activity will be implemented immediately. In both cases, the problem reporter must approve the problem solution before the problem can be closed.

All problems related information must be added to the free-form text section of the problem record before problem closure is finalized.

Service Level Document

The sections contained within this document are:

- Symptom,
- Problem Analysis,
- Details,
- Impact,
- Solution, and
- Future Prevention.

If problem resolution information was not available in the initial Post Mortem report, the Post Mortem document is updated until the problem solution is available (see Appendix 'A' for Post Mortem document and process).

Management Reports and Review

Problem reports are generated for a variety of business reasons, including:

- Open and/or closed problems,
- High impact/severity, problems,
- Problems by date/time range,
- Problems by functional area/department,
- Problems by component/vendor,
- Problems by type, frequency, duration, etc...

In all cases, problem reports can be used to isolate weaknesses in products, applications, standards, procedures, supportive documentation, and training. Through problem reports and periodic reviews, management and technical personnel can make adjustments to the functions they perform, thereby reducing problem events and improving performance.

Its data base design allows:

- Problem record searches for specific information,
- Grouping data in problem reports,
- Formatting output for hardcopy, fax, or e-mail,
- Routing reports and data to files for use by other products (i.e., it is possible to copy problem data to a file in spreadsheet format.

This information can then be used to generate graphs and other reports from Excel, Lotus 123, etc.). Reports can be produced on a periodic basis, or via ad-hoc requests.

The desired reporting scenario is that each level:

1st Level Managers receive Problem Reports (Open/Closed) for their areas,

2nd Level Managers receive Summary Reports for the areas reporting to them.

The reports should be generated via Apriori and distributed via cc:Mail (or some other electronic media like Fax) to the individual. A schedule for report generation and distribution should be created and adhered to. Responses to reported problems should be accomplished via cc:Mail/Fax, when information or resolutions are available.

The problem reports listed above should be for every manager in the Technology Operations organization. Application problem reports should be generated, as well.

The summary report for the Technology Operations executive should include all open/closed problem data for the areas under the executive's direct control. Trending analysis reports should be provided to allow the executive to pinpoint where problem most often occur, or where resolutions take the most time to develop. This information will allow the executive to direct his forces to concentrate efforts on eliminating problem areas, or to provide additional training to specified areas of operation.

3.9 CHANGE MANAGEMENT

Change management is the process of controlling modifications to configuration items so as to minimize incidents that disrupt normal operations.

Change management is the process during which the changes of a system are implemented in a controlled manner by following a pre-defined framework/model with, to some extent, reasonable modifications.

The term **change management** can refer to:

- Change management (engineering), a process in systems engineering
- Change Management (ITSM), an IT Service Management discipline
- Change management (people), a structured approach to change in individuals, teams, organizations and societies

- Change management (health), a systematic health-care reform
- Change management (documentation), a systematic process of managing the changes of official documents

The reason change management is so important is that one change can have ripple effects through multiple other assets.

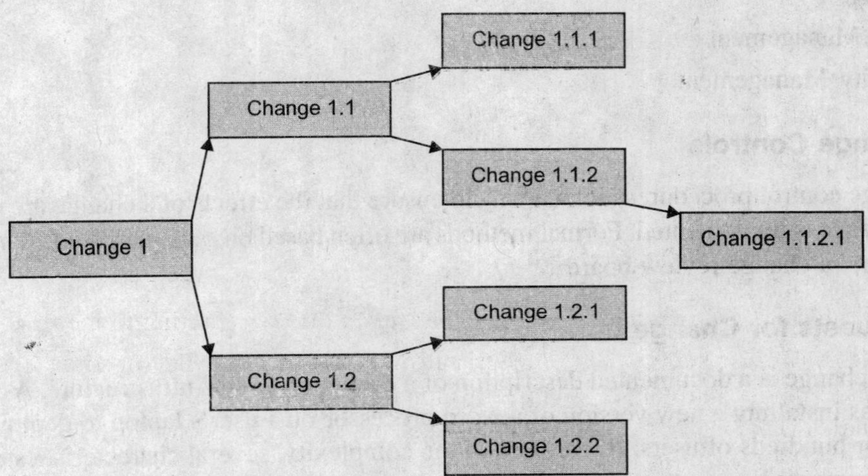

Fig. 3.3: Change Management Hierarchical overview

3.9.1 Ripple Effects of Change

Consider a change to a hypothetical management reporting system. Until now, managers have received static reports in Adobe PDF format once a week summarizing the business activity of their units. The IT department is deploying an interactive reporting system. Here are some of the changes related to the new system:

- Client software must be installed on power users' desktops and laptops; basic users will use a Web-based system to retrieve reports.
- The new client software for power users will have to be added to the patch management process to ensure clients receive all relevant security updates.
- Middleware software, including a downloadable applet, will have to be installed on Web servers.
- Firewall rules will be modified to allow traffic on a newly opened port to the Web component of the reporting system.
- New groups and roles will be added to the database access control system to allow managers to retrieve information using their network login ID.
- Additional database servers may be required to support the additional load of ad hoc querying.
- Failover servers may be added to ensure managers access to the database if a Web server should fail.

Clearly, what appears at first to be a software change can quickly propagate ripple effects to other software components, hardware devices, and network settings.

Large numbers of emergency change requests is an indication of failures in other processes, such as

- Planning,
- Testing,
- Patch Management
- Security Management

3.9.2 Change Controls

Formal change control procedures are one way to ensure that the effects of a change are understood before the change is implemented. Formal methods are often based on a standardized change request mechanism and a change review board.

3.9.3 Requests for Change

A request for change is a documented description of a change to the IT infrastructure. A change can be as simple as installing a new version of a word processor on a user's laptop to deploying a new application for hundreds of users. Regardless of the complexity, several characteristics of changes should be documented:

- Originator of request for change
- Configuration item to change
- Implementation plans
- Back out plans
- Type of change, such as a change in requirement, bug workaround, additional hardware for increased demand, and so on
- Reason for the change, such as compliance, policy change, defect, new business Requirement
- Priority, which can include emergency, urgent, or routine
- Detailed description of change
- Estimated time and resources required to implement
- Impact analysis for complex changes
- Approvals

Some of these items, such as the change description and the reason for change, are defined by the user or department making the request; others, such as the time and resource estimate and impact analysis, are determined by technical staff. The approvals required will depend on the priority and the complexity of the change. A relatively simple change, such as a desktop application installation, may require line manager approval, but a major software release will require approval from several managers, both on the business and technical sides of the organization.

3.9.4 Change Advisory Board (CAB)

A change advisory board (CAB), sometimes called a change control board, is responsible for reviewing complex requests for changes. A CAB should include managers responsible for business operations as well as technical staff familiar with systems administration, network operations, security and software development and management. The purpose of the CAB is to provide visibility to changes before they are made not to slow the change process.

CABs are sometimes seen as bureaucratic road blocks to getting work done — they should not be.

Their role is to provide a checkpoint to ensure that the implications of changes are thought through as completely as possible. Correcting a problem with a proposed change is much easier and less expensive when done at the planning stages than after the modification has been made.

In organizations with mature, functional IT operations, change is managed as a formal process. There is no avoiding change, but you can determine how we deal with it. After changes have been reviewed, revised and approved, the next step is implementation. This domain is addressed by release management practices.

Change Management is an IT Service Management discipline. The objective of Change Management in this context is to ensure that standardized methods and procedures are used for efficient and prompt handling of all changes to controlled IT infrastructure, in order to minimize the number and impact of any related incidents upon service. Changes in the IT infrastructure may arise reactively in response to problems or externally imposed requirements, e.g. legislative changes, or proactively from seeking imposed efficiency and effectiveness or to enable or reflect business initiatives, or from programs, projects or service improvement initiatives. Change Management can ensure standardized methods, processes and procedures are used for all changes, facilitate efficient and prompt handling of all changes, and maintain the proper balance between the need for change and the potential detrimental impact of changes.

Change Management within ITSM is often associated with ITIL, but the origins of change as an IT management process predate ITIL considerably, at least according to the IBM publication A Management System for the Information Business.

In the ITIL framework, change management is responsible for controlling change to all configuration items in the configuration management database within the live environment, test and training environments (all environments under the control of 'ICT Operations'. It is not typically responsible for change within development projects (see below).

3.10 CHANGE MANAGEMENT IN DEVELOPMENT PROJECTS

ITSM Change Management is not typically responsible for overseeing changes that occur within deployment or development projects which are typically delegated to a change management process dictated by the project management methodology adopted for the project. However close liaison between development project managers and the Change Manager is expected and the project manager may be required to utilize Change Management for items within the production or test environments that are required for testing or release.

3.10.1 Process Overview

Change Management would typically be composed of the raising and recording of changes, assessing the impact, cost, benefit and risk of proposed changes, developing business justification and obtaining approval, **managing** and co-ordinating change implementation, monitoring and reporting on implementation, reviewing and closing change requests.

ITIL defines the change management process this way:

The goal of the Change Management process is to ensure that standardized methods and procedures are used for efficient and prompt handling of all changes, in order to minimize the impact of change-related incidents upon service quality, and consequently improve the day-to-day operations of the organization. To ensure all changes are assessed, approved, implemented and reviewed in a controlled manner.

Change management is responsible for managing change process involving:

- Hardware
- Communications equipment and software
- System software
- All documentation and procedures associated with the running, support and maintenance of live systems.

Any proposed change must be approved in the change management process. While change management makes the process happen, the decision authority is the Change Advisory Board (CAB), which is made up for the most part of people from other functions within the organization. The main activities of the change management are:

- Filtering changes
- Managing changes and the change process
- Chairing the CAB and the CAB/Emergency committee
- Reviewing and closing of Requests for Change (RFCs)
- Management reporting and providing management information

3.10.2 Some of the Potential Issues Concerning the Successful Change Deployment Process

1. **The House (Of Quality) Needs Foundations :**Underestimating the need for a support structure can be a big mistake in the process of deploying Lean or Six Sigma. It is important to first assess the gap between your current state and the future, desired state. This activity produces a list of things that need to change and, in addition, those that need to be positively reinforced. In the change process, this is not an either/or proposition. Both need to be done. As an example, if one has the fortune of having an army of talented Black Belts but a broken

Champion support system, the program can fail in a heartbeat. Again, if both are present and yet, executive support is absent, then that can lead to disastrous results for a program as well.

The role of a consultant is potentially huge in this case. The superior knowledge base can be helpful in foreseeing roadblocks and addressing them at the very outset.

2. **Speed Can Be An Illusion:** One common trait of all change initiatives is that they go through a series of necessary steps that have their own lead times. Failing to recognize this fact often leads to skipping essential activities that only create an illusion of speed and never produces desired results.

   Sticking to an overall game plan and building steady momentum over time brings change that is more coherent and permanent than islands of excellence resulting from scattered activities.

3. **Sustaining A Shared Vision:** Most executives do a good job of communicating a strong sense of urgency to effect change and move people out of their comfort zones. This often launches a flurry of activities in the right direction to start with. However, sustaining the quality and level of activities is a different ball game. For the abstraction that is called business, it requires more than organizational structure, incentives and job descriptions to have a multitude of people work in a concerted manner towards a common objective — it requires a shared vision. It is one, in which everybody has a role to play, everybody clearly understands his or her role, and everyone knows "what is in it for me?"

   Having a shared vision and communicating it well are essential in galvanizing a workforce to come together and stay together, during the process of change.

4. **New Vision, Old Constraints:** Doing the same old thing and expecting different results is the definition of insanity. As much as new tools and a new roadmap empowers people to do things differently, systemic constraints — be it organizational structure or reward system — if not addressed adequately can seriously damage the credibility of the effort and make cynics out of employees.

   Actions to confront big roadblocks early in the deployment phase can do the magic of boosting morale and providing momentum to overcome psychological hurdles throughout the organization.

5. **Show Me the Money :**In all fairness to the shareholders, every initiative should aim at producing measurable economic benefit to a business. Care should be taken to ensure that there is correlation between the metrics used to monitor improvement efforts and the bottom line. This may warrant adjustments to the accounting procedures[2] to enable the identification of reform opportunities drive the right activities and calculate project benefits consistently. In many cases, gains are realized only after a series of project segments (like a step function).

   It is important in such cases to make sure that cost accounting doesn't disincentives the very activities that culminate into a breakthrough.

6. **Success Breeds Success:** Every large initiative can appear potentially daunting and overwhelming if not split into manageable chunks. A process always runs the risk of losing

steam if there are no short-term goals and short-term wins defined. Short-term wins create enthusiasm and confidence amongst people and aid in team building.

This makes the ultimate goal look realizable to participants and helps garner support even from those who have been erstwhile resisting change and sitting on the sidelines.

7. **Leaders Wanted:** More often than not, management is incentives to minimize risk and preserve the status quo. Change on the other hand requires creation of a new state of business, which naturally requires leadership. A paralyzed decision making process (often the biggest impediment to change) is a symptom of having too many managers and not enough leaders.

   Great leaders transform cultures and stimulate breakthroughs. It is vital to have a good number of them on one's side as champions of the renewal process.

3.11 RELEASE MANAGEMENT

Release management is a demanding operation. The goal of release management is to preserve the integrity and availability of production systems while deploying new software and hardware.

Release management defines the mechanisms of building and releasing software, and is included as a component of the Service Support Set in ITIL. The practice of Release Management continues to evolve while being applied to complex distributed software services such as in the SOA realm.

Release Management is proactive technical support focused on the planning and preparation of new services. Some of the benefits are:

- The opportunity to plan expenditure and resource requirements in advance.
- A structured approach to rolling out all new software or hardware, which are efficient and effective.
- Changes to software are 'bundled' together for one release, which minimises the impact of changes on users.
- Testing before rollout, which minimises incidents affecting users and requires less reactive support.

The need therefore exists for dedicated resources to oversee the integration and flow of development, testing, deployment and support of these systems. Although project managers have done this in the past, they generally are more concerned with high-level, "grand design" aspects of a project or application, and so often do not have time to oversee some of the more technical or day-to-day aspects. Release Managers (aka "RMs") address this need. They must have a general knowledge of every aspect of the Software Development Lifecycle (SDLC), various applicable operating systems and software application or platforms, as well as various business functions and perspectives

3.11.1 Introduction

The goal of release management is to protect the live environment. Release management controls the release of new configuration items into that environment.

This can apply to software and hardware. The process is more than creating a new version or update of a program. When a new release is needed there are various steps to follow. Gathering the requirements and gathering the dependencies with the existing components must be checked out in advance. After that a new version can be built, tested and the release can be prepared. Finally the release that is brought to the operations environment consists of a software file ready to be installed, complete with manuals. The company itself also saves the design and testing documents. A release rollback plan is also available on standby to safeguard against surprises during the release, or non-acceptance by the end users.

Several processes are included under the umbrella of release management:

- Planning software and hardware releases
- Testing releases
- Developing software distribution procedures
- Coordinating communications and training about releases

Release management is the bridge that moves assets from development into production.

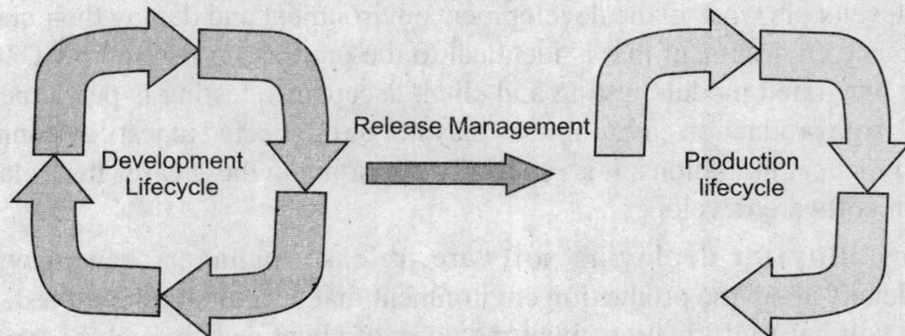

Fig.3.4: Release management is the bridge between two high-level IT life cycles: development and production.

3.11.2 Planning Releases

Planning releases is often the most time-consuming area of release management because there are so many factors that must be taken into consideration. For example, when deploying a new sales support system, the release managers must address:

- How to distribute client software to all current users
- How to migrate data from the current applications database to the new database with minimal disruption to database access
- How to verify the correct migration of data
- How to uninstall and decommission the applications replaced by the new system
- Verifying all change control approval are secured

Each of these issues breaks down into a series of more granular tasks. Consider distributing client software. Release managers must account for variations in OSs and patch levels of client devices, the need for administrative rights to update the registry if software is installed, and the possibility of conflicts or missing software on clients.

3.11.3 Testing and Verifying Releases

Release managers can play an important part in the testing phase of the software development life cycle; the key areas for testing and verification are:

- Software testing
- Data migration testing
- Integration testing

In each case, the testing process should constitute the final test and primary verification that the newly deployed applications operate as expected in the production environment.

3.11.4 Software Testing

It goes without saying that software should be thoroughly tested before it is released. In the ideal world, software developers work in the development environment and deploy their code to a testing and quality assurance environment that is identical to the production environment. It is in the test environment that integrated module testing and client acceptance testing is performed. This is not always possible. Large production environments may not be duplicated in test environments because of cost and other practical limitations. It is especially important in these cases that release managers work closely with software developers.

With responsibility for deploying software, release managers can provide valuable implementation details about the production environment that developers should test. For example, release managers will have information about the types of client devices and the types of network connectivity supported as well as other applications that may coexist with the system under development. Release managers may need to address data migration issues as well.

3.11.5 Data Migration Testing

In addition to supporting software developers on application testing and quality assurance processes, release managers may also have to support database administrators who are responsible for migrating data between applications. When the release of a new application entails shutting down one system, exporting data, transforming it to a new data model, and importing it into the new system, release managers will share responsibility for ensuring the data is extracted, transformed, and loaded correctly. Again, this process should be thoroughly tested prior to release, but realistic data loads are not always possible in test environments.

3.11.6 Integration Testing

Integration testing is the process of testing the flow of processing across different applications that support an operation. For example, an order processing system may send data to business partners' order fulfillment system, which then sends data to a billing system and an inventory management system. Certainly these would have been tested prior to deployment, but real-world conditions can vary and uncommon events can cause problems. For example, spikes in network traffic can increase the number of server response timeouts forcing an unacceptable number of transactions to rollback. In this case, it is not that the systems have a bug that is disrupting operations, but that the expected QoS levels are not maintained. Testing and verifying software functions, data migration, and integrated services can be easily overlooked as "someone else's job," but release managers have to share some of this responsibility.

3.12 SOFTWARE DISTRIBUTIONS

Software distribution entails several planning steps. At the aggregate level, release managers must determine whether a phased release is warranted, and if so, which users will be included in each phase. Phases can be based on several characteristics, including:

- Organizational unit
- Geographic distribution
- Role within the organization
- Target device

When deploying new software or major upgrades, a pilot group often receives the software first. This deployment method limits the risks associated with the release. (Even with extensive testing and evaluation, unexpected complications can occur—especially with end users' response to a new application).

When distributing software, several factors must be considered:

- Will all clients receive the same version of the application? Slightly different versions may be required for Windows 2000 (Win2K) clients and Windows XP clients.
- Will all clients receive the same set of modules? If a new business intelligence application is to be deployed, power users may need full functionality of an ad hoc query tool and analysis application, while managers and executives may require only summary reports and basic drill-down capability.
- How will installation recover from errors or failure? Downloads can fail and need to be restarted. There may be a power failure during the installation process. Disk drives can run out of space. In some cases, the process can restart without administrator intervention (for example, when the power is restored) but not in other cases (such as when disk space must be freed).
- How will the installation be verified? Depending on the regulations and policies governing IT operations, differing levels or verification may be required. At the very least, the CMDB must be updated with basic information about the changes.

Software distribution is the heart of release management, but the ancillary process of communication and training are also important.

3.13 COMMUNICATIONS AND TRAINING

The goal of communication in release management is to make clear to all stakeholders the schedule and impact of releases. This is the responsibility of release managers.

Training users and support personnel on the released system is not the responsibility of release managers, but both training and release managers should coordinate their activities. When training occurs too far in advance or too late following the release of software, it may be of little use; the users may forget what they are taught or have already learned the basics by the time training occurs.

Release management is a bridge from project-oriented software development and application selection to production operations. Although testing can be a well-defined and well-executed part of the development life cycle, release management still maintains a level of testing and verification responsibilities. In addition, the core operations of planning, software distribution, and communications constitute the bulk of what is generally considered release management.

3.14 CHALLENGES FOR RELEASE MANAGEMENT

Many new challenges have arisen in recent years. Software may be developed by geographically dispersed teams, and development may be distributed amongst fragmented teams and even across different companies. Designers must take pre-existing components into account, and the dependencies between them, especially with geographically dispersed development teams. Documentation must describe the software accurately. One of the most important aspects of this is the documentation of interdependencies with other systems. Locating, receiving and tracing various components can result in errors.

3.15 BENEFITS OF RELEASE MANAGEMENT

Improvements are necessary within software to keep up with requirements, bugs and technology. When one uses release management, a structured process, several benefits can be found over ad hoc programming of improvements. Release management:

- Gives the possibility to plan resource requirements in advance
- Gives a structured approach, leading to an efficient and effective process
- Changes are bundled together in a release, minimizing the impact on the user
- Helps to verify correct usability and functionality before release by testing
- Provides version control and central storage, which ensures correct version use.

3.16 RELEASE MANAGER

The need exists for a resource to oversee the development, testing, deployment, and support of these systems. This resource must have a general knowledge of every aspect of the software development lifecycle, various operating systems and software application platforms, together with an understanding of the different business functions and perspectives. Release Management addresses this need.

A Release Manager is:

- Facilitator – serves as a liaison between varying business units to guarantee smooth and timely delivery of software products or updates.
- Gatekeeper – "holds the keys" to production systems/applications and takes responsibility for their implementations.
- Server Application Support Engineer – help troubleshoot problems with an application (although not typically at a code level).
- Coordinator – utilized to coordinate disparate source trees, projects, teams and components.

Some of the challenges facing a Software Release Manager include the management of:

- Software Defects
- Issues
- Risks
- Software Change Requests
- New Development Requests (additional features and functions)
- Deployment and Packaging
- New Development Tasks
- Organizational Politics

As illustrated in the preceding paragraphs Release Management is not a turnkey process; it relies upon and feeds other processes. Though some organizations spend significant efforts building a Release Management process from scratch, others find more success in leveraging what tasks and abilities they already have and merely redirecting and formalizing them.

In getting your arms around Release Management, start with identifying your goals and ranking their priority. An example might be:

1. A High quality Releases
2. Repeatable process for deploying Releases
3. Quick and accurate Release builds
4. Cost-effective Releases

The goals above are not much different than those you may give to a construction contractor for a construction project. Keep the rule of 2 in mind "You have three attributes to choose from for your project Quick, Cheap and Quality." You can choose any two in regards to Release Management, choosing all three will not yield good results.

Embarking on a Release Management project is not for the faint of heart. Failing to find a dependable project sponsor will be your ticket to defeat. If you find that you do not have any Subject Matter Experts (SME) in the field of Release Management this is not the time to go it alone. Anyone with an ITIL background helping with Release issues should also be able to demonstrate previous experience with the Software Development Life Cycle, QA disciplines, or Software Configuration.

Release management is a software engineering process intended to oversee the development, testing, deployment and support of software releases. The practice of release management combines the general business emphasis of traditional project management with a detailed technical knowledge of the systems development lifecycle (SDLC) and IT Infrastructure Library (ITIL) practices.

Release management usually begins in the development cycle with requests for changes or new features. If the request is approved, the new release is planned and designed. The new design enters the testing or quality assurance phase, in which the release is built, reviewed, tested and tweaked until it is ultimately accepted as a release candidate. The release then enters the deployment phase, where it is implemented and made available. Once deployed, the release enters a support phase, where bug reports and other issues are collected; this leads to new requests for changes, and the cycle starts all over again.

3.17 SUMMARY

- Service support is about responding to change. The needs of users change. Configurations change. Unexpected events occur. The specific details of these changes will vary, but how systems managers' respond should not.
- The objective of automated configuration management is twofold. First, it is to obtain and maintain information about the state of devices and applications deployed throughout the IT infrastructure. The second objective is to support multiple IT operations, especially service support.
- Automated configuration management is a mechanism that supports all parts of service support, not just traditional configuration management. This mechanism should not be confused with early configuration management tools that provided limited information and provide little support for related service support operations.
- Data is gathered from devices using agents, or applications that collect information locally and transmit it to a central repository. These agents should be relatively lightweight and autonomous; once installed and configured, they should require little systems manager intervention.
- A centralized data repository for configuration management is one that supports multiple functions related to service delivery, including managing configurations, which, in turn, support both service delivery and security enforcement.
- Information retrieval sounds trivial — you simply want to display data that is stored in a database. What is not trivial is precisely specifying what data it is that you want displayed.
- Configuration management is the process of controlling changes to device configurations in an IT environment.

- The traditional software configuration management (SCM) process is looked upon as the best solution to handling changes in software projects. It identifies the functional and physical attributes of software at various points in time, and performs systematic control of changes to the identified attributes for the purpose of maintaining software integrity and traceability throughout the software development life cycle.
- software configuration management (SCM) is the task of tracking and controlling changes in the software. Configuration management practices include revision control and the establishment of baselines.
- Network configuration management (NCM) is the process of organizing and maintaining information about all the components of a computer network. When a network needs repair, modification, expansion or upgrading, the administrator refers to the network configuration management database to determine the best course of action. T
- Incident Management (IM) is the way that the Service Desk puts out the 'daily fires'. An 'Incident' is any event which is not part of the standard operation of the service and which causes, or may cause, an interruption or a reduction of the quality of the service.
- The objective of Incident Management is to restore normal operations as quickly as possible with the least possible impact on either the business or the user, at a cost-effective price.
- The Problem Management System has been established to capture and report on encountered problems. It employs the APRIORI Problem Management System product from Answer Systems, Inc. as a front-end and problem repository.
- The Problem Management System is used to record problem events, assign them to a resolve, and track problems until they are successfully resolved. If problems are of a high priority, or outstanding beyond an acceptable period of time, then the problem Management System will escalate the problem in priority.
- Change management is the process of controlling modifications to configuration items so as to minimize incidents that disrupt normal operations.

3.18 REVIEW QUESTIONS

1. Discuss the Service Delivery Process and how it is implemented.
2. Discuss the Service Level Management and how it is different from Financial Management.
3. Write short notes on the followings
   I. Service Management
   II. Capacity Management
   III. Availability Management
4. Discuss the Service Support Process.
5. Discuss the Configuration Management and explain different types of configuration management.

6. Discuss the Incident Management and explain its advantages and disadvantages.
7. Write short notes on the following:
   I. Problem Management
   II. Change Management
   III. Release Management.

CHAPTER 4

Storage Management

4.1 STORAGE MANAGEMENT

With the explosive growth of data, increasingly complex storage infrastructures, and shrinking IT budgets, storage management is a major issue today for the IT community. Complexity challenges include:

- Learning disparate storage management tools from multiple vendors with different interfaces to manage different classes of storage.
- Escalating capital and operating costs to manage storage.
- Coping with new issues when implementing a virtual storage infrastructure to complement server virtualization.
- Ability to provision storage across the enterprise in a heterogeneous storage environment.
- Managing a disaster recovery plan, whether local or remote data backup and replication, without draining IT and server resources.
- Application disruption, data migration time and expenses when adding storage or replacing technology. Managing a heterogeneous storage environment does not have to be difficult or expensive.

In an information environment, an organization's success is tightly coupled to its ability to store and manage information. Storage systems provide a critical part of an organization's network infrastructure. With the amount of data growing at an incredible rate, your storage strategy must keep pace. In designing a storage strategy for your organization, you must select the right technology for your primary storage system, implement solid backup procedures and ensure ongoing management of the system.

This chapter explores the critical issues related to data storage in a network and will guide you through the many options available for storage, whether yours is a small-scale departmental LAN or a massively large enterprisewide network. The available technologies differ in terms of capacity, performance, cost and reliability. The network architect's job involves selecting the right combination of hardware and software options that will meet the data storage needs of the organization.

4.2 THE NEED FOR STORAGE

A computer's main memory holds active programs, data and computational results. The computer's efficient operation depends on data held in memory being available in a few nanoseconds. A computer's main memory uses Dynamic RAM (DRAM): It stores data and provides almost instantaneous access to that data, but is limited in and is gone once the computer is turned off.

Permanent storage holds the data and software that must be preserved even when the computer is powered down. Permanent storage needs can be immense. An organization's library of software applications can easily exceed many gigabytes, and the quantity of data can range in the terabytes. Financial systems, customer databases, electronic documents, bitmap images, digital sound and video are but some examples of the data on which organizations rely. A key part of the network infrastructure involves the hardware and software that stores the organization's ever-growing data.

In designing a data storage strategy for an organization's network, the stakes are extremely high. The data stored on the network is a vital resource that cannot be re-created. Give care to provide adequate capacity, fast performance and reliable access, but at all means never allow data loss.

This chapter focuses on the hardware and software technologies that directly relate to data storage itself. We will not attempt to cover the technologies for providing access to storage on a network and will not argue the nuances of the competing network operating systems and network communications issues. Our concern lies in the hardware and software solutions that become the building blocks of a comprehensive data storage strategy.

4.3 STORAGE STRATEGY DESIGN ISSUES

As you construct a storage system, keep the following goals in mind:

- Prevent data loss
- Offer adequate capacity that can easy scale as storage needs grow
- Provide fast access to data without interruptions
- Be prepared for equipment failures
- Use cost-effective technologies

4.3.1 Data Policies

Not all issues that have an impact on an organization's data strategy can be solved with technology. Individuals must follow sound practices with institutional data. Be sure that the users place their data within the supported data structures. Users cannot, for example, store vital data files on the local drives of their computers if the organization's storage strategy assumes that all data resides on network servers. End users are unlikely to perform frequent backups of their data or follow other procedures that ensure that institutional data are secure. An important part of an organization's storage strategy involves training users to trust that the network storage facilities are secure and well-managed.

Part of the design of the storage strategy includes defining what constitutes the supported data environment. Will you support data storage on desktop computers? Or must all institutional data reside on servers? Although it is possible to include desktop computers in the storage strategy to a limited extent, this practice should be generally avoided. Most backup software products will archive the contents of distributed computer hard drives, however, few of the other requirements of a well-managed storage strategy can be met with this approach. In this chapter, we will focus on storage systems designed to be integrated with network servers.

4.3.2 General Considerations

Several factors come into play when selecting storage options. Following is a survey of the basic concerns that will be discussed in detail later in the chapter.

4.3.3 Capacity

Your storage system must be able to handle the appropriate quantity of data. Be aware of the organization's current data storage needs and the expected rates of growth. You cannot plan a storage strategy without detailed knowledge of the quantities s of data involved.

4.3.4 Scalability

The type of storage technology must be well-matched to the overall size of the organization's data needs and must be able to outpace its expected growth. Storage strategies implemented when the organization's network was relatively small often cannot be expanded beyond a certain point. Storage technologies designed for large-scale enterprise networks may be burdensome for a departmental LAN. The storage systems on the network must be designed from the beginning to scale to larger data capacities without major upheavals. Avoid the disruption and costs associated with redeploying a whole new data storage system because you outgrew the previous system. Rather, choose a system that will continue grow as your data needs grow.

4.3.5 Costs

Select the least-costly approach that effectively meets the objectives. Many cost issues must be considered: the initial purchase cost of the hardware; the productivity costs related to network down time; and ongoing hardware and software maintenance, for example. Do not ignore the personnel costs associated with each storage technology option. More complex solutions will demand the time and attention of network administrators, technicians and operators. Simpler approaches should require less ongoing support.

4.3.6 Performance

Storage technologies must be able to deliver information to the user rapidly. Fortunately, many current systems have very high performance capabilities. Designing a storage solution to service a relatively small number of users can be fairly straightforward. But a network with an extremely large user population will challenge the network architect to design a system that can handle an extremely high rate of simultaneous activity and still deliver rapid access.

4.3.7 Reliability

All storage systems rely on parts that will eventually break down. It is possible to develop a data storage environment with enough redundancy to ensure that no interruptions can occur, even if individual components fail or malfunction. Such high-availability comes at a price—both in terms of the cost of the equipment and in the complexity of its operation. Smaller-scale departmental networks may be satisfied with a data system that can potentially fail, provided that it can be restored with little or no data loss within a reasonable time. It is relatively simple and inexpensive to build a storage system that is available 99 percent of the time. Eliminating that last 1 percent or 2 percent of failure possibilities is complex and expensive.

4.3.8 Manageability

Once a storage system has been designed and implemented, the organization must maintain it. Aim for the system with the simplest operational concerns. As systems increase in complexity it becomes increasingly important to be able to monitor their performance, preempt failures and manage storage media with as little effort and interaction as possible. Also, this functionality must come without sacrificing the depth of management available to the administrator.

4.3.9 Cost Analysis

A vital part of designing a storage system involves a careful cost analysis. Be sure to include all cost components. The major ones include:

- Capital outlays for hardware: disk drives, controllers, enclosures, power supplies, jukeboxes, tape drives, CD-ROM drives, etc.
- Media costs: tape cartridges, optical platters
- Any required software: RAID utilities, backup software, HSM software, systems management utilities
- Installation costs: vendor installation costs, internal personnel costs
- Ongoing costs: hardware maintenance, software maintenance and upgrades, product/technical support

The development of the cost analysis may be an iterative process. Design a system with the highest performance and reliability possible with generous capacity in your initial analysis. If this package does not then fit within your budget allotment, then incorporate other lower-cost storage technologies for selected tiers of storage.

4.3.10 Risk Analysis

The security of your organization's data reigns supreme in the design of a storage system. It is important to assess the impact of the possible failure of your organization's storage system. Be sure to consider the following factors:

- Productivity losses. Many, if not most, individuals in the organization will not be able to carry out their normal activities when key components of the technical environment—such as the network storage system—are inoperable.
- Asset recovery costs. When data are lost, the organization must channel resources into its recreation. Recovering data from archives and backups requires effort of technical staff. The re-keying of irrecoverable data can be a massive undertaking. * Loss of active sales. Organizations that depend on their storage environment to support sales may not be able to process financial transactions during periods of failure.
- Loss of customers. Prolonged or frequent failures diminish confidence in an organization by its clients.

It is relatively cheap and easy to construct a storage system that works 98% of the time. Eliminating the last few points of downtime possibilities can double or triple the cost of a storage system. The investment you make toward enhancing reliability operates much like an insurance policy. The financial value of the organization's operation guides the expense that can be justified for reducing the likelihood of downtime and reducing the recovery time from failures.

As you design a storage system, carefully measure the risk of failure for each alternative. Consider a wider range of alternatives. Start with a mental model of a system that initially seems to match your organization, and then work through design changes that both increase and decrease reliability. Finally, weigh the cost implications of the design alternatives against their relative risk factors and the impact of downtime to the organization. No magic formulas apply to risk analysis, but considering all these factors will lead to a solution w ell-matched to your organizations needs.

4.3.11 Capacity Planning

The development of a storage strategy involves planning for the quantity of storage and the level of performance required. Although there are no iron-clad rules for planning the capacity of your storage system, here are some general guidelines.

Measure the amount and significance of current data. Determine the extent of your current data environment. It should not be difficult to measure of the amount of data in use. Look for ways to consolidate and simplify. Look for pockets of data not currently managed in your central storage system that should be. Are there important institutional data files currently being stored on local drives of desktop computers? Do you have departmental servers that have data that needs to be managed in a more secure environment? Work closely with your organization's management to clarify the scope of the project.

Plan for growth. Once you have carefully calculated current data needs, you must predict its growth rates for the next few years. Although historical information about past growth rates may be useful, if your organization is like most, plan for significantly faster data growth in the future than you experienced in the past. Make sure that you are aware of any special projects that units within your organization may be planning for the next few years. New databases, document management systems, archiving and digitizing projects and the like could all have massive implications for your future storage requirements.

Allocate excess capacity. How much excess capacity should you provide in the first year of a new storage system? You should plan for 20 percent to 30 percent reserve capacity for the first year, just to keep the system operating smoothly. You also will want to purchase additional capacity for your anticipated growth for the second and third year of the system. Depending on your growth rates, you will probably size the system for at least double your current needs. The system will need to grow beyond its initial configuration, so make sure that the components needed for expansion are likely to be available in the future.

Expect to expand later. Do not purchase capacity too far in advance. Storage hardware, like other computing components, will most certainly decline in costs over time. You will probably be able to purchase higher-capacity storage units for less cost in future years.

System longevity. What is the lifecycle for the storage system you are designing? Always hedge your bets for your storage system. New technologies constantly arise, and one may come along in the next few years that will offer benefits above the system you are designing today. Keep realistic expectations on how long your storage system will last before its replacement. A five-year life span is typical for these systems.

Tiers of Storage. While the majority of organizations can manage their data with a single media-usually magnetic storage-large data environments may require a tiered approach. It may be impractical to build a system large enough from the highest-performing hardware. If your environment falls into this category, then you will need to analyze the various data sets and determine how much of your system must be managed with high-performance storage and what might be relegated to lower-cost media. An example of a multitiered storage environment would be one with small store of solid state disks, a large set of magnetic disks organized in a RAID structure, a jukebox of optical discs and a tape drive for backups and archives. Budget considerations and performance demands factor into the proportion of storage allocated to each tier. The distribution of data files among a multi tiered storage system can be automated through a genre of software called Hierarchical Storage Management (HSM).

4.4 STORAGE OPTIONS: GENERAL GUIDELINES

A variety of technologies are available for network storage. Each of these hardware and software solutions forms the building b locks from which you will build a comprehensive storage solution. The size of your data environment, the kind of applications you run, the performance you expect, and the level of reliability required and the cost expectations each factor into the picture.

The storage environment will use a hierarchy of technologies. The technologies with the best performance come at the highest cost. Organizations with data sets of a certain scale can build their storage system completely from high-performance hardware. Others have such large data considerations that make it impractical and unaffordable to use all high-performance storage and must therefore place some data on slower and less expensive media. Those that can store completely on high-performance media may still want slow/removable technologies such as tape, so that they store backups of critical data off-site.

The fastest and most expensive storage technology is magnetic disk drives. The capacities of magnetic drives have historically risen faster than their costs, making this technology affordable for an increasingly larger portion of the information storage paradigm. Currently a 9-GB drive can be purchased for around $2,000, yielding a cost of $0.25 per MB. When these drives are combined into arrays, the costs expand to include redundant drives, controller hardware, redundant power supplies, specialized enclosures and management software.

Magneto-optical technologies offer a lower per megabyte cost, if you consider only the media costs. Magnetic discs offer a level of performance just a notch below that of magnetic storage and are popular in environments that have extremely large data sets. Less frequently used data can be transferred from fast/expensive magnetic storage to cheaper/slower optical platters for a more cost-effective storage environment. For this reason, MO technologies are popular in HSM environments. While optical media itself is relatively cheap, its use may involve some fairly expensive hardware. At the very least you will nee d optical drives that cost a few hundred dollars each. In most cases you will also need equipment to manage the optical media. An optical minichanger may cost less than a thousand dollars, but a full-blown optical jukebox that can manage 100 to 500 discs can cost tens of thousands of dollars. Make sure that you factor in the costs of the disc changing hardware and the additional software as you calculate the cost effectiveness of optical technologies.

Magnetic tape stands at the lower end of the storage technology spectrum in terms of performance—it is relatively slow and has a correspondingly low media cost for high capacity. Both magnetic and optical storage allows random access of information on the media. Tape, however, is a serial-access media. This is fine for applications that read and write data files sequentially, such as backup operations. The use of magnetic tape also comes with significant hardware costs, including the purchase of one or more tape drives, SCSI controllers and software. Several varieties of magnetic are available: Digital Audio Tape (DAT) of the 8-mm and 4-mm varieties and Digital Linear Tape (DLT).

4.5 HARDWARE OPTIONS

4.5.1 Magnetic Disk Drives

Magnetic disks offer high-performance permanent storage for computer systems. In general, we consider magnetic disks to offer excellent performance, but at a relatively high cost. Individual disk drives have a long, but finite, life expectancy. As mechanical devices, we have to assume that they can fail at any point. Magnetic drives can be combined into arrays to increase capacity and reliability.

How they work

The storage of data on magnetic disks is one of the most fundamental computer technologies. They use basically the same technology as audio recording—that of changing the magnetic polarity of ferrite particles. With disk drives the ferrite particles are platted onto aluminum platters. These platters are divided into concentric circles of data areas called tracks, and each track is divided into sectors. Drives will have a magneto-resistive head that traverses over the platter as the drive spins to read and write data.

Performance Considerations

The two main performance factors include the sustained data transfer rate and the average response time. The data throughput of the drive largely depends on the rotational speed of the platters. The faster that the drive spins, the faster that blocks of data can be written or read. Currently, drives are available that spin at 5,400 to 10,000 RPM. The average access speed is determined by how quickly the read/write head can find the required data block. The response time of the drive is a function of the quickness of the read/write head. High-performance magnetic drives have average response times of less than 12 milliseconds.

Capacity

The overall capacity of the drive depends on the number of platters, the number of tracks per platter, sectors per track and the overall density of the recording surface. Magnetic drives accommodate a wide range of storage capacity needs. Single drives range from 100 MB to 23 GB. Generally the smallest drive that would be used in a server-class storage system would be 2 GB.

Reliability

The reliability of computer components is measured in mean time between failures (MTBF). As mechanical devices, magnetic drives cannot be expected to last forever. Look for the largest possible MTBF ratings. For a network storage system, do not accept drives with less than 300,000 hours MTBF.

The MTBF ratings provide a relative benchmark for comparing the reliability of equipment. Don't expect this to be a guarantee, however. In most cases the manufacturer calculates the MTBF based on empirical failure data. Theoretical MTBF ratings make a very liberal set of assumptions. Manufactures collect data on component failures, discounting failures that occur through shipping, installation mishandling, and the like to predict the number of hours the equipment should run before it fails. Some vendors also provide an Operational MTBF that includes failures of all types, including DOA's and early-life failures.

Alternatives

Magnetic disks dominate as the primary technology used for permanent data storage. They offer relatively fast performance at moderate cost. Higher performance and higher-cost alternatives include solid-state "disks" that rely on static memory devices rather than magnetic recording technology. Optical technologies offer options for lower-performance, high-capacity data environments.

Magnetic disks require a set of controller circuits to communicate with the host computer. The controller, as its name suggests, manages the basic operation of the disk drive and transfers data from the drive to the computer's operating system. The controller circuits may reside as a separate adapter card, may be integrated on the computer's motherboard, or can be embedded inside the disk itself. The disk drive and the controller must be of the same type. Currently, two types of disk controllers prevail: ATA/IDE and SCSI.

4.5.2 Disk Attachment Technologies

One of the greatest technical issues related to storage hardware concerns the method used to connect the drives to the host computer. As you design a storage environment, don't let this part of the system become a bottleneck. Make sure that the method that you use to attach the storage devices to the server can handle the load. Large storage systems may require faster host adapters or spreading the peripherals across multiple controllers. SCSI and its enhanced variants are the standard for network storage systems. Avoid IDE drives. Fiber Channel attachment has recently emerged as the high-end approach.

ATA/IDE (AT Attachment with Integrated Device Electronics)

These drives are rarely used in network storage systems. This is the simpler approach for attaching magnetic disks to a computer, used primarily for desktop computers. With IDE, most of the electronics needed to control the device are imbedded on the disk itself. No separate controller hardware is required, and many computer motherboards provide connectors for IDE drives. This approach to magnetic drive attachment includes limitations that effectively prevent their use in large-scale network storage systems. In most cases only two IDE drives can be chained together. They deliver data at only about 3 MB per second, though with the newer Extended IDE architecture, the data transfer data increases up to 11 MB per second. Another major limitation is that only one data request at a time can operate on the drive chain, which is not acceptable in a multiuser envrionment. The original IDE specification supports drives up to 504 MB, but Enhanced IDE can now handle up to 8-GB units.

4.5.3 SCSI: The Small Computer Systems Interface

SCSI offers a more flexible environment for interconnecting storage devices with reasonably high performance.

Connection Technology Speed And Expandability		
Technology	**Maximum Data Transfer Speed (per second)**	**Number of Drives per Controller**
SCSI	5 MB	7
Narrow SCSI–2	10 MB	15
Wide SCSI –2	20 MB	15
Ultra SCSI	40 MB	15
Fibre Channel	100 MB	128

Almost all network storage systems use some type of SCSI to attach peripherals to the host computer. Magnetic disks, optical drives, and tape drives all connect to their servers via SCSI host adapters. The SCSI architecture allows multiple devices to be chained together off a single controller. With SCSI, peripherals of differing types can be connected together to form a single bus, with terminating resisters installed on each end. While the original SCSI implementation allowed only seven drives per SCSI bus, newer versions allow more. Each device, counting the SCSI host adapter, on the chain is configured with a Logical Unit address from 0 to 7. SCSI uses a parallel data transmission architecture-the initial implementation deals with 8 bits at a time. Extensions of SCSI increase the width of the data path up to 16 and 32 bits. The maximum data transfer rate in the original SCSI design is about 5 MB per second, a factor of the 5-MHz bus speed. Multiple requests can operate on the SCSI bus simultaneously, allowing a group of devices to work toget her. Enhancements to the original SCSI specification have been developed to yield increased capacities and performance.

SCSI-2

This initial enhancement to SCSI can deliver data up to 10 MB per second with an 8bit data path. This version includes data caching and other performance-enhancing features and extends the number of devices per bus to 15.

Wide Fast SCSI-2

By both increasing the bus speed and increasing the data path to a width of 16 bits, Wide Fast SCSI-2 can yield performance of up to 20 MB per second.

Ultra SCSI

This most recent enhancement to the SCSI architecture increases performance to 40 MB per second. Each of these enhanced SCSI implementations maintain backward compatibility with previous versions.

Fiber Channel

This peripheral connection technology offers a major improvement in data throughput beyond the previous versions of SCSI. Though Fiber Channel was initially designed for fiber optic technology, its use in connecting disk drives generally relies on non-optical connectors. While SCSI uses a bus architecture, Fiber Channel connects devices in a continuous loop. This method of connecting devices is thus called Fiber Channel Arbitrated Loop, or FC - AL, and can yield data transfers at speeds up to100 MB per second. While the connectivity model differs from SCSI, the low-level data access commands and methods are much closely related and is sometimes called SCSI-3 or SCSI -FCP (Fiber Channel Protocol). In addition to faster data transfer rates, fiber channel allows greater distances between peripherals (up to 30 meters) and can connect up to 126 devices. While fiber technology, now in its early stage, costs more than traditional SCSI attachment, its costs are expected to drop to a competitive level.

FC-AL, with its major advancement in performance and reliability, enables new opportunities for storage architectures. The ability to interconnect more devices and to deliver data at dramatically faster speeds facilitates the creation of much larger storage arrays than were previously possible. Through FC-AL these storage arrays can be defined as network devices, associated with multiple servers. Network-attached storage devices can be created that allow computers to access data at extremely high-speeds, completely bypassing servers. Applications that require extremely large bandwidth, such as streaming video, would benefit from such an architecture. New models of server clustering are emerging, and the possibilities for high-performance large-large scale storage systems that can be shared on the network in very flexible ways will help shape future of computing.

RAID

In the era of mainframe computing, the primary model of storage involved the use of very large disk drives. This refrigerator-sized Direct Access Storage Devices (DASD) were designed to offer high reliability and availability, but were expensive to own and operate. The magnetic drives designed for PCs offered lower capacities, and lacked the reliability of mainframe DASD. Beginning in the late 1980s, methods were developed for combining a number of smaller inexpensive disks to form logical storage units that exceeded the capacities and reliability of large disk structures. These multidisk arrays could be constructed for a fraction of the cost of the mainframe disk systems.

We know that basic magnetic disk drives can offer reasonable amounts of storage with high performance. The strengths of magnetic drives can be expanded through the use of RAID technologies. RAID, or Redundant Arrays of Inexpensive (or Independent) Disks, combines multiple magnetic disk devices in ways that increase capacity, reliability and performance.

The initial specification for RAID was developed at the University of California at Berkeley. This proposal defined five RAID levels, and compared the reliability performance and capacity of these systems to the large-scale mainframe disks commonly used at that time.

To implement RAID, additional intelligence must be introduced into the storage system. In the simple disk storage system data are written and read directly from a single disk. But with RAID, a more complex process is involved in reading and writing data. The management of the disk array can be handled either through software or through hardware in the form of specialized disk controllers. For RAID levels that involve the generation of parity information, software solutions may be less expensive, but require more system resources on the host. Hardware-based RAID implementations require expensive special-purpose disk controllers, but offer better performance and reliability.

The implementation of RAID involves a trade-off in that the the use of more storage devices doesn't directly scale the net usable storage capacity. (Some amount of space is used for redundancy of data.) Consequently, the relative hardware cost of a RAID system depends on the usable storage capacity percentage. For configurations that require complete redundancy, the usable storage capacity is only 50 percent of the gross hardware capacity. Some RAID options may offer 80 percent to 95 percent efficiency of the hardware's capacity.

Many RAID storage systems use a special controller that manages the distribution of data on the disks. The RAID controller can connect to the host computer as another SCSI device or it can connect directly into the bus of the host computer. Since most computer system busses operate at faster speeds than SCSI allows, expect some performance gains from controllers that connect this way. SCSI-attached RAID controllers are usually easier to configure, making the entire RAID system appear as a single SCSI device.

Another concern in RAID systems concerns data caching. Earlier RAID systems had performance problems, which have been largely been overcome in more modern systems through caching. Many RAID controllers offer a large data cache that allows the RAID subsystem to operate with significantly better performance. The main disadvantage concerns f ailure. If the storage system fails—especially if the failure is in the controller— there must be a way to save the data in the memory cache and get it written to disk. Otherwise, data lost is irretrievably lost.

RAID-based storage systems almost always rely on SCSI disks. These disks are widely used in both Unix and PC servers, both in conventional storage configurations and in RAID.

The use of RAID usually introduces a penalty in performance. The management of parity information requires additional processing. Some improvement in the performance of RAID systems can be gained through caching.

The official classification of storage devices is maintained by the RAB (Raid Advisory Board) established in 1992. Vendors of storage devices may submit their equipment to the RAB for classification for a fee. Once classified, the vendor may display a logo corresponding to their assigned RAID or EDAP (Extended Data Availability and Protection) level. (http://www.raid-advisory.com/index.html)

Below are the different options, or levels, available to implement RAID.

Level 0

Simple data striping. This storage strategy involves combining multiple drives into a single logical data volume. The data are then interleaved among multiple disks. Having multiple drives service data yields an increase in performance over nonarray disks, because the data is being written in parallel. Applications that use data sets larger than a physical disk benefit from the ability to create larger disk volumes through RAID 0. This RAID strategy offers no increased benefits for data availability over conventional disk storage.

Level 1

Data mirroring. This level of RAID involves a redundancy of storage devices. With RAID Level 1, data are written to two separate disk drives. If one fails, the other is available to service data requests. This method provides excellent data protection, but doubles the number of devices required for storage needs.

Level 3

This method involv es data striping as does Level 0, but it also uses an additional device that is dedicated to holding parity information that can be used to reconstruct the data stored on any of the other storage devices. RAID Level 3 stripes each byte of information across multiple disks and places a parity bit on an additional disk. In the event of the failure of one of the data disks, the information on the parity disk can be used to recreate the data on the failed drive onto a replacement drive. The cost of RAID 3 involves the purchase of one additional drive for each storage system beyond that needed for data only, plus the cost of the software that manages the RAID array. The overhead of RAID 3 introduces a performance penalty that make it unsuitable for applications with very intensive I/O activity, such as online transaction processing systems.

Level 5

This disk configuration also uses parity to reconstruct data on a failed drive, but distributes the parity information on the data drives. This distributed parity approach offers better performance than RAID 3, reduces the extra hardware needed and still offers redundancy. This implementation of RAID still suffers somewhat in disk writes compared to RAID 0, but is generally considered the fastest reliable RAID option.

Level 6

This RAID level was not part of the original Berkeley specification. While RAID 3 and 5 can handle the failure of a single disk in the array, they still are vulnerable to multiple failures. If two drives fail simultaneously or if a second drive fails during a data rebuild, the entire data structure is lost and will have to be restored from backups. Level 6 RAID was designed to accommodate the loss of two drives simultaneously or can handle a disk failure during a data rebuild after an initial failure. This additional failure resistance is accomplished through multiple parity devices, but the additional overhead introduces additional performance loss.

Other RAID Levels

Some vendors have extended the R AID Levels to higher numbers, indicating a combination of disk options. For example, RAID Level 30, would represent a system that combines Level 3 and duplexing. The use of these higher numbers is not supported by the RAB.

EDAP

While storage systems have historically been classified by RAID Levels, RAB has begun using new terminology to describe storage reliability. RAID describes particular technical implementations of data storage that protect the storage system from a disk failure. But may other components comprise the storage system. Disk controllers and their on-board cache memory can also fail and lead to data loss and unavailability. The language that describes highly reliable storage systems must encompass the entire storage system, not just the disks. For this reason, the RAB now emphasizes Extended Data Availability and Protection (EDAP), which considers all components of the storage system. There are three general EDAP levels:

The RAB classifies a device as Failure Resistant Disk System (FRDS) to systems which provide protection against the loss of data during a disk failure and maintain access to the data during the disk failure. The disk mirroring and parity RAID 3, 5 and 6 accomplish this degree of EDAP.

A Failure Tolerant Disk System (FTDS) represents a greater degree of EDAP capability, and applies to systems that can protect data and maintain access to data during the failure of any component of the storage system-disks, controllers, and power supplies. To achieve FTDS capability, systems must be equipped with redundancy on a wider scope than just the disks. FTDS-compliant storage systems will have redundant power supplies, redundant disk controllers, multiple cooling fans, and advanced environmental monitoring and control. Such systems take into account the relatively high percentage of failures that occur through non-disk failures.

The highest level of EDAP compatibility, Disaster Tolerant Disk System (DTDS), applies to systems that protect data in the ev ent of a complete failure of equipment in a given geographic area or "zone." Systems that meet this level of protection will have data distributed in separate physical locations.

When selecting a RAID system look for some of these features.

- Hot-swappable components. To maintain high-availability, the ability to replace components without shutting down the server is critical.
- Redundant power. Power supply failures comprise a fairly high percentage of storage system failures. Look for systems that include redundant power sources.
- Temperature controls. Excessive heat can lead to storage system failures. Not only should you consider redundant cooling fans, but you should also look for systems that monitor operating temperature and automatically generate alerts. An overheated unit can lead to multiple simultaneous failures—the worst possible scenario for a storage system.

4.6 OPTICAL STORAGE

Optical storage technologies can play a part in an organization's storage strategy. They offer a lower-cost alternative to magnetic disks for extremely large data sets. Magnetic disks offer significantly higher performance, and their costs per storage unit consistently decline. But for extremely large storage environments, it becomes impractical to rely solely on magnetic disks. Optical technologies, as removable media, can offer a lower cost solution for large-scale data.

Optical media come in several flavors-MO, Phase Change and CD-Recordable. Each of these different variations offer differences in cost, performance, capacity and number of times the media can be rewritten.

4.7 MEDIA MANAGEMENT

You will need to select a process for managing your optical discs. All the optical technologies involve discs of removable media. Cost efficiency comes through the use of multiple media units per drive—contrasting to magnetic drives which have fixed media. Several options prevail for handling the removable media.

Manual operation. If you expect to have only a few op tical platters, then you might use one or more basic optical drives and change media manually. This option suits only environments that use magnetic media for archiving data for safekeeping. If your volume of data is small enough that it fits on one or two platters that can be left in the drive constantly, you should probably consider sticking with magnetic drives.

Optical disc changers. These devices manage optical discs, storing the disks in cartridges or magazines and loading them into a drive when needed. A minichanger might handle a dozen platters or less, and jukeboxes will manage hundreds. The number of optical discs that can be mounted at a time corresponds to the number of optical drives imbedded in a jukebox or minichanger. The jukebox can house a large storehouse of discs, mounting discs on demand for users and applications.

The structure of an optical disc changer includes one or more optical drives, a set of slots for storing discs and a robotic mechanism that selects and loads discs into a drive. Optical disc changers store and manage a large number of discs, but include a limited number of drives. The number of embedded drives defines the number of discs that can be read simultaneously. A large capacity optical disc changer, for example, would hold 150 optical discs and include four internal optical drives. Such a unit would allow any four of the 140 discs to be accessed by users on the network simultaneously.

The optical jukebox uses a robotic mechanism to transfer discs from their standby location to the drives. The changer locates the desired disc and loads it into an available drive and returns it once the data request is satisfied. Expect the optical disc changers to find and mount an optical disc in about five seconds.

4.7.1 Typical Applications

Optical technologies fit within a storage environments that include requirements for large data sets, relatively modest performance and a low cost per storage unit costs. Consider optical media for the part of your storage environment that requires "near-online" access. Most implementations of optical technologies involve hardware that requires a few seconds to mount the disc into a drive, and the data transfer rates are slower than magnetic drives. Rarely would an organization use optical technologies for their primary storage environment.

Organizations that implement Hierarchical Storage Management (see below) typically use optical media to off-load data from their primary storage system. Other applications for optical media include those that involve large document or image libraries. An organization might digitize a large collection of documents, for example, and store the images on optical discs, which would be called up out of a jukebox as needed.

Data archiving often involves optical technologies. Information that has reached its final [illegible] may be deposited on WORM discs to ensure that no further alterations occur.

4.7.2 Media Options

Optical storage comes in several varieties. CD-ROM/Recordable (CD-R) and Write Once Read Many (WORM), support only a single write to the media. Other optical media, such as those using magneto optical and phase change technologies allow data to be re-written multiple times. CD-ROM, a read-only media, fits into the storage strategy for data or software distribution.

MO (Magneto Optical)

One of the most popular optical technologies uses the magneto optical process. Magneto optical drives use both magnets and lasers to read and write data. To write a bit of data, the laser first heats a spot on the disc to its Curie point (the temperature at which a material looses its magnetic properties) and then a magnet changes its polarity. The process of writing data takes two passes. During the first pass the laser is turned on to high power and the magnet is set to change all points to magnetic north, or zeros. On the second pass the laser is set to fire on only for the points to be set as one, or magnetic south . During this second pass the magnet is set to constant south polarity. For reading data, the laser fires at lower power. Differences in polarity cause slight differences in angular deflection, called the Kerr effect, causing the points to be read as ones or zeros.

Phase Change

The other multiple-write process, called phase change, writes data with a single pass. Phase change drives use only lasers and write in a single pass. Both methods offer similar performance for reading data.

WORM

Write Once Ready Many drives allow data to be written to a disk only once. This type of technology works well for those who rely on optical media for data archiving. CD-ROM/Recordable, one of several WORM implementations, employs a purely optical process. A laser fires at high power to heat microscopic crystals imbeded in the media. Differences in reflectivity cause each spot to register as a one or a zero. The same laser fires at low power to read data.

CD-ROM

CD-ROM fits into a storage strategy for distribution of prepared data. Organizations may purchase data that is delivered on this media, or they may master and produce CD-ROMs internally. While the equipment for creating CD-ROMs is fairly expensive, drives for reading this media are quite inexpensive and each new generation of CD-ROM drives offers remarkable improvements in performance. You can now purchase 10X or 12X drives that offer very impressive data throughput abilities. A number of products are available that provide shared network access to CD-ROM discs.

4.7.3 Solid State Disks (SSD)

If you must store data with extremely fast performance, you might consider Solid State Disks. These devices, not really disks at all, use large arrays of DRAM to store data. Since no mechanical limitations apply, SSDs can offer incredible performance-almost instantaneous writing and reading of data. Expect response times of at least 40 times that of magnetic disks. SSD's emulate SCSI magnetic disks. They use the same ca bles and connectors and appear the host computer's operating system as a conventional SCSI device.

SSD's main challenge concerns the fact that they rely on volatile memory—when the unit loses power the data is lost. To be made nonvolatile, these devices must be equipped to ensure that this can't happen. Most will have battery backup and will have embedded magnetic drives that can receive the data when the unit must be powered down. A nonvolatile SSD can be used for applications that have extremely harsh performance demands, and where a finite number of files can be identified that require this performance boost. It would be completely impractical to construct a disk storage system completely from SSD.

Volatile devices without data preservation safeguards are available, but must be used only with applications that do not involve critical data. Some applications, for example, might need extremely fast temporary storage for intermediate results sets or indexes. Make sure not to use volatile SSD with data that cannot be easily reconstructed.

The performance advantage of SSD comes at a price. You will only use this storage technology if you need a storage tier of extremely fast performance. Plan to pay $65 per megabyte for a large-scale system (950 MB) or $80 for a smaller system (132 MB). Few organizations have applications that justify this level of expense for high-performance storage.

4.8 HARDWARE SCOREBOARD

4.8.1 Single Magnetic Drive

A single drive connects to a single controller in a network server.

- **Pros:** Inexpensive, simple to manage
- **Cons:** Limited capacity
  Single drive or controller failure causes system unavailability and possible data loss
- **Best suited for:** small departmental networks.
- **Tips:** Perform frequent backups, use SCSI drives for expandability, consider implementing mirrored drives or RAID.

4.8.2 Multiple Magnetic Drives

Several drives conne ct to a single controller in a network server.

- **Pros:** Inexpensive, simple to manage
- **Cons:** Moderate capacity
  Single drive or controller failure causes system unavailability and possible data loss
- **Best suited for:** departmental networks
- **Tips:** Perform frequent backups, use SCSI drives for expandability, consider implementing mirrored drives or RAID

4.8.3 Mirrored Drives (or RAID Level 1)

All data are written to two separate magnetic drives.

- **Pros:** High failure tolerance. In the event of a failure, the storage system relies on the remaining functional drive set. Performance is about the same as nonmirrored system
- **Cons:** Expensive-mirroring doubles the number of drives required for data storage. Vulnerable to multiple simultaneous failures. A controller failure may cause system unavailability

- **Best suited for:** Networks with relatively small data sets that require high performance
- **Tips:** Consider duplexed drives for increased reliability or RAID to decrease the number of drives

4.8.4 Duplexed Drives

All data are written to two separate magnetic drives that connect to separate controllers

- **Pros:** High failure tolerance. In the event of a failure, the storage system relies on the remaining functional drive set. Performance is about the same as nonmirrored system
- **Cons:** Expensive. Duplexing doubles the number of drives required for data storage. Vulnerable to multiple simultaneous failures.
- **Best suited for:** Networks with relatively small data sets that require high performance
- **Tips:** Consider RAID to decrease the number of drives, though this might result in a slight performance penalty. Use hot-swappable components to recover from failures without scheduled downtime

4.8.4.1 RAID Level 0

Data stripped across multiple drives

- **Pros:** Increased capacity with high performance. Efficient use of disk drives—all drives used for active storage
- **Cons:** No increased resistance to failure. Single drive or controller failure can result in system unavailability or data loss.
- **Best suited for:** Large data sets that demand high performance storage
- **Tips:** Consider implementing Parity RAID or mirroring the drives

4.8.4.2 RAID Level 3

Data striping with a dedicated parity drive

- **Pros:** High failure tolerance. In the event of a failure the storage system can rely on the parity drive. After the replacement of the failed drive, the data can be automatically regenerated. If the parity drive fails, the parity information can be reconstructed
- **Cons:** The calculation of the parity information introduces a performance loss. Even more performance degradation can occur during and after a failure.
- **Best suited for:** Environments that require high availability
- **Tips:** Use hot-swappable components in the storage system

4.8.4.3 RAID Level 5

Data striping with distributed parity

- **Pros:** High failure tolerance. In the event of a failure the storage system can rely on the parity drive. After the replacement of the failed drive, the data can be automatically regenerated. If the parity drive fails, the parity information can be reconstructed

- **Cons:** The calculation of the parity information introduces a performance loss. Even more performance degradation can occur during and after a failure.
- **Best suited for:** Environments that require high availability
- **Tips:** Use hot-swappable components in the storage system

4.9 BACKUP STRATEGIES

No storage system can be guaranteed never to fail. We learned that even though most RAID systems can withstand the loss of a single drive, multiple simultaneous failures can result in complete data loss. Even though you have implemented the most failure resistant storage system available, you must also be prepared for both minor and catastrophic failures. Storage systems also fall prey to human failures. Users will inevitably accidentally delete a file or directory and you will be expected to recover it.

Most organizations cannot even to begin to calculate the costs of data loss. If your company trusts its data to your network, then you must guarantee that you can preserve it under all circumstances.

Your storage system must include a solid backup strategy. If your primary storage system fails, then you must be able to repair it and restore all data back to its original state.

The most common backup strategy involves routinely copying data from your primary storage system to a slower, less-expensive medium. While most organizations use magnetic tape, other possibilities include the various optical storage technologies.

4.9.1 Full Backup

At selected intervals, you will need to make a full and complete backup of your storage system. This is your starting point if you must rebuild your data from scratch. In cases of catastrophic system failure where all data is lost or corrupted, you may need to reinitialize your storage devices and copy all data from your most recent backup set.

4.9.2 Incremental Backup

Storage strategies also usually include incremental backups. It may not be practical to perform a full backup every day. You will want to archive all the files added or changed since the last full backup as frequently as possible. Two approaches are possible here. You might want to catch all the files modified each day in an incremental backup run. If you must rebuild your data, you would put restore the last full backup plus each of the incremental runs. Alternately, you could set your incremental backups to copy all new and modified files since the last full backup. This way restoring the server will take only two tapes—the last full backup plus the last differential. Whether you use daily or cumulative incremental backups will depend on the volume of new and changed data versus the time available for the backup runs. Media costs may be a minor factor—the cumulative approach will consume more space.

4.9.3 Scheduling Issues

Schedule your backup jobs to run at the most frequent interval possible. Typically, organizations plan full backups at least once a week and incremental backups at least daily. How fast your data changes and the value of the data also come into play. Some shops will need to perform full backups daily and incremental backups several times per day. If your system is basically inactive for some period of time each night, then scheduling backups is a breeze. But most of our lives are more complicated than that. If your system must be available 24x7, then establishing an effective backup schedule can be quite a challenge.

One of the biggest issues in creating a backup strategy involves whether or not backups can be performed while the storage system is active. If you have a run-of-the-mill NetWare server, for example, and most of the data consists of word processing files, spreadsheets, and the like, then you can most likely perform backups during off-peak hours without problem. Here, open files pose the greatest problem. If a user has a file in active use, the backup system may not be able to open it to make a backup. You would expect the backup system to keep track of which files it failed to archive, retry them at a given interval and report any files missed to the system manager, who would archive them manually. Some backup systems have advanced capabilities for automatically archiving open files.

The more difficult problem for backup strategies concerns transactional databases. Here the entire database may be a single file, but with millions of records. In the simplest case, you would close the database and perform the backup. If this is your strategy, you would want to use the fastest backup hardware possible to minimize the time your system must be inactive. Many organizations require constant availability of their online transaction processing systems. Here, the backup system must be able to more directly interact with your database. In some cases the database application can be placed into read-only, or maintenance, mode so that the backup system can get control of the files long enough to archive them.

4.9.4 Gaps of Vulnerability

Disk failures rarely occur immediately after a backup. No matter how frequently you backup your storage system, there will be a gap between the failure and your most recent backup set.

How much data can you really afford to lose? Some operations can risk the potential loss of a day's work, provided that the chances of that actually happening are very small. But many can't afford that level of risk. For organizations with extremely valuable data, you will build as must failure resistance into the primary storage system. The odds of having a data-losing failure in a RAID system are quite small indeed, but possible. You can reduce your gap of potential data loss by performing incremental backups frequently. Incremental backups don't necessarily have to use slow media. One option might involve performing incremental backups to a separate magnetic disk system hourly, and gathering the hourly backups to tape daily. Many online transaction-based systems support journalling. Each transaction not only updates the database, but it also writes the transaction to a log file. If the database must be recreated, you can restore it from the last full backup and replay all the subsequent transactions from the log file.

4.10 MANAGING BACKUPS

The safety of your organization's data depends on backup tasks being performed on schedule. The operation of backup tasks requires a high level of discipline. In general, you should rely on software that automatically schedules backup tasks and not depend on network managers or operators to manually perform them. Modern backup software should be expected to automate almost all aspects of your backup strategy.

4.10.1 Device Management

Expect your backup software to recognize and manage all the devices used in your backup system. If you have multiple tape drives, or tape changers, you should be able to direct the data to the appropriate device and media.

4.10.2 Media Management

Most backup strategies involve many media units—tapes, platters or cartridges. The backup set might include monthly archives, weekly full backups and daily incrementals. Most backup software systems will keep track of the media involved, tell you how to label each unit and specify whic h one to load.

4.10.3 File Management

Advanced backup systems will track the status of each file on the storage system. These systems maintain a database that includes information on when each file was backed up, what tape it is on, and the like. This information is critical for file restorations. If a user accidentally deletes a file, you should be able to find it in the backup system's database and have it tell you which tape includes the most recent version. If a file becomes corrupted, you may be asked to restore an older version.

4.10.4 Error Reporting

Expect the backup system to provide reports on the status of each backup run. Did it run completely? Were there files missed? Were whole server volumes missed? You may want status and error reports printed or sent by e-mail. There may be some errors where you need the system to send a message to your pager or trigger an alarm to an SNMP console.

4.10.5 Error Recovery

When problems occur in a backup operation, some can be recovered from automatically. If files are missed on the initial pass of the backup run, set the system to retry them at the end of the run. If the backup system fails to login to a server, it may automatically create a make-up job to run later.

4.11 BACKUP SOFTWARE PLATFORMS

Where do you expect to run your backup software? Will it run from a workstation on the network or will it operate on a server? There are some low-end solutions where the backup software runs on a client computer, archiving data from servers to a local tape drive. Most of the more advanced systems, however, run on network servers. Backup management requires a high-performance, multitasking environment, with scheduling capabilities. Servers offer these capabilities better than client computers. You will need to ensure that the backup software you choose is compatible with your server platform. Most of the systems available will operate under NetWare, Windows NT and the various flavors of Unix.

4.11.1 Agents

The backup process can be made to operate more efficiently with the cooperation of the target system. It is common for backup systems to use programs called agents which manage the communication between the target system and the backup host. Agents can be used to give the backup host access to workstations on the network so that their local drives can participate in the backup system. You may also need an agent to backup target systems that differ from the platform of your backup host. For example, if your backup host is a NetWare server, you may need an agent on Unix and NT hosts to backup their file systems. Agents can also optimize the performance of backups by taking advantage of the processor on the target system to pump data to the backup server.

4.11.2 Media Options

The primary concerns in selecting a backup media for your storage system involve increasing the volume of data that can be transferred to each tape and boosting performance. The more data that can be placed on tapes reduces the number of tape changes that must occur for each backup session. The speed of the data transfer is especially important for those systems that must be offline for backups. Faster backups mean less time offline, which can make a big difference for the organization's data center operations.

The vast majority of storage systems rely on tape-based backup systems. The two main competing tape technologies are 8 mm Digital Audio Tape (DAT) and Digital Linear Tape (DLT). Through advancements in tape density and compression, 8mm DAT has achieved capacities of up to 24GB per tape and can transfer data at 2.2 MB/Second. Even more recently, Exabyte—the leader in tape backup solutions—has increased its 8mm technology to one that supports 40 GB per tape with 6MB/second sustained throughput. Digital Linear Tape has offered capacity and performance advantages over DAT. In its current form, it can sustain 5MB/second data transfer and store up to 35GB per tape. While 8mm technologies have recently surpassed these measurements, we can expect DLT to make its own improvements and sustain its competitiveness.

Optical technologies such as MO or CD-R may suit some environments. For especially high-performance backups, you may want to use another set of magnetic disks, but this would be an extremely expensive alternative. The relative capacities of each of these media constantly increases, and the cost per MB varies. When calculating the costs, be sure to include the hardware costs as well as the media itself.

4.12 HSM: HIERARCHICAL STORAGE MANAGEMENT

One of the fundamental problems for data storage involves the constantly growing size of the data environment. There comes a point when the cumulative volume of data exceeds the hardware's ability to accommodate it. You can deal with the problem by adding capacity to your storage system or coaxing network users to deleted unneeded files. But such efforts cannot necessarily be sustained indefinitely. Organizations with large-scale storage environments should consider a more advanced storage management system.

One approach to controlling data growth involves automatic file grooming. Many of the advanced backup packages include the ability to automatically remove files that have not been accessed after a prescribed interval. The backup system would ensure that any file removed from the storage system would exist on multiple archive tapes. When users need groomed files, they would be manually restored. While this process may somewhat reduce the files on the network, it may leave users uncertain about the status of their files and involves considerable manual work in restoring files.

Hierarchical Storage Management (HSM) deals with the problem of rapid data growth in a more sophisticated way by automatically transferring data files to secondary and tertiary storage systems. HSM operates completely transparently to the user—files continue to appear in directory listings even if they have been moved. The key to HSM lies in migrating the files that are least likely to be n eeded again. Generally, HSM systems assume that the longer a file is idle, the lower the probability it will be accessed again. The secondary and tertiary storage systems can store infrequently used files at a low cost and free up space on the primary storage system for files in active use. Data may be stored online, near online or offline depending on their frequency of use.

Let's consider a typical HSM implementation. Three levels of storage are available: a RAID system of 100 GB, an optical jukebox and a 8-mm tape system. Once the RAID system reaches a certain threshold of capacity, say 90 percent, the HSM software begins scanning the storage system for files that are candidates for migration. We might specify that any file that has not been touched for at least 90 days can be transferred to secondary storage. The files are written to optical platters in the jukebox and deleted from the RAID system. The HSM system replaces the original file with a stub that occupies little space, but maintains the directory entry. As users browse their directories, they are unaware that any files have been deleted. If a user actually needs to use a file that has been migrated, the HSM software intercepts the request and automatically restores the file to primary storage. The user will notice a delay while the optical disk is selected and mounted in the jukebox and the file is copied back to its original location. The delay should be as little as a few seconds, depending on the size of the file. Some HSM systems can use a tertiary storage option. If the migrated data exceeds the capacity of the secondary storage system, then the data might be migrated down another level. In our example, files that had not been accessed on the optical platters for a year might be deleted and archived to magnetic tape and deleted.

The implementation of HSM involves several hardware and software components. On the hardware level, you will need equipment to manage your secondary storage. In most cases this will be an optical disc ch anger or jukebox. One could use a tape drive with an automatic media changer, but only if long file-restoration times are acceptable. The secondary storage device would connect to the same server as the primary storage system. With most HSM implementations, users do not access the secondary storage directly. The HSM software interacts with the secondary storage to place migrated files back to primary storage when needed. This configuration contrasts with a networked optical jukebox where users would access data directly. In most cases a tertiary storage media such as magnetic tape would be used for an additional level of data migration or to perform backups of data on both the primary and secondary storage systems.

The implementation of HSM requires specialized software. Storage management involves a number of complex tasks. The HSM application software must be tightly integrated into the server's operating system. To operate transparently to end users, the HSM software must manipulate the file system and directory structure to make all files appear to be present, even when some reside elsewhere. Some means must be provided to keep track of the location of all migrated files so that they can be efficiently retrieved when needed again. The HSM software will manage capacity issues for both the primary and secondary storage system. All data must be carefully tracked.

4.13 ACHIEVE DATABASE

An **archive** is a collection of historical records, and the location in which the collection is kept.Archives consist of records which have been selected for permanent or long-term preservation, due to their enduring research value.

1. An archive is a collection of computer files that have been packaged together for backup, to transport to some other location, for saving away from the computer so that more hard disk storage can be made available, or for some other purpose. An archive can include a simple list of files or files organized under a directory or catalog structure (depending on how a particular program supports archiving).

   On personal computers with the Windows operating system, WinZip is a popular program that lets you create an archive (a single file that holds a number of files that you plan to save to another medium or send someone electronically) or extract its files. WinZip also compresses the files that are archived, but compression is not required to create an archive. A WinZip archive has the file name suffix ".zip".

   In Unix-based operating systems, the tar(tape archive) utility can be used to create an archive or extract files from one. On mainframe operating systems such as IBM's MVS and OS/390, procedures for archiving or backing up files are often automated as a daily operation.
2. On Web sites as well as in libraries, an archive is a collection of individual publications that are often cataloged or listed and made accessible in some way. Magazines, journals, and newspapers with Web sites sometimes refer to their back issues as an archive.
3. Web and File Transfer Protocol sites that provide software programs that can be downloaded sometimes refer to the list of downloadable files as an archive or as archives.

   The intricate process of creating and administrating relational Databases and spawned Database-driven Archives is a task that not many Web Development Companies dare to pursue. Our Ecom Solutions expertise allows us to leverage the skills needed to deploy such complex operations successfully at the Enterprise Level. We are available to discuss your Database & Archive needs, and help you implement your Project based on your vision, strategy, and further consultation.

4.14 DATABASE WORKS

When delivering a data-driven Application or Website, our Team has the right understanding and appreciation for the intricacies of Database Design and Development. Ecom Solutions has been writing complex database queries that power high traffic Websites, across all major database vendors: MySQL, MSSQL, Oracle, or Sybase.

Our relational data experts have created many custom Website Search Engines, reporting systems, and tools for import/export, data-mining, and data sanitization. We have also provided DB consultation, and worked with clients to develop data management strategies based on their preferences and following logical processes.

We are accustomed to complex requests for Database Works, are ready to answer your questions, offer consulting, and deploy resources for Database Projects.

4.14.1 Archive Works

Database-driven Archives are one of the key features of the a Website, and can serve as the backbone to bringing income for an Organization. The Archive, or Archive / E-Commerce combination Solutions implemented by EcomSolutions will allow for multi-optional purchasing directly from a Website, will be streamlined with the appropriate transaction forms, and the current Financial Fulfillment Company.

Upon digitizing and converting your data into searchable files, the content and objects will carefully be uploaded and find permanent residence in a Database Server of choice (Relational Database Management System).

The vending of the items contained in the Archive can be managed from a custom designed back-end CMS, will offer detailed information, and will automatically create and avail full reports about transactions, amounts, fees, client account information, and taxes for individual items or packs.

The further customizable set-up can allow for purchasing of individual items, or packages, as per the client's preference. One example of tiered vending of Publication / Magazine issues and articles for a fee can be:

- Purchase Individual Article
- Purchase Article Pack (set amount of articles)
- Purchase Issue
- Purchase Issue Pack (set amount of issues)
- Purchase Individual reviews

- Purchase reviews Pack
- Purchase Individual Book Reviews
- Purchase Donation – and receive free item
- Purchase Gift – receive free item
- Unlimited access to Archive for a specific time period

4.14.2 Database & Archive Works

It is the competency of our client to set prices, time intervals, structure, and itemize the multi-vending packs based on their strategic, marketing, tactical, and financial goals. Our technical ability, flexibility, and expertise will help creating the multi-functional Archive upon the client's preferences and further consultancy.

4.14.3 Timed Archive and Access

A Magazine subscriber - for example, and individuals who purchase Articles, Issues, Reviews, or any combination item packs can have timed access to the Archive. A specific time-frame such as 6 Months or One Year can be implemented before password-secure individual account access to download items expires. If an account holder purchases an 8 Article Pack, for example, they will have access to the Archive for a full calendar year.

4.15 DISASTER RECOVERY

Disaster recovery is the process, policies and procedures related to preparing for recovery or continuation of technology infrastructure critical to an organization after a natural or human-induced disaster. Disaster recovery planning is a subset of a larger process known as business continuity planning and should include planning for resumption of applications, data, hardware, communications (such as networking) and other IT infrastructure. A business continuity plan (BCP) includes planning for non-IT related aspects such as key personnel, facilities, crisis communication and reputation protection, and should refer to the disaster recovery plan (DRP) for IT related infrastructure recovery / continuity.

4.15.1 Introduction

With the increasing importance of information technology for the continuation of business critical functions, combined with a transition to an around-the-clock economy, the importance of protecting an organization's data and IT infrastructure in the event of a disruptive situation has become an increasing and more visible business priority in recent years.

It is estimated that most large companies spend between 2% and 4% of their IT budget on disaster recovery planning, with the aim of avoiding larger losses in the event that the business cannot continue to function due to loss of IT infrastructure and data. Of companies that had a major loss of business data, 43% never reopen, 51% close within two years, and only 6% will survive long-term.

4.15.2 Classification of Disasters

Disaster can be classified in two broad categories. Viz, 1) Natural disasters- Preventing a natural disaster is very difficult, but it is possible to take precautions to avoid losses. These disasters include flood, fire, earthquake, hurricane, etc 2) Man made disasters- These disasters are major reasons for failure. Human error and intervention may be intentional or unintentional which can cause massive failures such as loss of communication and utility. These disasters include accidents, walkouts, sabotage, burglary, virus, intrusion, etc.

4.15.3 Security Holes

Security holes are the vulnerabilities in computing hardware or software. They indirectly invite malicious hackers to work on and exploit them. Security holes are flaws in the network software that allow unintended control within the network. Network components such as PCs and routers can hold these holes in their operating systems. Therefore, the technical details of any system should not be made public unless absolutely necessary. Once security holes are discovered, information about them should be immediately passed to the security professional responsible for the system. On the other hand, this information is often quickly passed to hackers who might want to intercept the network. Security professionals should always work to fix such holes to eliminate a possible attack.

4.15.4 General steps to follow while creating BCP/DRP

1. Identify the scope and boundaries of business continuity plan. First step enables us to define scope of BCP. It provides an idea for limitations and boundaries of plan. It also includes audit and risk analysis reports for institution's assets.
2. Conduct a business impact analysis (BIA). Business impact analysis is study and assessment of financial losses to institution resulting from destructive event as unavailability of important business services.
3. Sell the concept of BCP to upper management and obtain organizational and financial commitment. Convincing senior management to approve BCP/DRP is key task. It is very important for security professional to get approval for plan from upper management to bring it to effect.
4. Each department will need to understand its role in plan and support to maintain it. In case of disaster, each department has to be prepared for the action. To recover and to protect the critical systems each department has to understand the plan follows it accordingly. It is also important to maintain and help in creation of plan for each individual department.
5. The BCP project team must implement the plan. After approval from upper management plan should be maintained and implemented. Implementation team should follow the guidelines procedures in plan.
6. NIST tool set can be used for doing BCP. National Institute of standards and Technologies has published tools which can help in creating BCP.

4.16 CONTROL MEASURES IN RECOVERY PLAN

Control measures are steps or mechanisms that can reduce or eliminate computer security threats. Different types of measures can be included in BCP/DRP Types of measures:

1. **Preventive measures:** These controls are aimed at preventing an event from occurring.
2. **Detective measures:** These controls are aimed at detecting or discovering unwanted events.
3. **Corrective measures:** These controls are aimed at correcting or restoring the system after disaster or event.

These controls should be always documented and tested regularly.

4.16.1 Strategies

Prior to selecting a disaster recovery strategy, a disaster recovery planner should refer to their organization's business continuity plan which should indicate the key metrics of recovery point objective (RPO) and recovery time objective (RTO) for various business processes (such as the process to run payroll, generate an order, etc). The metrics specified for the business processes must then be mapped to the underlying IT systems and infrastructure that support those processes.

Once the RTO and RPO metrics have been mapped to IT infrastructure, the DR planner can determine the most suitable recovery strategy for each system. An important note here however is that the business ultimately sets the IT budget and therefore the RTO and RPO metrics need to fit with the available budget. While most business unit heads would like zero data loss and zero time loss, the cost associated with that level of protection may make the desired high availability solutions impractical.

The following is a list of the most common strategies for data protection.

- Backups made to tape and sent off-site at regular intervals (preferably daily)
- Backups made to disk on-site and automatically copied to off-site disk, or made directly to off-site disk
- Replication of data to an off-site location, which overcomes the need to restore the data (only the systems then need to be restored or synced). This generally makes use of storage area network (SAN) technology
- High availability systems which keep both the data and system replicated off-site, enabling continuous access to systems and data
- Wide Area network Optimization technology - helps improve disaster recovery and increases network response time. This type of technology will also make sure data still comes through the network even when it's down..

In many cases, an organization may elect to use an outsourced disaster recovery provider to provide a stand-by site and systems rather than using their own remote facilities.

In addition to preparing for the need to recover systems, organizations must also implement precautionary measures with an objective of preventing a disaster in the first place. These may include some of the following:

- Local mirrors of systems and/or data and use of disk protection technology such as RAID
- Surge protectors — to minimize the effect of power surges on delicate electronic equipment
- Uninterruptible power supply (UPS) and/or backup generator to keep systems going in the event of a power failure
- Fire preventions — alarms, fire extinguishers
- Anti-virus software and other security measures

For many organizations, messaging services are mission-critical or business-critical. If the messaging system is not available, productivity can be lowered, and business and revenue opportunities can be lost. Even if e-mail is neither mission-critical nor business-critical to your organization, chances are that the loss of messaging services would create a substantial disruption to your organization.

All of the redundancy, security and fault tolerance in the world cannot help you when it comes to a damaged, corrupt, or lost database. Backing up the critical data in your Microsoft Exchange Server 2007 organization is a necessary operational task for all organizations.

As part of your disaster recovery planning, it is important that you understand how to correctly back up Exchange 2007, how to restore Exchange 2007, and how to repair corrupt databases when no backups are available. Disaster recovery planning is a complex process that relies on many decisions that you make regarding the planning for Exchange 2007. Generally, to start the planning process, you must first consider the following concepts that relate to Exchange 2007 disaster recovery:

- Knowing what you may have to recover from
- Considering your service level agreement requirements
- Understanding the importance of deploying Exchange 2007 with disaster recovery in mind
- Understanding how Exchange relies on the Active Directory directory service
- Understanding Exchange database technology

Disaster recovery for Exchange 2007 is enhanced by or is also available as a service from Microsoft Exchange Hosted Services. Microsoft Exchange Hosted Services is a set of four distinct hosted services:

- Hosted Filtering, which helps organizations protect themselves from e-mail-borne malware
- Hosted Archive, which helps them satisfy retention requirements for compliance
- Hosted Encryption, which helps them encrypt data to preserve confidentiality
- Hosted Continuity, which helps them preserve access to e-mail during and after emergency situations

These services integrate with any on-premise Exchange servers that are managed in-house or Hosted Exchange e-mail services that are offered through service providers.

4.16.2 What You May Have To Recover From

Many types of failures and disasters may require that you repair or restore one or more parts of your messaging system. It is important that you have a strategy in place to recover from the following situations:

- Lost mail item (permanently deleted mail)
- Lost mailbox
- Lost database or storage group
- Lost server that is running Exchange 2007 (Exchange databases and transaction log files intact)
- Lost server that is running Exchange 2007 (Exchange database and transaction log files also lost)
- Lost computer in an Exchange 2007 Network Load Balancing cluster
- Lost computer in an Exchange 2007 back-end Microsoft Windows Server failover cluster
- Lost database or storage group for a Windows failover cluster
- Lost entire Exchange 2007 back-end Windows Server failover cluster
- Lost external services (including domain controller services, global catalog services, certificate services, DNS, etc.)
- Lost site (including all Exchange servers and all servers that provide external services)

A company that does not backup enough data on the servers in their messaging organization has not carefully considered its backup strategy. For example, if your organization experiences a disaster, such as a lost mailbox server (including its Exchange databases and transaction log files), and only has backups of the Exchange databases and transaction log file basic server elements, you may be able to recover the Exchange 2007 database files and some Exchange configuration data. However, with such limited backups, you may not be able to recover all the data and information that existed on the original server. Data and information on the original server could include cluster configuration information, management scripts, or system management software that resided on the server before it was lost. We recommend that you document all configuration settings and changes you make to a server starting immediately after Setup is completed, so that you can manually redo them after a disaster.

Conversely, if you take time to backup everything in your Exchange 2007 organization, you will likely be able to restore completely all critical data and configuration settings. However, if you back up all the data in your organization, your backup and restore processes will be more complex, more time-consuming, and will require more tapes or disk space than if you did not back up all the data.

To determine exactly what data that you need to back up to successfully recover from a disaster, we recommend that you practice disaster recovery procedures in a test environment before you implement a backup strategy on your production servers. Additionally, after you have implemented a backup and recovery strategy, you should consider conducting test restore operations regularly to make sure that you will be able to recover from various disasters that may occur.

4.16.3 Impact of the Full Server Recovery Strategy

The data that you need to back up depends on the type of full server recovery strategy you select. A full server recovery is when a disaster damages one of your servers to a point where you must take steps to, at a minimum, rebuild or restore the operating system and Exchange installation. Additionally, you may have to restore other information such as Exchange databases. You can categorize full server recovery strategies as either a full computer backup and restore, or a clean operating system install and Exchange disaster recovery.

Each server recovery strategy has its own set of backup and restore procedures:

- The full computer backup strategy must include the Exchange binaries. Restores require a System State restore, which should be performed using similar hardware.
- The clean operating system installation method includes recovering Microsoft Windows by running Windows Setup, restoring a Windows backup set, and then running Exchange 2007 in Disaster Recovery mode to retain your Exchange configuration.

4.16.4 Recovering Mailboxes and Individual Items

Exchange 2007 provides additional flexibility with regard to how you can recover mailboxes. This flexibility is made possible using features such as the recovery storage group. You can also help protect mailbox data on the client side with the Cached Exchange Mode feature of Microsoft Office Outlook 2007.

Consider implementing one or more of the following strategies to help you be prepared to recover individual mailboxes or individual items:

- *Server-side deleted item retention:* In this method, you help protect mailboxes from accidental item deletion through the clients by saving deleted items before purging them from a mailbox. You can customize the deleted item retention period for your users.
- Server-side reconnect of a deleted or orphaned mailbox In the case of deleted or orphaned mailboxes, you can reconnect them to a user account using the Exchange Management Console or by using the Exchange Management Shell. You can customize the time that deleted or orphaned mailboxes can be retained on the server..
- Restoration of backups performed at the mailbox level In the case of a damaged mailbox, you can restore a user's individual mailbox from backup.
- *Recovery storage group:* With the recovery storage group feature in Exchange 2007, you can mount a second copy of an Exchange mailbox database on the same server as the original database or on any other server that is running Exchange in the same Exchange administrative group. This action can be performed while the original database is still running and serving clients. With this capability, you can recover data from an older backup copy of the database without disturbing user access to current data. The recovery storage group can also be useful in various disaster recovery scenarios, most notably the messaging dial tone scenario.
- *Third-party brick-level backups:* Some third-party backup tools let you back up and restore Exchange at the level of individual mailboxes.

- Alternate server method This method requires that you restore an entire database to a server outside of your production environment and that you extract the mailbox data that you want. Although this method is still valid, whenever possible, you should use the recovery storage group method.

4.16.5 Recovering Exchange Databases

When your Exchange data becomes damaged or is lost in a disaster, you must recover it from backup. There are several cases in which restoring from backup may be necessary, including:

- Corruption of one or more databases in a storage group In this case, the native single-database restore functionality of Exchange can usually be used to restore the damaged databases without interrupting access to other databases on the same server.
- Hardware failure that causes loss of access to transaction logs or databases. In this case, you may have to recover all storage groups, including their associated logs and database files.
- Failure or damage to a mailbox or public folder server that requires the server to be rebuilt In this case, disaster recovery frequently requires rebuilding the underlying server and its operating system.

4.16.6 Recovering Exchange Databases from Exchange Streaming Backups Sets

Individual databases in a storage group may be restored while all other databases remain online. This method is the preferred means of replacing a single failed database. When the database is remounted, pertinent transactions are automatically played back from the storage group's log files to bring the restored database back to the time of the disaster.

When you use Backup to restore Exchange databases, API calls are made to the Exchange Extensible Storage Engine (ESE) to restore Exchange database files and their associated log files. You can use Exchange database backups to restore one or more damaged mailbox stores or public folder stores. You can also use Exchange database backups to restore every mailbox and public folder on the server. In a disaster recovery scenario that involves rebuilding a server, use Backup to restore your Exchange databases after you run Exchange Setup and any Exchange service packs in Recover Server mode (assuming that Active Directory is still available).

4.16.7 Recovering Exchange Databases By Using Hardware-Based Snapshot Backup Sets

Exchange 2007 supports hardware-based snapshots using the Volume Shadow Copy Service (VSS) implemented in Microsoft Windows Server 2003. Generally, it takes much less time to restore a backup that was taken using a hardware-based snapshot. Therefore, depending on the hardware and software that was used in the solution, restoring Exchange data from these types of backups may make it easier to meet the elements of your service level agreement (SLA) requirements that relate to the time that it takes to restore Exchange databases. Additionally, because larger databases can be restored more quickly, hardware-based snapshot restores can help you support larger database sizes and still let you meet your SLAs for restoring Exchange data.

4.16.8 Recovery Storage Group Restore Considerations

To provide more flexibility when restoring mailboxes and mailbox stores, Exchange 2007 provides a feature named the recovery storage group. The recovery storage group is a specialized storage group that can exist alongside the regular storage groups in Exchange, even if the server already has the maximum number of regular storage groups. You can restore Exchange 2007 mailbox stores from any storage group in the Exchange organization.

After you restore a mailbox store to the recovery storage group, move the recovered mailbox data from the recovery storage group to the regular storage group. With this method, you can recover an entire mailbox store, which includes all the database information, including the log data, or just a single mailbox. Mailboxes in the recovery storage group are disconnected and are not accessible to users who have mail clients.

The recovery storage group also makes it possible to offer dial-tone service quickly after a failure. This capability means that users can create and receive mail while their existing data is being restored. Frequently this approach is the fastest way to restore mail service to users. Because the volume of data generated by the users is likely to be less than the amount of data in the existing database, merging the dial-tone mail data into the original store after it is recovered is faster than moving the original database contents to a new store. When correctly used, the recovery storage group can be a powerful tool for reducing outage times.

4.17 DATABASE RECOVERY CONSIDERATIONS

Consider the following information before you perform specific recovery procedures in the Exchange 2007 organization:

- Determine the time that is required to restore and play transaction log files. Performance in your environment may vary significantly from the average, and you should consider log replay in addition to restore time. If you perform weekly Normal backups and daily Incremental backups, you may have thousands of transaction log files that require replay after a restoration.
- To minimize the time that it takes to recover an individual database, configure storage limits for the mailbox and public folder stores to constrain databases to a maximum size limit.
- To back up Exchange data using the ESE streaming backup APIs or a VSS-based solution, the database must be online. You can still back up an offline database manually. However, in that event, manual checksum verification is required. In addition, performing an offline backup of Exchange involves an interruption of service to clients.
- You can back up and restore databases in a storage group individually or simultaneously. As long as you do not exceed the data bandwidth capacity of your hard drives, controllers, and backup hardware, you can save time by simultaneously running multiple instances of Backup to back up or restore databases.

4.17.1 Database Backup and Restore on Windows Server 2008

Windows Server Backup in Windows Server 2008 no longer supports Exchange-aware backups or restores. Unlike earlier versions of Windows Backup, you cannot make or restore streaming backups of Exchange by using Windows Server Backup. To back up and restore Exchange Server 2007 Service Pack 1 (SP1) on Windows Server 2008, you must use an Exchange-aware application that supports the Volume Shadow Copy Service (VSS) writer for Exchange 2007, such as Microsoft System Center Data Protection Manager, a third-party Exchange-aware VSS-based application, or a third-party Exchange-aware application that uses the streaming backup APIs locally on the Exchange server to make a backup locally on the Exchange server. An application that uses a backup agent that runs locally on the Exchange server and streams the backup remotely to a backup application is considered a local backup.

4.17.2 Disaster Recovery Terminology

(ESE) Database

An Extensible Storage Engine (ESE) database used by Exchange.

(ESE) Logs

The logs used by ESE to provide atomicity, consistency, isolation, and durability (ACID) characteristics.

(Remote) copy

A storage group or database copy that is maintained by another server in the cluster.

Active copy

The master, mountable copy for the storage group. This copy represents current content of the other copies of the same storage group.

Back up

(verb) To create a copy of a database or other system component by preserving the actual files that make up that component. These files are typically stored in a different location, such as on specialized storage media.

Backup

(noun) The file or other media, typically compressed, that stores files that have been backed up.

Backup job

The act of backing up a set of files at the same time.

Boot partition

The hard disk partition where the Windows Server 2003 operating system is installed. This partition contains the %systemroot% folder and the %programfiles% folder.

Checkpoint file

A file that tracks the progress of transaction logging. The checkpoint file has a pointer to the oldest log file that contains data that has not yet been written to the database. The name of the checkpoint file is Enn.chk, where Enn is the log file prefix of the storage group.

Clean shutdown

Whenever a database is shut down, a flag in the database header keeps track of whether the database did the required maintenance to put the database in a consistent state. A database that was shut down in a consistent state is referred to as being shutdown clean.

Clone

A Volume Shadow Copy Service (VSS) concept where a complete copy is created of a set of files. The content of files reflects a particular point in time.

Consistent state

If the database is in a consistent state, the database can be remounted without any kind of transaction log replay. The database successfully detached from the log file stream when it was shut down. Such a database can be mounted and attached again to the log stream without requiring additional transaction log replay. Changing a database from an inconsistent state to a consistent state generally involves two processes: Restoring the database from a backup that was completed while the database was online, and replaying the transaction log files into the restored database.

Continuous replication

An asynchronous replication-like technology that creates a copy of a storage group and maintains its currency through change propagation. This feature includes local continuous replication and clustered continuous replication.

Copy

A replica of one or more files. In the context of disaster recovery, the term copy applies to a storage group.

Database

In the context of disaster recovery, database is a generic term that refers to either a mailbox store or a public folder store. An Exchange database is composed of both information in memory and the database files on the disk. If the information in memory is lost before it is written to the database files on the disk, it can be replayed from the transaction log files.

Dirty shutdown

When a database is shut down before you have performed required maintenance, it is put into an inconsistent state. This kind of shutdown is flagged as a dirty shutdown. This term means that some transaction log files must be replayed before the database can be considered consistent. You cannot mount a database that was shut down in this state until the transaction logs have been replayed and the database has correctly detached from the current log stream.

Extensible Storage Engine (ESE)

The database engine that Exchange uses. ESE is a multi-user Indexed Sequential Access Method (ISAM) table manager with full data manipulation language (DML) and data definition language (DDL) capabilities. Applications such as Exchange use ESE to store records and create indexes.

Full computer backup set

You create a full computer backup set when you back up your Windows Server 2003 operating system files, including the System State data and ail the applications that you have installed on the server. You must back up these files as part of the same backup job.

Hard recovery

Hard recovery is the process that changes a restored database back to a consistent state by playing transactions into the database from transaction log files. To initiate hard recovery, you select the Last Backup Set check box in Backup when you restore your last database, or you can uses the eseutil /cc command. The hard recovery process uses a RESTORE.env file that is generated during the recovery process to determine how to restore the database files and what transaction log files must be replayed from the temp directory that the backup was restored to. After the databases are copied to their original location, and the transaction log files from the temp directory are replayed into them, hard recovery continues to replay any additional transaction log files that it finds in the transaction log file path specified for the storage group of the restored database. The soft recovery process also replays any additional transaction log files that it finds.

Healthy copy

A state of a storage group copy that indicates that logs are being applied to reflect changes into the storage group. A copy that is fully seeded, has a valid, non-corrupted log stream, and can have successful log replay operations performed.

Inconsistent state

If the database is in an inconsistent state, which is referred to as a dirty shutdown, it cannot be remounted. A database in an inconsistent state has not been detached from the transaction log stream, and it can be mounted only after the appropriate transaction log replay has been performed. After the replay, the database is detached from the log stream and left in a consistent and mountable state.

Local copy

A copy that is maintained by the same server as the production storage group.

Mailbox store

A database for storing mailboxes in Exchange. Exchange mailbox stores contain data that is private to a user, and they also contain mailbox folders generated when a new mailbox is created for a user.

Mounted drive

A mounted drive is a drive that is mapped to an empty folder on a volume that uses the NTFS file system. Mounted drives function like other drives function, but they are assigned drive paths instead of drive letters. You can use a mounted drive to add another drive to a computer with all 26 possible drive letters already used, or to extend the size of a volume without having to re-create the volume on a larger disk.

Offline backup

A backup made while the Exchange services are stopped. When you perform an offline backup, users do not have access to their mailboxes.

Online backup

A backup made while the Exchange services are running.

Physical corruption

The data content of a file that does not read or correctly validate.

Point-in-time copy

A particular version of a copy created by a VSS snapshot or clone operation for the purposes of verification or data access.

Public folder store

The part of the Exchange store that maintains information in public folders.

Recovery

When it refers to Exchange databases, recovery means to replay transaction log files into a restored database. This action brings the database up-to-date. There are two distinct forms of recovery: soft recovery and hard recovery.

Replay

A process in which Exchange examines the transaction log files for a storage group to identify transactions that have been logged, but they have not been incorporated into the databases of that storage group. This process, also known as playing back log files, brings the databases up-to-date with the transaction log files. The operation of applying log files to a database to advance its content to a different state.

Resource groups

In a cluster, resource groups are collections of resources that are managed as a single unit. During failover, the whole resource group is moved from the failed node to an available node.

Restore

To return the original files that were previously preserved in a backup to their location on a server.

Seed

The baseline content of a storage group used to start replay processing.

Snapshot

A VSS concept where a copy on a write version of a set of files is created. The content of files reflects a particular point in time.

Soft recovery

An automatic transaction log file replay process that occurs when a database is remounted after an unexpected stop.

The soft recovery process only replays logs from the transaction log file path specified for the storage group that contains the affected databases. Affected databases are described as having been shut down in a dirty state. Soft recovery uses the checkpoint file to determine which transaction log file to start with when it sequentially replays transactions into databases. This process makes the databases up-to-date with all recorded transactions.

Storage group

An Exchange concept that identifies a set of databases.

System partition

The disk partition from which your computer starts. This partition contains files in the root directory such as NTLDR and BOOT.ini.

Transaction log files

Files that contain a record of the changes that were made to an Exchange database. All changes to the database are recorded in the transaction log files before they are written into the database files. If a database shuts down unexpectedly, unfinished transactions can be restored by replaying the transaction log files into the database.

Volume Shadow Copy Service

The Volume Shadow Copy Service (VSS) is a service in Windows Server 2003 and Windows Server 2008. It is a framework that facilitates communication between applications such as Exchange 2007, storage subsystems, and storage management applications (including backup applications) in order to define, persist, and exploit point-in-time copies of storage data.

VSS

See Volume Shadow Copy Service.

Windows backup set

The most basic collection of files and folders that is required to preserve a backup of the Windows Server 2003 operating system. This collection includes all the files and folders that Windows created in both the boot and system partitions. The collection also includes the System State data that are preserved together with the Windows Server 2003 operating system files and folders in the same backup.

4.18 DISASTER RECOVERY STRATEGIES

Having familiarized yourself with the various disaster recovery concepts, it is important to select a disaster recovery strategy. The disaster recovery strategy you select also influences your backup strategy. If your Microsoft Exchange Server 2007 organization encounters a problem that requires the recovery of a server that is running Exchange 2007 (for example, if a fire destroys one of your servers), there are three recovery options from which you can select:

- **Restore the server:** You can restore the server from a full computer backup set, and then restore your Exchange databases. A full backup set includes a backup of System State data, the Exchange binary files, and most of the data on your hard disks.
- **Rebuild the server:** You can rebuild the server completely. This option involves performing a new installation of Windows Server running Exchange 2007 in Disaster Recovery mode,

and then restoring your Exchange databases. This option assumes that Active Directory directory service is still available in Exchange 2007 in Disaster Recovery mode.

- **Use a standby server:** You can use a standby recovery server as part of the rebuild the server strategy. This option involves keeping recovery servers available with the operating system and other software installed. Having standby recovery servers available reduces the time it takes to rebuild a damaged server.

In addition to choosing a server recovery strategy, to maximize your flexibility of recovery options when you must perform a full server recovery, consider the following issues:

- **Priority of Protecting Active Directory and Exchange Database Data:** Take extra precautions to make sure of the safety of your Active Directory data and Exchange databases, which include both Exchange database files and transaction log files. If you have protected both of those sets of data, you will have additional options for recovering your Exchange data. Focus your resources on making sure that you protect those two items. Everything else is secondary.
- **Preparedness for being able to re-create configuration data manually if it becomes necessary:** Although running Setup /mode:RecoverServer can help you bring up a functional server, it may not preserve every custom setting or leave connectors functional. Therefore, you should be prepared to re-create any Exchange configuration settings in the event that you cannot recover those settings stored in Active Directory. If you can manually reconfigure the server, you have additional recovery options if a disaster occurs. Reconfiguring the server involves such tasks as reconfiguring your connectors, making metabase modifications, and making registry modifications.

In addition to the strategies discussed earlier, there are new features in Exchange 2007 that enable more recovery options and scenarios, including:

- **Improved backup and restore:** When you use local continuous replication (LCR) or cluster continuous replication (CCR), Exchange 2007 enables you to offload Exchange-aware Volume Shadow Copy Service (VSS) backups from the active copy of a database to a passive copy of a database.
- **Database portability:** Database portability provide several features, including the ability to port and recover a database on another server in the Exchange organization. Database portability enables faster disaster recovery strategies to be implemented for both site-level disasters and hardware failures for Exchange 2007 servers.
- **Dial tone portability:** When a database, server, or datacenter is lost, you can use dial tone portability to provide access to a new dial tone database on another server in the Exchange organization.

The following tools are included with Microsoft Exchange Server 2007:

- Database Recovery Management
- Database Troubleshooter
- Exchange Server Database Utilities (Eseutil.exe)

- Information Store Integrity Checker (Isinteg.exe)

These tools comprise the core disaster recovery applications for Exchange 2007.

. Tools Available in the Exchange Management Console Toolbox

You can find the Database Recovery Management tool and the Database Troubleshooter in the Toolbox of the Exchange Management Console. These tools provide a graphical user interface (GUI) for many of the command-line tools used to troubleshoot Exchange databases. The wizards in each tool make use of knowledge gained from Microsoft Product Support Services, the Exchange Server product team, and industry best practices. Web updates for the tools are available frequently. You can use the wizards to recover from a database disaster, work with a recovery storage group, recover a mailbox from a backup, and several other tasks.

4.19 DATABASE RECOVERY MANAGEMENT

The Database Recovery Management tool uses the same engine as the Exchange Troubleshooting Assistant to programmatically execute a set of troubleshooting steps to identify issues with the database that you specify. It then provides multiple wizards to guide you through possible solutions for already identified issues.

4.19.1 Database Troubleshooter

The Database Troubleshooter also uses the same engine as the Exchange Troubleshooting Assistant (ExTRA) to programmatically execute a set of troubleshooting steps to identify the root causes of database mounting issues. The tool automatically determines the set of data that is required to troubleshoot the identified symptoms and collects configuration data, performance counters, event logs, and live tracing information from Exchange Server and other appropriate sources. Then, it provide guidance for possible solutions with links to related database recovery management wizards.

4.19.2 Exchange Server Database Utilities

Exchange Server Database Utilities (Eseutil.exe) is a command-line tool that works with the Extensible Storage Engine (ESE), database files, and log files that are associated with an Exchange database. You can use Eseutil to verify, modify, and repair an Exchange database file. When a database is corrupt or damaged, you can restore data from backup or repair it using Eseutil.

4.19.3 Information Store Integrity Checker

The Information Store Integrity Checker (Isinteg.exe) finds and eliminates errors from the public folder and mailbox databases at the application level. Isinteg is not intended for use as a part of routine information store maintenance; it is provided to assist in disaster recovery situations. Because the Isinteg tool works at the logical schema level, it can recover data that Eseutil cannot recover. This is because data that is valid for the Eseutil tool at the physical schema level can be semantically invalid at the logical schema level.

The Isinteg tool performs two main tasks:

- It patches the information store after a restore from an offline backup.
- It tests and optionally fixes errors in the information store.

4.20 DATA RETENTION

Data retention defines the policies of persistent data and records management for meeting legal and business data archival requirements. A data retention policy weighs legal and privacy concerns against economics and need to know concerns to determine both the retention time, archival rules, data formats, and the permissable means of storage, access, and encryption.

Data retention issues plagued recovery of essential data of many early computer systems, notably the Data Recovery for Viking lander.

In the field of telecommunications, **data retention** (or **data preservation**) generally refers to the storage of call detail records (CDRs) of telephony and internet traffic and transaction data (IPDRs) by governments and commercial organisations. In the case of government data retention, the data that is stored is usually of telephone calls made and received, emails sent and received and web sites visited. Location data is also collected.

The primary objective in government data retention is traffic analysis and mass surveillance. By analysing the retained data, governments can identify the locations of individuals, an individual's associates and the members of a group such as political opponents. These activities may or may not be lawful, depending on the constitutions and laws of each country.

In the case of commercial data retention, the data retained will usually be on transactions and web sites visited.

Data retention also covers data collected by other means (e.g. by automatic numberplate recognition systems) and held by government and commercial organisations.

Home Office Voluntary Code of Practice on Data Retention

Subscriber Information-retention period 12 months

Subscriber details relating to the person e.g. Name, date of birth, installation and billing address, payment methods, account/credit card details Contact information (information held about the subscriber but not verified by the CSP) e.g. Telephone number, email address Identity of services subscribed to (information determined by the communication service provider) Customer reference/ account number, list of services subscribed to Telephony: telephone number(s), IMEI, IMSI (s) Email: email address(es), IP at registration Instant messaging: Internet Message Handle, IP at registration ISP - dial-in: Log-in, CLI at registration (if kept) ISP - always-on: Unique identifiers, MAC address (if kept), ADSL end points, IP tunnel address

Telephony Data-retention period 12 months

All numbers (or other identifiers e.g. name@bt) associated with call (e.g. physical/presentational/ network Assigned CLI, DNI, IMSI, IMEI, exchange/divert numbers) Date and time of start of call Duration of call/date and time of end of call Type of call (if available) Location data at start and/or end of call, in form of lat/long reference. Cell site data from time cell ceases to be used. IMSI/MSISDN/IMEI mappings. For GPRS & 3G, date and time of connection, IMSI, IP address assigned. Mobile data exchanged with foreign operators; IMSI & MSISDN, sets of GSM triples, sets of 3G quintuples, global titles of equipment communicating with or about the subscriber.

In addition it has been reported that the UK police and security services have the following additional capabilities on mobile telephones, provided by telephone operators, but not covered by the voluntary code.

1. The capability to record to the content of selected conversations.
2. The capability to determine the location of a mobile telephone to within a few yards by using triangulation and multiple base stations.
3. The capability to remotely activate the microphones of some mobile telephones. The UK Financial Times of the 2nd August 2005 [page 4 of the UK edition] reported that the UK police can ask mobile phone operators to download special spying software to a mobile telephone without the user's knowledge or permission. When this has been done the authorities can turn on the microphone of a mobile telephone and listen to any conversations in its vicinity. This capability only exists for mobile telephones which can accept downloaded software. The telephone must be turned on for the microphone to be activated, but the user does not have to be making a call.

SMS, EMS and MMS Data – Retention period 6 months

Calling number, IMEI - Called number, IMEI - Date and time of sending - Delivery receipt - if available - Location data when messages sent and received, in form of lat/long reference.

Email Data – Retention period 6 months

Log-on (authentication user name, date and time of log-in/log-off, IP address logged-in from) - sent email (authentication user name, from/to/cc email addresses, date and time sent) - received email (authentication user name, from/to email addresses, date and time received).

ISP Data – Retention period 6 months

Log-on (authentication user name, date and time of log-in/log-off, IP address assigned, Dial-up: CLI and number dialed, Always-on: ADSL end point/MAC address (If available).

Web Activity Logs – Retention period 4 days

Proxy server logs (date/time, IP address used, URL's visited, services. The data types here will be restricted solely to Communications Data and exclude content of communication. Web browsing information is retained to the extent that only the host machine or domain name (web site name) is disclosed. For example, within a communication, data identifying www.homeoffice.gov.uk would be traffic data, whereas data identifying www.homeoffice.gov.uk/kbsearch?qt=ripa+traffic=data would be content and not subject to retention.

Other Services – Retention period relative to service provided

Instant Message Type Services (log-on/off time) if available.

Collateral Data – Retention period relative to data to which it is related

Data needed to interpret other communications data, for example the mapping between cell mast identifiers and their location, and the translation of dialing (as supported by IN networks).

4.20.1 Retention of Other Data

Postal Data – Retention period unknown

Information written on the outside of a postal item (such as a letter or parcel, online tracking of postal items, records of postal items, such as records of registered, recorded or special delivery postal items, records of parcel consignment, delivery and collection

Banking Data – Seven years

It has been reported in the UK Economist magazine that UK banks are required to retain data on all financial transactions for seven years. This has not been verified. It is not clear whether data on credit card transactions is also retained for seven years.

Vehicle Movement Data – Two years

Leaked documents from the Association of Chief Police Officers [ACPO] have revealed that the UK is planning to collect data from a nationwide network of automatic numberplate recognition cameras and store the data for two years in a controversial new centre being built at Hendon. This data could then be linked with other data held by the government and watchlists from the police and security services.

4.20.2 Access to Retained Data

The bodies which are able to access retained data in the United Kingdom are listed in the Regulation of Investigatory Powers Act 2000 (RIPA). These are -

- Police forces (as defined in section 81(1) of RIPA)
- National Criminal Intelligence Service
- National Crime Squad
- HM Customs and Excise
- Inland Revenue
- Security Service
- Secret Intelligence Service
- Government Communications Headquarters

4.20.3 Reasons for Accessing Retained Data

The justifications for accessing retained data in the United Kingdom are set out in the Regulation of Investigatory Powers Act 2000 (RIPA). They are -

- in the interests of national security;
- for the purpose of preventing or detecting crime or of preventing disorder;
- in the interests of the economic well-being of the United Kingdom;
- in the interests of public safety;
- for the purpose of protecting public health;
- for the purpose of assessing or collecting any tax, duty, levy or other imposition, contribution or charge payable to a government department;
- for the purpose, in an emergency, of preventing death or injury or any damage to a person's physical or mental health, or of mitigating any injury or damage to a person's physical or mental health;
- for any purpose (not falling into the above) which is specified for the purposes of this subsection by an order made by the Secretary of State.

Italy

In July 2005 new legal requirements on data retention came into force in Italy.

Subscriber information

Internet cafes and public telephone shops with at least three terminals must seek a license permit within 30 days from the Ministry of Home Affairs. They must also store traffic data for a period which may be determined later by administrative decree. WIFI hotspots and locations that do not store traffic data have to secure ID information from users before allowing them to log on. For example, users may be required to enter a number from an ID card or driving license. It is not clear how this information is validated. Mobile telephony users must identify themselves before service activation, or before a SIM may be obtained. Resellers of mobile subscriptions or pre-paid cards must verify the identity of purchasers and retain a photocopy of identity cards.

Telephony data

Data, including location data, on fixed line and mobile telephony must be retained for 29 months. There is no requirement to store the content of calls. Telephony operators must retain a record of all unsuccessful dial attempts.

ISP data

Internet service providers must retain all data for at least six months. The law does not specify exactly what traffic data must be retained. There is no requirement to store the content of internet communications.

Legality

The legislation of July 2005 enables data retention by outlawing all the relevant data protection provisions until 31 December 2007. Under the data protection provisions, service providers are obliged to anonymise or delete traffic data when they no longer need it to process the communication or to send bills (with a maximum of six months). The traffic data which will now be retained can be used for anti-terrorism purposes and for general penal enforcement of criminal offences.

Italy already required the retention of telephony traffic data for 48 months, but without location data. Italy has adopted the EU Directive on Privacy and Electronic Communications 2002 but with an exemption to the requirement to erase traffic data.

Denmark

Denmark has implemented the EU data retention directive and much more, by logging all internet flow or sessions between operators and consumers.

1. "2.2.1. Session logging (section 5(1) of the Executive Order) Providers of access to the internet must, in respect of the initiating and terminating package of an internet session, retain data that identifies the sending and receiving internet protocol address (in the following called IP address), the sending and receiving port number and the transmission protocol."
2. "2.2.2. Sampling (section 5(4) of the Executive Order) The obligation to retain data about the initiating and terminating package of an internet session does not apply to providers in case such retention is not technically feasible in their systems. In that case, data must instead be retained for every 500th package that is part of an end user's communication on the internet."
3. "2.2.5. Hot spots (section 5(3) of the Executive Order) In addition to the internet data that must otherwise be retained, the provider must retain data that identifies the precise geographic or physical location of a hot spot and the identity of the communication equipment used. This means that a provider of internet access via a hot spot must retain data on a user's access to the internet and, at the same time, retain data that identifies the geographic location of the hot spot in question."

4.20.4 Commercial Data Retention

Amazon is known to retain extensive data on customer transactions. Google is also known to retain data on searches, and other transactions. If a company is based in the USA the FBI can obtain access to such information by means of a National Security Letter (NSL). The Electronic Frontier Foundation states that "NSLs are secret subpoenas issued directly by the FBI without any judicial oversight. These secret subpoenas allow the FBI to demand that online service providers or ecommerce companies produce records of their customers transactions. The FBI can issue NSLs for information about people who haven't committed any crimes.

NSLs are practically immune to judicial review. They are accompanied by gag orders that allow no exception for talking to lawyers and provide no effective opportunity for the recipients to challenge them in court. This secret subpoena authority, which was expanded by the controversial

USA PATRIOT Act., could be applied to nearly any online service provider for practically any type of record, without a court ever knowing."

4.20.5 Arguments on Data Retention

It is often argued that data retention was necessary to combat terrorism. However, data retention cannot prevent any terrorist attacks. At best it may, as its proponents claim, assist the police to find the culprits and their accomplices after an attack has already taken place. The authorities in Spain and the United Kingdom have claimed that retained telephony data made a significant contribution to police enquires into the 11 March 2004 Madrid train bombings and the 7 July 2005 London bombings.

The opponents of data retention make the following arguments –

1. The Madrid train bombings can also be seen as proof that the current data retention level is sufficient and hence the EU directive is not necessity.
2. Schemes for data retention do not make provisions for adequate regulation of the data retention process and for independent judicial oversight.
3. Data retention is an invasion of privacy and a disproportionate response to the threat of terrorism.
4. It is easy for terrorists to avoid having their communications recorded. The Home Office Voluntary Code of Practice of Data Retention admits that there are some internet protocols which cannot be effectively monitored. It would be possible for terrorists to avoid monitoring by using peer to peer technologies, internet cafes, anonymous proxies or several other methods. The police forces of the EU are sceptical about the value of data retention. Heinz Kiefer, president of Eurocop [European Confederation of Police] issued a press statement saying "it remains easy for criminals to avoid detection through fairly simple means, for example mobile phone cards can be purchased from foreign providers and frequently switched. The result would be that a vast effort is made with little more effect on criminals and terrorists than to slightly irritate them. Activities like these are unlikely to boost citizens' confidence in the EU's ability to deliver solutions to their demand for protection against serious crime and terrorism.'
5. The hardware and software required to store all the retained data would be extremely costly. The costs of retaining data would not only fall on Internet Service Providers and telephone companies, but also on all companies and other organisations which would need to retain records of traffic passing through their switchboards and servers.
6. Data retention gives excessive power to the state to monitor the lives of individual citizens.
7. Data retention may be abused by the police to monitor the activities of any group which may come into conflict with the state; including ones which are engaged in legitimate protests. The UK police have used anti-terrorism powers against groups opposed to the ware in Iraq and protestors at an arms fair. The definition of terrorism in the UK Terrorism Act 2000 includes not only action, but the threat of action, involving serious violence against a person,

or serious damage to property, for the purposes of advancing a "political, religious or ideological cause". There is concern that the definition is vaguely worded and could be applied to supporters of animal liberation, anti-war demonstrators and many others.

8. Even if data retention may be justified, the retention periods proposed in some cases are excessive. It has been argued that a period of five days for web activity logs and ninety days for all other data would be adequate for police purposes.

4.20.6 Protection Against Data Retention

The current directive proposal (see above) would force ISPs to record the internet communications of its users. The basic assumption is that this information can be used to identify with whom someone, whether innocent citizen or terrorist, communicated throughout a specific timespan. Believing that such as mandate would be useful is ignoring that some very committed community of crypto professionals has been preparing for such legislation for decades. Below are some strategies available today to anyone to protect themselves, avoid such traces, and render such expensive and legally dubious logging operations useless.

VPNs

Several organizations have set up VPNs so their employees can safely access the private data of the company. In this case the only data retained is the connection to the VPN server, that will contain all the data served to the EU citizen encrypted.

The connections, if the company is in the EU, will be recorded as a company access, mixed with all the other employees access. To single out any user, the company would have to be tapped and that the citizen would have to use it after it's been tapped. In practice that would mean that data retention would be of the same use that the present tapping legislation, so it presents only a cost with no benefit.

If the company is outside the EU, not even tapping can be done. Google created a public use VPN with their Google Wifi project. While their client software isn't provided by Google anymore, it can still be downloaded in sites like Softpedia. In this situation, any EU citizen can simply download their software and use the Internet without worrying about data retention in the EU.

Anonymizing proxy services: Web

There are anonymizer proxies that provide anonymous web access, using standard e-commerce cryptography to communicate with the final user and cloaking the Internet address of the user. As in the case above, the data retained is only the connection to the server.

Webmail

Most hosting companies (Pair Networks, Inc. in the US, for instance), provide a secure interface to their webmail system. This means that any EU citizen that pays for their services can read and send email without any information about it being recorded, other than a secure (e-commerce like) connection to the hosting company.

P2P Communications

Some P2P services, being it file transfer or voice over IP, use other computers to allow communication between computers behind firewalls. This means that trying to follow a call between two citizens might, mistakenly, identify a third citizen unaware of the communication.

Privacy Enhancing Tools

For security conscious citizens, using tools like I2P, Tor, mixmaster and the cryptography options integrated into any major mail client these days is always an option. Though, in practice, not everyone has the knowledge to employ the techniques described above.

I2P is an international peer-to-peer anonymizing network, which aims at not only evade data retention, but also make spying by other parties impossible. The structure is similar to the one TOR (see next paragraph) uses, but there are substantial differences. It protects better against traffic analysis and offers strong anonymity and for net-internal traffic end-to-end encrpytion. Due to unidirectional tunnels it is less prone to timing attacks as tor. In I2P several services are available: anonymous brwosing, anonymous e-mails, anonymous instant messenger, anonymous filesharing, **Tor** is a project of the US non-profit Tor Project to develop and improve an onion routing network to shield its users from traffic analysis. Mixmaster is a remailer service that allows anonymous email sending.

JAP is a project very similar to Tor. It is designed to route web requests through several proxies to hide the end users Internet address. Tor support has been included into JAP.

4.20.7 Making use of Dynamic IP Addresses

Almost since the beginning of commercial Internet dynamic IP address were given out to consumers out of a pool of a set of addresses. Every connection is logged to a central database. When broadband DSL made PPPoE popular one would still be given dynamic IP addresses but disconnecting the session and calling back was now a matter of seconds instead of waiting a minute for an analog modem to retrain. If a large number of computers disconnected and reconnected every minute this would cause a lot of logs to be retained until it becomes uneconomic to retain this data of logins. Web usually still works with this and so does email. In calculation: if 1 million users at an ISP connected and disconnected every minute and did this 24/7 an ISP would need 11 terabytes of storage, for 365 days of retention, if they sign a 4 byte field for logon/logoff time, a 4 byte field for customer number and a 4 byte field for IP address used.

4.21 SPACE MANAGEMENT

Businesses are becoming more and more dependant on the vailability of corporate databases and the business information they hold. To ensure that databases are constantly available and can grow as required, incurring only minimal performance penalties, administration of the database must include space management.

4.21.1 Importance of Space Management

Space management is important in all Oracle databases to some degree. One or more of the following aims will usually be applicable.

4.21.2 Aims of Space Management

Handle Data Growth

The most critical deliverable of good space management is the assurance that all the databases' functions will be performed without failures that are caused by a lack of capacity.

Maintain Data Density

Space management can have a significant influence over the performance of an active database, by maintaining the density of the data stored in the various database structures.

Reduce Administration Effort

The workload of the DBA can be reduced by using sensible space management policies and monitoring software. Various tools and database features can make detecting and correcting capacity problems easier. Avoiding outages and large reorganisations should also be an aim of space management.

Increase Efficiency of Data Storage / Retrieval

If disk capacity is a restricted resource, then space management policies can be used to control the size of a database. The way that objects are stored in the database can affect the efficiency of I/O and caching.

4.21.3 Space Management Theory Provision for the Growth of Data

Most live databases grow over time.

The three challenges that growth presents are

- To ensure the availability of the application by providing adequate capacity
- To maintain acceptable performance levels
- To keep the database manageable in regards to administration tasks databases allow space for growth at a number of levels
- Tablespaces have free blocks for new extents
- Extents have free (unused) blocks for new data
- Blocks have free bytes for new (or growing) rows
- Rows may have allocated space for new data (depending on the datatypes and order of the columns)

Pre-allocating space to avoid growing pains can have the side effects of decreased data density, wasted space and increased effort & resource requirements when performing administration tasks, such as backups.

Therefore, if space or performance is an important factor, then some care should be taken when managing space to create an efficient database.

4.21.4 Application Protection

Application Protection is a catchall term, applied generically to all security measures that protect application services. URL-based attacks, script exploits, malicious data injection to SQL, ORACLE, IBM DB2 and other databases, mail server attacks and DNS poisoning are all examples of application level attacks.

The distinction between application and network-based protection is a fuzzy one, since network-based is interpreted both as "attacks attempted across a network" as well as "attacks against the networking protocols (TCP, IP, ...)". But the distinction is not arbitrary, nor is it entirely market spin. Network, and specifically, Internet-based attacks attempt to compromise a system through a flaw in a Internet protocol standard or implementation; if successful, attackers often gain administrator privileges for the system and applications, and access to data. Fortunately, the set of Internet protocols we use is finite, and after nearly two decades, firewall technology, combined with improvements and patches to implementations of Internet protocols, has matured to where we can provide very good protection against network attacks (proper configuration notwithstanding).

But the set of applications, especially web-based applications, is essentially infinite.

While standards exist for web protocols and services, for security purposes, each web presence - the combination of server application and OS platform, pages served, scripts, databases, and forms employed, and of course, the configuration of all these elements - is unique. Accordingly, attackers have infinite attack vectors, and so, too, are suitable locations for the deployment of defenses and countermeasures. Hence, the question, "Where is application protection best applied?"

4.21.5 Internet Firewalls & Network IDS

Many enterprise class firewalls and inline intrusion detection systems apply stateful packet inspection beyond traditional TCP/IP protocols, and examine application data streams. Through this *deep packet inspection* process, the best of application protection firewalls and inline IDS can distinguish known network-based attacks from legitimate traffic. Firewall and inline IDS hybrids - Intrusion Prevention Systems, or IPS - provide advanced intrusion and denial of service detection by distinguishing anomalous from normal traffic patterns and behavior.

The best of these breeds can identify and block long lists of known attacks against web applications, including malicious URL encoding, CodeRed and Nimbda worms, WebDAV, and chunked data encoding attacks. Several also protect SMTP server applications from flooding/DOS, worm, and relay attacks; FTP server applications from malicious operator and bounce attacks; and DNS server applications from protocol and database (zone) poisoning attacks. Depending on the product, protection is available for other services, from database (SQL. Oracle) to secure tunneling protocols (SSH, SSL), and even Voice over IP.

4.21.6 Proxies

Proxies, either standalone or integrated within firewall or VPN appliances, terminate application streams and police the contents of that stream. For example, an SMTP mail proxy will collect all the application data that comprises a single email message, inspect the message, and apply whatever measures a security policy dictates: e.g., remove or modify unknown or potentially dangerous mail headers, block the delivery of potentially dangerous attachment and content types, etc. SMTP, FTP and DNS proxies customarily check for protocol anomalies. HTTP proxies check for protocol anomalies, strip scripts, active controls and other active code or content prohibited by security policy. Whether marketed as proxies or *(Web) Application firewalls*, these systems validate incoming and outgoing HTTP traffic, to prevent client-based attacks, web defacements, server mis-operation and other "web perversions" (this cleverism is courtesy of Sanctum, Inc.).

4.22 INTERDEPARTMENTAL IPS AND SERVER FIREWALLS

Application Protection at the Internet firewall has the benefit of performing security checks at a familiar aggregation point, the Internet access circuit. But increasingly, clients operating within the protected and trusted network are proven vectors for attack. This is particularly true in organizations with mobile and roaming workforces. Servers themselves are also vectors for attack against "fellow" servers. Application streams that form these internal attacks do not pass through Internet Firewalls so are not subject to inspection and prevention.

Adding interdepartmental firewalls or placing firewall-capable switches directly in front of (literally, adjacent to) server farms provides a means of collapsing the perimeter around the assets (principally, servers) deemed most critical. This is commonly described as layered defense, or defense in depth. A variation on this theme does not require discrete and separate hardware appliances: application-level inspection and filtering on the target server platform itself - in a network adapter form factor, software, or embedded OS service (e.g., Microsoft ICF) - can be used to create very granular, compartmented borders. Both of these solutions act like water-tight hatches on a naval vessel, e.g., a submarine.

4.23 HOST INTRUSION PREVENTION

Philosophically, it makes sense to protect applications, the platforms on which they run, and the data they use, as close to "the asset" as possible. Host Application Protection measures wrap a protective shell around applications, databases, Operating Systems and file systems. These act like intrusion detection systems, to block attacks at the system call level and protect critical system files (e.g., Windows Registry, *nix .conf files). Such products also provide additional access controls to protect web-accessible information from unauthorized access and modification. In some cases, policy synchronization across large server farms (and distributed server environments) proves difficult. These solutions can be construed as complementary to vulnerability assessment and mitigation, but are also commonly claimed to compensate for inherently weak security features available in server platforms. Whether you regard them as supplementary or complementary, they provide another layer of defense, close to the asset.

4.24 VULNERABILITY ASSESSMENT AND MITIGATION (HARDENING)

Vulnerability assessment and mitigation are processes organizations can employ to thoroughly test all elements of a web presence, and systematically identify, then eliminate or minimize each threat until the web presence meets the intended security requirements and satisifies the desired risk profile. Vulnerability Assessment systems automate the process. System-level scanners search for overly-generous access permissions, weak passwords, default accounts, and missing web server patches, while web application vulnerability assessment scanners may look for exploitable cookie implementations, vulnerable forms, cross-site scripting, etc. The best of this breed provide detailed reports explaining the vulnerabilities discovered and methods to eliminate or minimize them. The actual process of configuring systems and applications following a vulnerability assessment is called "hardening", and it is labor-, knowledge-, and skills-intensive. In the case of (web) application vulnerability assessment, vulnerability assessment may reveal fundamental flaws in development; for example, a persistent failure to validate (data) input in web forms and database queries. These may lead an organization to conclude that a secure code review is required for all application code.

Given these choices, where is application protection best applied?

A strategy I believe to be efficient and effective is one in which coarse- and network-level policy enforcement is done at the outer ("loose") perimeters. Increasingly stringent and application specific policies are enforced close to or at the location where a web or application presence is deployed. This is similar in principle to the "choke and screen" early firewall deployments used to create DMZs many years ago. You can apply application protection at Internet firewalls and proxies, but do not rely entirely on these. In the choke and screen deployment, your outermost firewall should implement the coarsest of policies. Implement more stringent application protection measures in firewalls, proxies and switches that protect server farms, to defend against attacks from external and internal hosts. Collapsing perimeters around server farms and enforcing per client security measures is a practical concession and reponse to the now omni-present and worrisome mobile workplace.

Investing in host application protection to complement security measures you employ at the server and applications themselves is one of those "iffy" areas. Some security experts question, "how much better off is an organization that invests in these solutions than one that rigorously assesses risk, identifies vulnerabilities, and hardens servers and applications?" Perhaps your systems administrators are capable of hardening and configuring secure systems; your programming staff develops and maintaining securely written applications; and your daily operations staff are monitoring ninjas.

Perhaps you need some backup. If you do, one or even several of the several dozen companies listed in the sidebar may have an application protection solution that meets your needs.

4.25 SUMMARY

- The security of your organization's data reigns supreme in the design of a storage system.

- The development of a storage strategy involves planning for the quantity of storage and the level of performance required. Although there are no iron-clad rules for planning the capacity of your storage system, here are some general guidelines.
- A variety of technologies are available for network storage. Each of these hardware and software solutions form the building b locks from which you will build a comprehensive storage solution.
- The strengths of magnetic drives can be expanded through the use of RAID technologies. RAID, or Redundant Arrays of Inexpensive (or Independent) Disks, combines multiple magnetic disk devices in ways that increase capacity, reliability and performance.
- An **archive** is a collection of historical records, and the location in which the collection is kept.Archives consist of records which have been selected for permanent or long-term preservation, due to their enduring research value.
- **Disaster recovery** is the process, policies and procedures related to preparing for recovery or continuation of technology infrastructure critical to an organization after a natural or human-induced disaster. Disaster recovery planning is a subset of a larger process known as business continuity planning and should include planning for resumption of applications, data, hardware, communications (such as networking) and other IT infrastructure.
- Data retention defines the policies of persistent data and records management for meeting legal and business data archival requirements.
- A data retention policy weighs legal and privacy concerns against economics and need to know concerns to determine both the retention time, archival rules, data formats, and the permissable means of storage, access, and encryption.
- Businesses are becoming more and more dependant on the vailability of corporate databases and the business information they hold. To ensure that databases are constantly available and can grow as required, incurring only minimal performance penalties, administration of the database must include space management.

4.26 REVIEW QUESTIONS

1. Discuss the term STORAGE MANAGEMENT and what are the uses of Backup & Storage.
2. Discuss the Archive & Retrieve for storage management.
3. What do you mean by Disaster Recovery and it is implemented.
4. Discuss the role of space Management and its technique.
5. Discuss the term protection and differentiate Database & Application Protection.
6. Write short notes on the following

   I. Bare Machine Recovery

   II. Data Retention

CHAPTER 5

Security Management

Security Management is a broad field of management related to asset management, physical security and human resource safety functions. It entails the identification of an organization's information assets and the development, documentation and implementation of policies, standards, procedures and guidelines.

In network management it is the set of functions that protects telecommunications networks and systems from unauthorized access by persons, acts, or influences and that includes many subfunctions, such as creating, deleting, and controlling security services and mechanisms; distributing security-relevant information; reporting security-relevant events; controlling the distribution of cryptographic keying material; and authorizing subscriber access, rights, and privileges.

Management tools such as information classification, risk assessment and risk analysis are used to identify threats, classify assets and to rate system vulnerabilities so that effective control can be implemented.

5.1 SECURITY

Security is the degree of protection against danger, loss, and criminals. Security has to be compared and contrasted with other related concepts: Safety, continuity, reliability. The key difference between security and reliability is that security must take into account the actions of people attempting to cause destruction.

Definitions

The word security is derived from the Ancient Greek "Se-Cura" and literally translates to "without fear". 'Security' is therefore the state of being secure, or the actions employed to achieve that state, i.e. to be secure is to be without fear of harm.

The definition of security provided by the Institute for Security and Open Methodologies is geared towards operations and how we interact with security. It states security is:

- A form of protection where a separation is created between the assets and the threat. This includes but is not limited to the elimination of either the asset or the threat. In order to be secure, either the asset is physically removed from the threat or the threat is physically removed from the asset.

The definition given in a UN study, in 1986, is interesting as a contribution to the understanding of the concept of security, "Security is a state at which countries think that there is no danger of military attack, political pressure, or economic coercion, so that they can develop and progress freely.

- With respect to classified matter, the condition that prevents unauthorized persons from having access to official information that is safeguarded in the interests of national security.
- Measures taken by a military unit, an activity or installation to protect itself against all acts designed to, or which may, impair its effectiveness.

5.1.1 Perceived Security Compared to Real Security

It is very often true that people's perception of security is not directly related to actual security. For example, a fear of earthquakes is much more common than a fear of slipping on the bathroom floor; however, the latter kills far more people than the former.

The tool may be mistaken for the effect, for example when multiple computer security programs interfere with each other, the user assumes the computer is secure when actual security has vanished. Another side of this is a phenomenon called security theatre where ineffective security measures such as screening of airline passengers based on static databases are introduced with little real increase in security or even, according to the critics of one such measure - Computer Assisted Passenger Prescreening System - with an actual decrease in real security.

Conversely, if it is perceived that there is security then there will be an increase in actual security, even if the perception of security is mistaken. Sometimes a sign may warn that video surveillance is covering an area, and even if there is no actual visual surveillance then some malicious agents will be deterred by the belief that there may be.

Also, often when there is actual security present in the area, such as video surveillance, an alarm system in a home, or an anti-theft system in a car such as a LoJack, signs advertising this security will increase its effectiveness, protecting the value of the secured vehicle or area itself. Since some intruders will decide not to attempt to break into such areas or vehicles, there can actually be less damage to windows in addition to protection of valuable objects inside. Without such advertisement, a car-thief might, for example, approach a car, break the window, and then flee in response to an alarm being triggered. Either way, perhaps the car itself and the objects inside aren't stolen, but with perceived security even the windows of the car have a lower chance of being damaged, increasing the financial security of its owner(s).

However, the non-profit, security research group, ISECOM, has determined that such signs may actually increase the violence, daring, and desperation of an intruder This claim shows that perceived security works mostly on the provider and is not security at all. It is important, however, for signs advertising security not to give clues as to how to subvert that security, for example in the case where a home burglar might be more likely to break into a certain home if he or she is able to learn beforehand which company makes its security system.

5.1.2 Security Concepts

Certain concepts recur throughout different fields of security:

- **Assurance -** assurance is the level of guarantee that a security system will behave as expected
- **Countermeasure -** a countermeasure is a way to stop a threat from triggering a risk event
- **Defense in depth -** never rely on one single security measure alone
- **Exploit** - a vulnerability that has been triggered by a threat - a risk of 1.0 (100%)
- **Risk -** a risk is a possible event which could cause a loss
- **Threat -** a threat is a method of triggering a risk event that is dangerous
- **Vulnerability -** a weakness in a target that can potentially be exploited by a threat

5.1.3 Security Management in Organizations

In the corporate world, various aspects of security were historically addressed separately - notably by distinct and often noncommunicating departments for IT security, physical security, and fraud prevention. Today there is a greater recognition of the interconnected nature of security requirements, an approach variously known as holistic security, "all hazards" management, and other terms.

Inciting factors in the convergence of security disciplines include the development of digital video surveillance technologies and the digitization and networking of physical control systems. Greater interdisciplinary cooperation is further evidenced by the February 2005 creation of the Alliance for Enterprise Security Risk Management, a joint venture including leading associations in security, information security, and IT audit.

5.2 COMPUTER SECURITY

Computer security is a branch of technology known as information security as applied to computers and networks. The objective of computer security includes protection of information and property from theft, corruption, or natural disaster, while allowing the information and property to remain accessible and productive to its intended users.

5.2.1 Security by Design

The technologies of computer security are based on logic. As security is not necessarily the primary goal of most computer applications, designing a program with security in mind often imposes restrictions on that program's behavior. There are several approaches to security in computing, sometimes a combination of approaches is valid:

1. Trust all the software to abide by a security policy but the software is not trustworthy (this is computer insecurity).

2. Trust all the software to abide by a security policy and the software is validated as trustworthy (by tedious branch and path analysis for example).
3. Trust no software but enforce a security policy with mechanisms that are not trustworthy (again this is computer insecurity).
4. Trust no software but enforce a security policy with trustworthy mechanisms.

Many systems have unintentionally resulted in the first possibility. Since approach two is expensive and non-deterministic, its use is very limited. Approaches one and three lead to failure. Because approach number four is often based on hardware mechanisms and avoids abstractions and a multiplicity of degrees of freedom, it is more practical. Combinations of approaches two and four are often used in a layered architecture with thin layers of two and thick layers of four.

There are various strategies and techniques used to design security systems. However there are few, if any, effective strategies to enhance security after design. One technique enforces the principle of least privilege to great extent, where an entity has only the privileges that are needed for its function. That way even if an attacker gains access to one part of the system, fine-grained security ensures that it is just as difficult for them to access the rest.

Furthermore, by breaking the system up into smaller components, the complexity of individual components is reduced, opening up the possibility of using techniques such as automated theorem proving to prove the correctness of crucial software subsystems. This enables a closed form solution to security that works well when only a single well-characterized property can be isolated as critical, and that property is also assessable to math. Not surprisingly, it is impractical for generalized correctness, which probably cannot even be defined, much less proven. Where formal correctness proofs are not possible, rigorous use of code review and unit testing represent a best-effort approach to make modules secure.

The design should use "defense in depth", where more than one subsystem needs to be violated to compromise the integrity of the system and the information it holds. Defense in depth works when the breaching of one security measure does not provide a platform to facilitate subverting another. Also, the cascading principle acknowledges that several low hurdles does not make a high hurdle. So cascading several weak mechanisms does not provide the safety of a single stronger mechanism.

Subsystems should default to secure settings, and wherever possible should be designed to "fail secure" rather than "fail insecure". Ideally, a secure system should require a deliberate, conscious, knowledgeable and free decision on the part of legitimate authorities in order to make it insecure.

In addition, security should not be an all or nothing issue. The designers and operators of systems should assume that security breaches are inevitable. Full audit trails should be kept of system activity, so that when a security breach occurs, the mechanism and extent of the breach can be determined. Storing audit trails remotely, where they can only be appended to, can keep intruders from covering their tracks. Finally, full disclosure helps to ensure that when bugs are found the "window of vulnerability" is kept as short as possible.

5.2.2 Early History of Security by Design

The early Multics operating system was notable for its early emphasis on computer security by design, and Multics was possibly the very first operating system to be designed as a secure system from the ground up. In spite of this, Multics' security was broken, not once, but repeatedly. The strategy was known as 'penetrate and test' and has become widely known as a non-terminating process that fails to produce computer security. This led to further work on computer security that prefigured modern security engineering techniques producing closed form processes that terminate.

5.2.3 Security Architecture

Security Architecture can be defined as the design artifacts that describe how the security controls (security countermeasures) are positioned, and how they relate to the overall information technology architecture. These controls serve the purpose to maintain the system's quality attributes, among them confidentiality, integrity, availability, accountability and assurance." A security architecture is the plan that shows where security measures need to be placed. If the plan describes a specific solution then, prior to building such a plan, one would make a risk analysis. If the plan describes a generic high level design (reference architecture) then the plan should be based on a threat analysis.

5.2.4 Hardware Mechanisms that Protect Computers and Data

Hardware based or assisted computer security offers an alternative to software-only computer security. Devices such as dongles may be considered more secure due to the physical access required in order to be compromised.

While many software based security solutions encrypt the data to prevent data from being stolen, a malicious program may corrupt the data in order to make it unrecoverable or unusable. Hardware-based security solutions can prevent read and write access to data and hence offers very strong protection against tampering.

5.2.5 Secure Operating Systems

One use of the term computer security refers to technology to implement a secure operating system. Much of this technology is based on science developed in the 1980s and used to produce what may be some of the most impenetrable operating systems ever. Though still valid, the technology is in limited use today, primarily because it imposes some changes to system management and also because it is not widely understood. Such ultra-strong secure operating systems are based on operating system kernel technology that can guarantee that certain security policies are absolutely enforced in an operating environment. An example of such a Computer security policy is the Bell-La Padula model. The strategy is based on a coupling of special microprocessor hardware features, often involving the memory management unit, to a special correctly implemented operating system kernel. This forms the foundation for a secure operating system which, if certain critical parts are designed and implemented correctly, can ensure the absolute impossibility of penetration by hostile elements.

This capability is enabled because the configuration not only imposes a security policy, but in theory completely protects itself from corruption. Ordinary operating systems, on the other hand, lack the features that assure this maximal level of security. The design methodology to produce such secure systems is precise, deterministic and logical.

Systems designed with such methodology represent the state of the art of computer security although products using such security are not widely known. In sharp contrast to most kinds of software, they meet specifications with verifiable certainty comparable to specifications for size, weight and power. Secure operating systems designed this way are used primarily to protect national security information, military secrets, and the data of international financial institutions. These are very powerful security tools and very few secure operating systems have been certified at the highest level (Orange Book A-1) to operate over the range of "Top Secret" to "unclassified" (including Honeywell SCOMP, USAF SACDIN, NSA Blacker and Boeing MLS LAN.) The assurance of security depends not only on the soundness of the design strategy, but also on the assurance of correctness of the implementation, and therefore there are degrees of security strength defined for COMPUSEC. The Common Criteria quantifies security strength of products in terms of two components, security functionality and assurance level (such as EAL levels), and these are specified in a Protection Profile for requirements and a Security Target for product descriptions. None of these ultra-high assurance secure general purpose operating systems have been produced for decades or certified under the Common Criteria.

In USA parlance, the term High Assurance usually suggests the system has the right security functions that are implemented robustly enough to protect DoD and DoE classified information. Medium assurance suggests it can protect less valuable information, such as income tax information. Secure operating systems designed to meet medium robustness levels of security functionality and assurance have seen wider use within both government and commercial markets. Medium robust systems may provide the same security functions as high assurance secure operating systems but do so at a lower assurance level (such as Common Criteria levels EAL4 or EAL5). Lower levels mean we can be less certain that the security functions are implemented flawlessly, and therefore less dependable. These systems are found in use on web servers, guards, database servers, and management hosts and are used not only to protect the data stored on these systems but also to provide a high level of protection for network connections and routing services.

5.2.6 Secure Coding

If the operating environment is not based on a secure operating system capable of maintaining a domain for its own execution, and capable of protecting application code from malicious subversion, and capable of protecting the system from subverted code, then high degrees of security are understandably not possible. While such secure operating systems are possible and have been implemented, most commercial systems fall in a 'low security' category because they rely on features not supported by secure operating systems (like portability, et al.). In low security operating environments, applications must be relied on to participate in their own protection. There are 'best effort' secure coding practices that can be followed to make an application more resistant to malicious subversion.

In commercial environments, the majority of software subversion vulnerabilities result from a few known kinds of coding defects. Common software defects include buffer overflows, format string vulnerabilities, integer overflow, and code/command injection.

Some common languages such as C and C++ are vulnerable to all of these defects (see Seacord, "Secure Coding in C and C++"). Other languages, such as Java, are more resistant to some of these defects, but are still prone to code/command injection and other software defects which facilitate subversion.

Recently another bad coding practice has come under scrutiny; dangling pointers. The first known exploit for this particular problem was presented in July 2007. Before this publication the problem was known but considered to be academic and not practically exploitable.

In summary, 'secure coding' can provide significant payback in low security operating environments, and therefore worth the effort. Still there is no known way to provide a reliable degree of subversion resistance with any degree or combination of 'secure coding.'

5.2.7 Capabilities vs. ACLs

Within computer systems, the two fundamental means of enforcing privilege separation are access control lists (ACLs) and capabilities. The semantics of ACLs have been proven to be insecure in many situations (e.g., Confused deputy problem). It has also been shown that ACL's promise of giving access to an object to only one person can never be guaranteed in practice. Both of these problems are resolved by capabilities. This does not mean practical flaws exist in all ACL-based systems, but only that the designers of certain utilities must take responsibility to ensure that they do not introduce flaws.

Capabilities have been mostly restricted to research operating systems and commercial OSs still use ACLs. Capabilities can, however, also be implemented at the language level, leading to a style of programming that is essentially a refinement of standard object-oriented design. An open source project in the area is the E language.

First the Plessey System 250 and then Cambridge CAP computer demonstrated the use of capabilities, both in hardware and software, in the 1970s. A reason for the lack of adoption of capabilities may be that ACLs appeared to offer a 'quick fix' for security without pervasive redesign of the operating system and hardware.

The most secure computers are those not connected to the Internet and shielded from any interference. In the real world, the most security comes from operating systems where security is not an add-on, such as OS/400 from IBM. This almost never shows up in lists of vulnerabilities for good reason. Years may elapse between one problem needing remediation and the next.

5.2.8 Applications

Computer security is critical in almost any technology-driven industry which operates on computer systems. The issues of computer based systems and addressing their countless vulnerabilities are an integral part of maintaining an operational industry.

5.2.9 In Aviation

The aviation industry is especially important when analyzing computer security because the involved risks include human life, expensive equipment, cargo, and transportation infrastructure. Security can be compromised by hardware and software malpractice, human error, and faulty operating environments. Threats that exploit computer vulnerabilities can stem from sabotage, espionage, industrial competition, terrorist attack, mechanical malfunction, and human error.

The consequences of a successful deliberate or inadvertent misuse of a computer system in the aviation industry range from loss of confidentiality to loss of system integrity, which may lead to more serious concerns such as data theft or loss, network and air traffic control outages, which in turn can lead to airport closures, loss of aircraft, loss of passenger life. Military systems that control munitions can pose an even greater risk.

A proper attack does not need to be very high tech or well funded; for a power outage at an airport alone can cause repercussions worldwide. One of the easiest and, arguably, the most difficult to trace security vulnerabilities is achievable by transmitting unauthorized communications over specific radio frequencies. These transmissions may spoof air traffic controllers or simply disrupt communications altogether. These incidents are very common, having altered flight courses of commercial aircraft and caused panic and confusion in the past. Controlling aircraft over oceans is especially dangerous because radar surveillance only extends 175 to 225 miles offshore. Beyond the radar's sight controllers must rely on periodic radio communications with a third party.

Lightning, power fluctuations, surges, brown-outs, blown fuses, and various other power outages instantly disable all computer systems, since they are dependent on an electrical source. Other accidental and intentional faults have caused significant disruption of safety critical systems throughout the last few decades and dependence on reliable communication and electrical power only jeopardizes computer safety.

5.2.10 Notable System Accidents

In 1994, over a hundred intrusions were made by unidentified hackers into the Rome Laboratory, the US Air Force's main command and research facility. Using trojan horse viruses, hackers were able to obtain unrestricted access to Rome's networking systems and remove traces of their activities. The intruders were able to obtain classified files, such as air tasking order systems data and furthermore able to penetrate connected networks of National Aeronautics and Space Administration's Goddard Space Flight Center, Wright-Patterson Air Force Base, some Defense contractors, and other private sector organizations, by posing as a trusted Rome center user. Now, a technique called Ethical hack testing is used to remediate these issues.

Electromagnetic interference is another threat to computer safety and in 1989, a United States Air Force F-16 jet accidentally dropped a 230 kg bomb in West Georgia after unspecified interference caused the jet's computers to release it.

A similar telecommunications accident also happened in 1994, when two UH-60 Blackhawk helicopters were destroyed by F-15 aircraft in Iraq because the IFF system's encryption system malfunctioned.

5.2.11 Terminology

The following terms used in engineering secure systems are explained below.

- Authentication techniques can be used to ensure that communication end-points are who they say they are.
- Automated theorem proving and other verification tools can enable critical algorithms and code used in secure systems to be mathematically proven to meet their specifications.
- Capability and access control list techniques can be used to ensure privilege separation and mandatory access control. The next sections discuss their use.
- Chain of trust techniques can be used to attempt to ensure that all software loaded has been certified as authentic by the system's designers.
- Cryptographic techniques can be used to defend data in transit between systems, reducing the probability that data exchanged between systems can be intercepted or modified.
- Firewalls can provide some protection from online intrusion.
- Mandatory access control can be used to ensure that privileged access is withdrawn when privileges are revoked. For example, deleting a user account should also stop any processes that are running with that user's privileges.
- Secure cryptoprocessors can be used to leverage physical security techniques into protecting the security of the computer system.
- Microkernels can be reliable against errors, e.g. EROS and Coyotos.

Some of the following items may belong to the computer security are:

- Access authorization restricts access to a computer to group of users through the use of authentication systems. These systems can protect either the whole computer - such as through an interactive logon screen - or individual services, such as an FTP server. There are many methods for identifying and authenticating users, such as passwords, identification cards, and, more recently, smart cards and biometric systems.
- Anti-virus software consists of computer programs that attempt to identify, thwart and eliminate computer viruses and other malicious software (malware).
- application with known security flaws should not be run. Either leave it turned off until it can be patched or otherwise fixed, or delete it and replace it with some other application. Publicly known flaws are the main entry used by worms to automatically break into a system and then spread to other systems connected to it. The security website Secunia provides a search tool for unpatched known flaws in popular products.
- Backups are a way of securing information; they are another copy of all the important computer files kept in another location. These files are kept on hard disks, CD-Rs, CD-RWs, and tapes. Suggested locations for backups are a fireproof, waterproof, and heat proof safe, or in a separate, offsite location than that in which the original files are contained. Some individuals and companies also keep their backups in safe deposit boxes inside bank vaults. There is also a fourth option, which involves using one of the file hosting services that backs up files over the Internet for both business and individuals.

- Backups are also important for reasons other than security. Natural disasters, such as earthquakes, hurricanes, or tornadoes, may strike the building where the computer is located. The building can be on fire, or an explosion may occur. There needs to be a recent backup at an alternate secure location, in case of such kind of disaster. Further, it is recommended that the alternate location be placed where the same disaster would not affect both locations. Examples of alternate disaster recovery sites being compromised by the same disaster that affected the primary site include having had a primary site in World Trade Center I and the recovery site in 7 World Trade Center, both of which were destroyed in the 9/11 attack, and having one's primary site and recovery site in the same coastal region, which leads to both being vulnerable to hurricane damage (e.g. primary site in New Orleans and recovery site in Jefferson Parish, both of which were hit by Hurricane Katrina in 2005). The backup media should be moved between the geographic sites in a secure manner, in order to prevent them from being stolen.
- Encryption is used to protect the message from the eyes of others. It can be done in several ways by switching the characters around, replacing characters with others, and even removing characters from the message. These have to be used in combination to make the encryption secure enough, that is to say, sufficiently difficult to crack. Public key encryption is a refined and practical way of doing encryption. It allows for example anyone to write a message for a list of recipients, and only those recipients will be able to read that message.
- Firewalls are systems which help protect computers and computer networks from attack and subsequent intrusion by restricting the network traffic which can pass through them, based on a set of system administrator defined rules.
- Honey pots are computers that are either intentionally or unintentionally left vulnerable to attack by crackers. They can be used to catch crackers or fix vulnerabilities.
- Intrusion-detection systems can scan a network for people that are on the network but who should not be there or are doing things that they should not be doing, for example trying a lot of passwords to gain access to the network.
- Pinging The ping application can be used by potential crackers to find if an IP address is reachable. If a cracker finds a computer they can try a port scan to detect and attack services on that computer.
- Social engineering awareness keeps employees aware of the dangers of social engineering and/or having a policy in place to prevent social engineering can reduce successful breaches of the network and servers.
- File Integrity Monitors are tools used to detect changes in the integrity of systems and files.

5.3 INTERNET SECURITY

When a computer connects to a network and begins communicating with others, it is taking a risk. **Internet security** involves the protection of a computer's internet account and files from intrusion of an unknown user.Basic security measures involve protection by well selected passwords, change of file permissions and back up of computer's data.

Security concerns are in some ways peripheral to normal business working, but serve to highlight just how important it is that business users feel confident when using IT systems. Security will probably always be high on the IT agenda simply because cyber criminals know that a successful attack is very profitable. This means they will always strive to find new ways to circumvent IT security, and users will consequently need to be continually vigilant. Whenever decisions need to be made about how to enhance a system, security will need to be held uppermost among its requirements. Internet security professionals should be fluent in the four major aspects:

- Penetration testing
- Intrusion Detection
- Incidence Response
- Legal / Audit Compliance

5.4 INFORMATION SECURITY

Information Security

means protecting information and information systems from unauthorized access, use, disclosure, disruption, modification or destruction.

The terms information security, computer security and information assurance are frequently incorrectly used interchangeably. These fields are interrelated often and share the common goals of protecting the confidentiality, integrity and availability of information; however, there are some subtle differences between them.

These differences lie primarily in the approach to the subject, the methodologies used, and the areas of concentration. Information security is concerned with the confidentiality, integrity and availability of data regardless of the form the data may take: electronic, print, or other forms.

Computer security can focus on ensuring the availability and correct operation of a computer system without concern for the information stored or processed by the computer.

Governments, military, corporations, financial institutions, hospitals, and private businesses amass a great deal of confidential information about their employees, customers, products, research, and financial status. Most of this information is now collected, processed and stored on electronic computers and transmitted across networks to other computers.

Should confidential information about a business' customers or finances or new product line fall into the hands of a competitor, such a breach of security could lead to lost business, law suits or even bankruptcy of the business. Protecting confidential information is a business requirement, and in many cases also an ethical and legal requirement.

For the individual, information security has a significant effect on privacy, which is viewed very differently in different cultures.

The field of information security has grown and evolved significantly in recent years. As a career choice there are many ways of gaining entry into the field. It offers many areas for specialization including: securing network(s) and allied infrastructure, securing applications and databases, security testing, information systems auditing, business continuity planning and digital forensics science, to name a few.

5.5 PHYSICAL SECURITY

Physical Security

Describes both measures that prevent or deter attackers from accessing a facility, resource, or information stored on physical media and guidance on how to design structures to resist various hostile acts. It can be as simple as a locked door or as elaborate as multiple layers of armed Security guards and Guardhouse placement.

Physical security, by no means, is a modern phenomenon. Physical security, as a field, exists in order to deter persons from entering a physical facility. Thus, as long as the need to defend physical facilities has existed, a need to provide for their security has also been needed. Historical examples of physical security include city walls, moats, booby traps, etc.

The key factor is the technology used for physical security has changed over time. While in past eras, there was no PIR-based technology, electronic access control systems, or VSS cameras, the essentially methodology of physical security has **not** altered over time.

5.5.1 Elements and Design

The field of security engineering has identified the following elements to physical security:

- Explosion protection;
- Obstacles, to frustrate trivial attackers and delay serious ones;
- Alarms, security lighting, security guard patrols or closed-circuit television cameras, to make it likely that attacks will be noticed; and
- Security response, to repel, catch or frustrate attackers when an attack is detected.

In a well designed system, these features must complement each other. There are at least four layers of physical security:

- Environmental design
- Mechanical and electronic access control
- Intrusion detection
- Video monitoring

The goal is to convince potential attackers that the likely costs of attack exceed the value of making the attack.

The initial layer of security for a campus, building, office, or physical space uses Crime Prevention Through Environmental Design to deter threats. Some of the most common examples are also the most basic - barbed wire, warning signs and fencing, concrete bollards, metal barriers, vehicle height-restrictors, site lighting and trenches.

The next layer is **mechanical** and includes gates, doors, and locks. Key control of the locks becomes a problem with large user populations and any user turnover. Keys quickly become unmanageable forcing the adoption of electronic access control. **Electronic access control** easily manages large user populations, controlling for user lifecycles times, dates, and individual access points. For example a user's access rights could allow access from 0700 to 1900 Monday through Friday and expires in 90 days.

An additional sub-layer of mechanical/electronic access control protection is reached by integrating a **key management system** to manage the possession and usage of mechanical keys to locks or property within a building or campus.

The third layer is **intrusion detection** systems or alarms. Intrusion detection monitors for attacks. It is less a preventative measure and more of a response measure, although some would argue that it is a deterrent. Intrusion detection has a high incidence of false alarms. In many jurisdictions, law enforcement will not respond to alarms from intrusion detection systems.

5.1: Closed-circuit television sign

The last layer is **video monitoring** systems. Like intrusion detection, these are not much of a deterrent. Video monitoring systems are more useful for incident verification and historical analysis. For instance, if alarms are being generated and there is a camera in place, the camera could be viewed to verify the alarms. In instances when an attack has already occurred and a camera is in place at the point of attack, the recorded video can be reviewed. Although the term closed-circuit television (CCTV) is common, it is quickly becoming outdated as more video systems lose the closed circuit for signal transmission and are instead transmitting on computer networks. Advances in information technology are transforming video monitoring into video analysis. For instance, once an image is digitized it can become data that sophisticated algorithms can act upon. As the speed and accuracy of automated analysis increases, the video system could move from a monitoring system to an intrusion detection system or access control system. It is not a stretch to imagine a video camera inputting data to a processor that outputs to a door lock. Instead of using some kind of key, whether mechanical or electrical, a person's visage is the key.

Fig. 5.2: Private Factory Guard

Intertwined in these four layers are people. Guards have a role in all layers, in the first as patrols and at checkpoints. In the second to administer electronic access control. In the third to respond to alarms. The response force must be able to arrive on site in less time than it is expected that the attacker will require to breach the barriers. And in the fourth to monitor and analyze video. Users obviously have a role also by questioning and reporting suspicious people. Aiding in identifying people as known versus unknown are identification systems. Often photo ID badges are used and are frequently coupled to the electronic access control system. Visitors are often required to wear a visitor badge.

5.5.2 Examples of Physical Security

Instances of physical security in everyday life are numerous.

Many installations, serving a myriad of different purposes, have physical obstacles in place to deter intrusion. This can be high walls, barbed wire, glass mounted on top of walls, etc.

The presence of PIR-based motion detectors are common in many places, as a means of noting intrusion into a physical installation. Moreover, VSS/CCTV cameras are becoming increasingly common, as a means of identifying persons who intrude into physical locations.

ATMs (cash dispensers) are protected, not by making them invulnerable, but by spoiling the money inside when they are attacked. Money tainted with a dye could act as a flag to the money's unlawful acquisition.

Safes are rated in terms of the time in minutes which a skilled, well equipped safe-breaker is expected to require to open the safe. These ratings are developed by highly skilled safe breakers employed by insurance agencies, such as Underwriters Laboratories. In a properly designed system, either the time between inspections by a patroiling guard should be less than that time, or an alarm response force should be able to reach it in less than that time.

Hiding the resources, or hiding the fact that resources are valuable, is also often a good idea as it will reduce the exposure to opponents and will cause further delays during an attack, but should not be relied upon as a principal means of ensuring security

5.6 NETWORK SECURITY

A security threat is defined as a circumstance, condition or event with the potential to cause economic hardship to data or network resources in the form of destruction, disclosure, modification of data, denial of service and fraud waste and abuse. Security concerns in e-commerce can be divided into two broad types –

(i) **Client server security** – uses various authorization methods to make sue that only valid users and programs have access to information resources as databases. Such mechanism includes password protection, encrypted smart cards, biometrics and firewalls.

(ii) **Data and transaction security** – ensures the privacy and confidentially in electronic messages and data packets, including the authentication of remote users in network transactions for activities such as on line payments. Preventive measures include data encryption using various cryptographic methods.

5.6.1 Client – Server Network Security

Network security on the Internet is a major concern for commercial organizations, especially top management. Recently the Internet has raised many new security concerns. By connecting to the internet, a local network organizations may be exposing itself to the entire population on the internet.

An Internet connection effectively breaches the physical security perimeter of the corporate network and opens itself to access from other network comprising the public Internet. For many commercial operations, security will simply be a matter of making sure that existing system features, such as password and privileges are configured properly. They need to audit all access to the network.

Hackers can use password guessing, password trapping, security holes in programs, or common network access procedures to impersonate users and thus pose a threat to the server. Client server network security problem manifest themselves in three ways –

(i) **Physical Security Holes** – Result when individuals gain unauthorized physical access to a computer. A good example would be a public workstation room, where it would easy for a wandering hacker to reboot a machine into single user mode and tamper with the files, if precautions are not taken. On the network, this is also a common problem, a hackers gain access to network systems by guessing passwords of various users.

(ii) **Software Security Holes** – result when badly written programs or privileged software are compromised into doing things they should not the most famous example of this category is the send mail hole. This is the highest level of access possible and could be used to delete the entire file system or create a new account or password file resulting in incalculable damage.

(iii) In Consistent Usage Holes – result when a system administrator assembles a combination of hardware and software such that the system is seriously flawed from a security point of view. The incompatibility of attempting two unconnected but useful things creates the security holes.

Problems like this are difficult to isolate once a system is set up and running, so it is better to carefully build the system with them in mind. This type of problem is becoming common as software becomes more complex.

To reduce these security threats, various protection methods are used.

- Trust based security
- Security through obscurity
- Password schemes
- Biometric systems.

5.6.1.1 Trust based security

Trust based security means to trust everyone and do nothing extra for protection. It is possible not to provide access restriction of any kind and to assume that all users are trust worthy and competent in their use to the shared network. This approach worked in the past, when the system administrator had to worry about a limited threat.

5.6.1.2 Security through obscurity – (less know)

Any network can be secure as long as nobody outside its management group is allowed to find out any thing about its operational details and users are provided information on a need to know basis. Hiding accounts passwords in binary files or scripts with the presumption that "nobody will never find them" is a prime case of STO.

In short, STO provides a false sense of security in computing systems by hiding information. In reality, however better pay from competitor's means that the knowledge goes with employees reducing the effectiveness of the method. Many users today have advanced knowledge of how their operating system works and through experience can guess at the bits of knowledge considered confidential. This bypasses the whole basis of STO and makes this method of security useless.

5.6.1.3 Password schemes

This scheme often works because users tend to choose relatively simple or familiar word as passwords. To beat the dictionary comparison method, experts often recommend using a minimum of eight-character length mixed case passwords containing at least one non-alphanumeric character and changing passwords every 60 to 90 days.

Because passwords in a remote log in session usually pass over the network in unencrypted form, any eavesdropper on the network can simply record the password any time it is used. Having distinct passwords for distinct devices is sometimes a problem, because people will write them down share them or include them in automatic scripts.

5.6.1.4 Biometric system

Biometric systems, the most secure level of authorization, involve some unique aspects of a person's body. Past biometric authentication was based on comparisons of fingerprints, palm prints, retinal patterns or on signature verification or voice recognition.

Disadvantage

Biometric systems are very expensive to implement. They may be better suited for controlling physical access – where one biometric unit can serve for many workers – than for network or workstation access.

5.6.1.5 Emerging client – Server security threats

Another security threats that are emerging in the electronic commerce world are mobile code (software agent), which in many ways resembles a more traditional virus threats. Mobile code is an executable program that has the ability to move from machine to machine and also to invoke itself without external influence. These threats can be divided into two major categories –

1. Threats to local computing environment from mobile software.
2. Access control and threats to servers that include impersonation, denial of service, packet relay and packet modification.

Software agents and malicious code threat

The major threats to security from running client software results because of the nature of the Internet client programs interpret data download from arbitrary servers on the internet.

The security threats arises when the downloaded data passes through local interpreters on the client system without the user's knowledge the potential security breach has been plugged in most of the new mail system.

The client threats arise from malicious data or code malicious code refers to viruses, worms, Trojan horses and other deviant S/W programs clients must scan for malicious data and executable program fragments that are transferred from the server to client.

Threats to servers

Threats to server consists of authorized modification of server data, unauthorized eavesdropping or modification of incoming data packets and compromise of a server system by exploiting bugs in the server S/W.

Compared to stand alone systems, network servers are much more susceptible to attacks where legitimate users are impersonated.

For example – Hackers have potential access to a large number of systems. Hackers can use popular Unix programs liker finger, rsh or ruser to discover account names and then try to guess simple passwords using a dictionary or more sophisticated password guessing methods.

Note: Hackers can use electronic eavesdropping to trap user names and unencrypted passwords sent over the network. They can monitor the activity on a system continuously and impersonate a user when the impersonation attack is less likely to be detected.

Hackers can eavesdrop using S/W that monitors packets sent over the network. Many networks programs, such as Telnet and ftp are vulnerable to eavesdroppers who obtain passwords, who are often sent across the network encrypted.

Three types of effects:

- Service overloading
- Message overloading
- Packet overloading

5.6.2 Data and Transaction Security

Data security is concerned with four aspects—Privacy authenticationl integrity and non-repudiation. If are have implemented these four aspects of data security then our data as well as transactions are served the four aspects are described below:

(i) **Privacy:** Data should be private, only limited user can access it.

(ii) **Authentication:** After proper verification, user can access data.

(iii) **Integrity:** Data should be boundup into packet.

(iv) **Non-repudiation:** After transaction starts, no one can deny neither sender or receiver of data.

5.7 FIREWALLS AND NETWORK SECURITY

The most commonly accepted network protection is a barrier – a firewall between the corporate network and the outside world. The term firewall can mean many things to many people, but basically it is a method of placing a device – a computer or a router between the network and the internet to control and monitor all traffic between the outside world and the local network.

In the context of the internet – "A Firewall is a system – a router, a personal computer, a host or a collection of hosts – set up specifically to shield a site or subnet from protocols and services that can be abused from hosts on the outside of the subnet".

A firewall system is usually located at a gateway point, such as a site's connection to the internet, but can be located at internal gateways to provide protection for smaller collection of hosts or subnets. Firewalls come in several types and offer various levels of security.

The firewall can be though of as a pair of mechanism –

(ii) To block incoming traffic.

(iii) To permit outgoing traffic.

Without a firewall, network security is a function of each host on the network and all hosts must cooperate to achieve a uniformly high level of security. The larger, the subnet, and the less manageable it is to maintain all hosts at the same level of security.

Firewalls in Practice—Firewalls range from simple traffic logging systems, that record all network traffic flowing through the firewall in a file or database for auditing purposes to more complex method.

(i) **Service Overloading:** Servers are especially vulnerable to service overloading. One can easily overload a www server by writing a small loop that sends requests continually for particular file. Example – home page.

(ii) **Message Overloading:** Message overloading occurs when someone sends a very large file to message box every few minutes. The message to occupy all the space on the disk and increases the number of receiving processes on the recipient machine trying it even more and often causing a disk crash. The best way to avoid message overloading is to provide separate areas for different programs and to make provisions for graceful failures.

(iii) **Packet Overloading:** The packet relay refers to the recording and retransmission of message packets in the network. This is a significant threat for programs that require authentication sequences because a hacker could replay legitimate authentication sequence messages to gain access to a secure system.

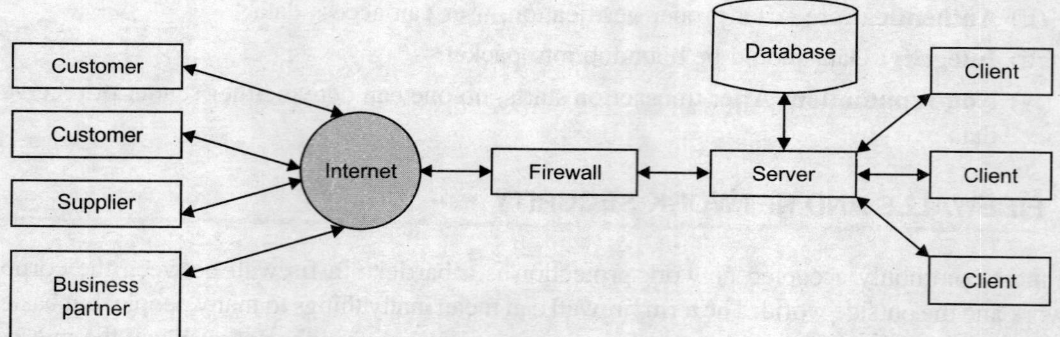

Fig. 5.3: Firewall

Such as

(i) IP Packet screening routers

(ii) Hardened firewall hosts.

(iii) Proxy application gateways.

The simplest firewall is a packet-filtering gateway or screening router more complex and secure are application gateways.

5.7.1 IP Packet Screening Routers

This is a static traffic routing service placed between the network service provider's router and the internal network. The traffic routing service may be implemented at an IP level via screening rules in a router or at an application level via proxy gateways and services.

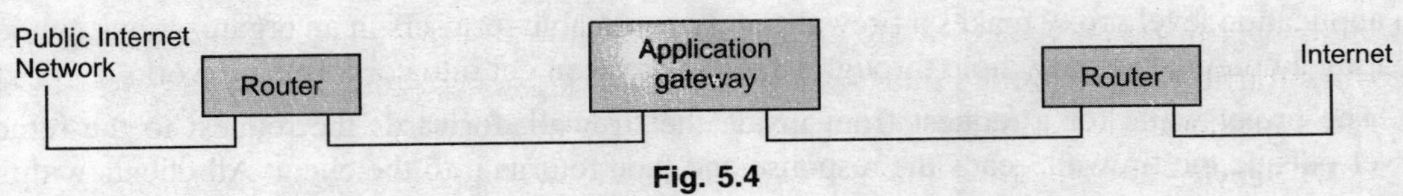

Fig. 5.4

The firewall router filters incoming packets to permit or deny IP packets based on several screening rules. These screening rules, implemented into the router are automatically performed.

Rules include target interface to which the packet is routed, known source IP address and incoming packet protocol (TCP, UDP, ICMP).

5.7.2 Hardened Firewall Hosts

A hardened firewall host is a stripped down machine that has been configured for increased security. This type of firewall requires inside or outside users to connect to the trusted applications on the firewall machine before connecting further.

These firewall are configured to protect against unauthenticated interactive logins from the external world.

Creating a hardened host requires:

- Removing all user accounts except those necessary for operation of the firewall ie. If users can not log in to the firewall host, they can not subvert the security measures.
- Removing all non crucial files and executable especially network server programs and client programs like FTP and telnet.
- Extending traffic logging and monitoring to check remote access.
- Disabling IP forwarding to prevent the firewall from forwarding unauthorized packets between the internet and the enterprise network.

Advantage

(i) Provide a greater level of audit & security

(ii) Information hiding.

(iii) Centralized and simplified network services management.

Disadvantage

(i) Increased Configuration cost.

(ii) Decreased level of service.

5.7.3 Proxy Application Gateways

A Proxy application gateway is a special server that typically runs on a firewall machine. Their primary use is access to applications such as the world wide web from within a secure parameter.

Instead of talking directly to external www servers, each request from the client would be routed to a proxy on the firewall that is defined by the user. The proxy knows how to get through the firewalls.

An application level proxy makes a firewall safely permeable for users in an organizations, without creating a potential security hole through which halkes can get into corporate networks.

The proxy waits for a request from inside the firewall, forwards the request to the remote server outside the firewall, reads the response and then returns it to the client. All clients within a given subnet use the same proxy.

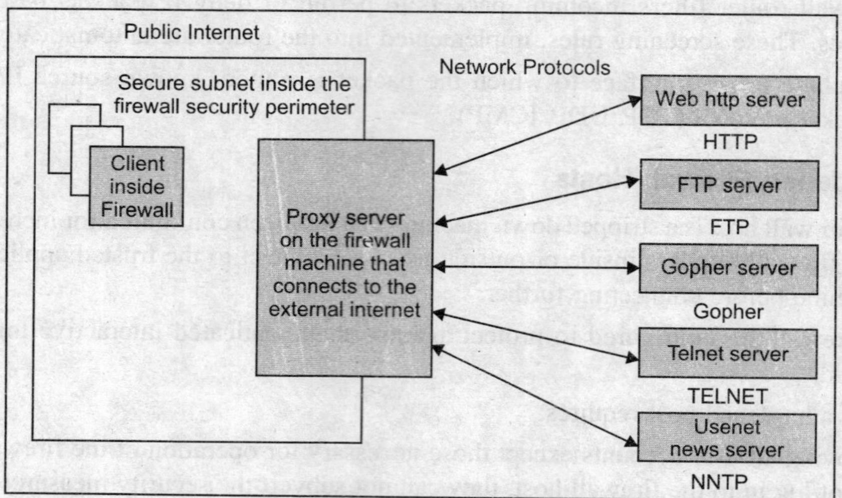

Fig. 5.5: Proxy servers on the World Wide Web

Advantage

(i) Allow browser programmers to ignore the complex networking code necessary to support every firewall protocol

(ii) Concentrate on important client issues.

(iii) Proxies can manage network functions.

(iv) Control access to services for individual methods, host and domain and the like.

(v) The proxy must be in a position to filter dangerous URLS and malformed commands.

5.8 IDENTITY MANAGEMENT

Identity management (ID management) is a broad administrative area that deals with identifying individuals in a system (such as a country, a network, or an enterprise) and controlling their access to resources within that system by associating user rights and restrictions with the established identity. The driver licensing system is a simple example of identity management: drivers are identified by their license numbers and user specifications (such as "can not drive after dark") are linked to the identifying number.

In an IT network, identity management software is used to automate administrative tasks, such as resetting user passwords. Enabling users to reset their own passwords can save significant money and resources, since a large percentage of help desk calls are password-related. Password synchronization (p-synch) enables a user to access resources across systems with a single password; a more advanced version called single signon enables synchronization across applications as well as systems.

In an enterprise setting, identity management is used to increase security and productivity, while decreasing cost and redundant effort. Standards such as Extensible Name Service (XNS) are being developed to enable identity management both within the enterprise and beyond.

In a wider context, industry groups such as the World Wide Web Consortium (W3C) and The Open Group are developing standards that would enable global identity management, in which each individual would be uniquely identified, and all applicable data would be linked to that identity. A position paper on the W3C Web site, Requirements for a Global Identity Management Service, maintains that establishing global identity management is crucial for the development of the Web and Web services. The W3C position paper stipulates, among other things, that such a system that must be universally portable and interoperable; that it must support unlimited identity-related attributes; that it must provide adequate mechanisms for privacy and accountability; and that it must be overseen by an independent governing authority.

In information systems, **identity management** is the management of the identity life cycle of entities (subjects or objects).

Identity management is multidisciplinary and covers many dimensions such as:

- **Technical.** With identity management systems.
- **Legal.** Such as legistation for data protection.
- **Police.** For instance for dealing with identity theft.
- **Social and humanity.** Dealing with issues such as privacy.
- **Security.** With elements such as access control.
- **Organizations**

5.8.1 History

Identity Management or IDM is a term related to how humans are identified and authorized across computer networks. It covers issues such as how users are given an identity, the protection of that identity and the technologies supporting that protection such as network protocols, digital certificates, passwords and so on.

Digital identity: Personal identifying information (PII) selectively exposed over a network.

While the term management requires little explanation, the term identity is a more abstract concept that will always be difficult to define in a way that satisfies everyone. It is a concept that is fluid and contextual depending on a number of factors including culture.

Thus the term management is appended to "identity" to indicate that there is technological and best practices framework around a somewhat intractable philosophical concept. Digital identity can be interpreted as the codification of identity names and attributes of a physical instance in a way that facilitates processing. In each organisation there is normally a role or department that is responsible for managing the schema of digital identities of their staff and their own objects, these represented by object identities or object identifiers (OID)

5.8.2 Three Perspectives on IdM

In the real-world context of engineering online systems, identity management can involve three perspectives:

1. The pure identity paradigm: Creation, management and deletion of identities without regard to access or entitlements;
2. The user access (log-on) paradigm: For example: a smart card and its associated data used by a customer to log on to a service or services (a traditional view);
3. The service paradigm: A system that delivers personalized, role-based, online, on-demand, multimedia (content), presence-based services to users and their devices.

5.8.3 The Pure Identity Paradigm

A general model of identity can be constructed from a small set of axiomatic principles, for example that all identities in a given abstract namespace are unique and distinctive, or that such identities bear a specific relationship to corresponding entities in the real world. An axiomatic model of this kind can be considered to express "pure identity" in the sense that the model is not constrained by the context in which it is applied. In general, an entity can have multiple identities, and each identity can consist of multiple attributes or identifiers, some of which are shared and some of which are unique within a given name space. The diagram below illustrates the conceptual relationship between identities and the entities they represent, as well as between identities and the attributes they consist of.

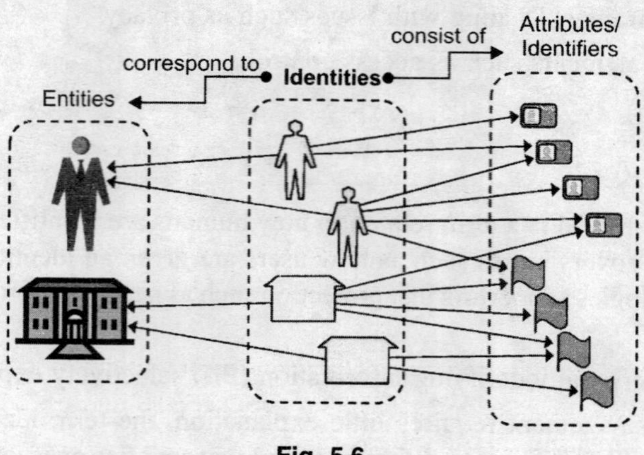

Fig. 5.6

In most theoretical and all practical models of digital identity, a given identity object consists of a finite set of properties. These properties may be used to record information about the object, either for purposes external to the model itself or so as to assist the model operationally, for example in classification and retrieval. A "pure identity" model is strictly not concerned with the external semantics of these properties.

The most common departure from "pure identity" in practice occurs with properties intended to assure some aspect of identity, for example a digital signature or software token which the model may use internally to verify some aspect of the identity in satisfaction of an external purpose. To the extent that the model attempts to express these semantics internally, it is not a pure model.

Contrast this situation with properties which might be externally used for purposes of information security such as managing access or entitlement, but which are simply stored and retrieved, in other words not treated specially by the model. The absence of external semantics within the model qualifies it as a "pure identity" model.

Identity management, then, can be defined as a set of operations on a given identity model, or as a set of capabilities with reference to it. In practice, identity management is often used to express how identity information is to be provisioned and reconciled between multiple identity models.

5.8.4 The User Access Paradigm

Identity management in the user "log-on" perspective may involve an integrated system of business processes, policies and technologies that enable organizations to facilitate and control access by their users to critical online applications and resources — while protecting confidential personal and business information from unauthorized access. It represents a category of interrelated solutions which system administrators employ towards managing user authentication, Access rights and restrictions, account profiles, passwords, and other attributes supportive of the roles/profiles of user in relation to applications and/or systems. Organizations have traditionally been less concerned with how users can verify the identity of service providers. The emergence of phishing attacks demonstrated that this must be considered as an integral part of the user access paradigm, otherwise users can not know which services they access. Petname systems have been proposed as a general approach to providing service provider identity management solutions.

5.8.5 The Service Paradigm

In the service paradigm perspective, where organizations evolve their systems to the world of converged services, the scope of identity management becomes much larger, and its application more critical. The scope of identity management includes all the resources of the company deployed to deliver online services. These may include devices, network equipment, servers, portals, content, applications and/or products as well as a user's credentials, address books, preferences, entitlements and telephone numbers.

Today[update], many organizations face a major clean-up in their systems if they are to bring identity coherence into their influence. Such coherence has become a prerequisite for delivering unified services to very large numbers of users on demand — cheaply, with security and single-customer viewing facilities.

5.8.6 Emerging Fundamental Points

- IdM provides significantly greater opportunities to online businesses beyond the process of authenticating and granting access to authorized users via cards, tokens and web access control systems.

- User-based IdM has started to evolve away from username/password and web-access control systems toward those that embrace preferences, parental controls, entitlements, policy-based routing, presence and loyalty schemes.
- IdM provides the focus to deal with system-wide data quality and integrity issues often encountered by fragmented databases and workflow processes.
- IdM embraces what the user actually gets in terms of products and services and how and when they acquire them. Therefore, IdM applies to the products and services of an organization, such as health, media, insurance, travel and government services. It is also applicable to means by which these products and services are provisioned and assigned to (or removed from) "entitled" users.
- IdM can deliver single-customer views that include the presence and location of the customer, single products and services as well as single IT infrastructure and network views to the respective parties. Accordingly, IdM relates intrinsically to information engineering, security and privacy.
- IdM covers the machinery (system infrastructure components) that delivers such services because a system may assign the service of a user to: a particular network technology, content title, usage right, media server, mail server, soft switch, voice mailbox, product catalog set, security domain, billing system, CRM, help desk etc.
- It is equally important for users to correctly identify and authenticate service providers as it is for service providers to identify and authenticate users. This aspect has largely been ignored during the early development of identity management, but will have to be taken seriously in the future.
- Critical factors in IdM projects include consideration of the online services of an organization (what the users log on to) and how they are managed from an internal and customer self-care perspective.

5.8.7 Issues

The management of identity raises a certain number of issues, such as privacy issues that may lead to the implementation of a surveillance society, or risk related to the stealing of identity (identity theft).

The advent of the social web, and in particular the important development of online social networking services, for which the management of their identities of their members represent a core element of these systems, also create a certain number of risks related to the disclosure of personal information, and in particular in losing an individual's privacy.

5.8.8 Addressing the Identity Issues

First, it is important to note that the people, and in particular the young people (15-25), are well aware of the risks towards eID enabled services. More specifically young people:

- are often very knowledgeable about these systems that they use frequently and for a long time

- have a high level of perception of risk associated to these tools

Addressing these different issues may be done only by legislation or via the use of technical systems, but have to combine the different dimensions such as:

- **Legal:** With the data protection legislation or human rights legislation.
- **Technical:** Using for instance with the use of Privacy enhancing technologies.
- **Security:** Including socio-psychological aspects (social engineering).
- **Police** (i.e. Forensics).

5.9 IDENTITY MANAGEMENT SYSTEMS

An **identity management system** refers to an information system, or to a set of technologies that can be used to support the management of identities.

An identity management system

1. Establishes the identity
   (a) Links a name (or number) with the subject or object;
   (b) Re-establishes the identity (i.e. links a new or additional name, or number, with the subject or object);
2. Describes the identity:
   (a) Optionally assigns one or more attributes applicable to the particular subject or object to the identity;
   (b) Re-describes the identity (i.e. changes one or more attributes applicable to the particular subject or object);
3. Follows identity activity:
   (a) Record and/or provide access to logs of identity activity
   (b) Optionally auto-analyze behaviour patterns of the identity
4. Destroys the identity

5.9.1 Electronic Identity Management

Several interpretations of identity management (IdM) have been developed in the IT industry. Computer scientists traditionally associate the phrase with the management of user credentials and the means by which users might log on to an online system. With the emergence of phishing attacks it became obvious that service provider identities also need to be managed. Phishing precisely exploits the difficulty of properly identifying and authenticating service providers on the web due to poor management of service provider identities. With relation to online government services the term National Identity Management[j] has been used. In general, electronic IdM can be said to cover the management of any form of digital identites. The focus on identity management goes back to the development of directories, such as X.500, where a namespace serves to hold named objects that represent real-life "identified" entities, such as countries, organizations, applications, subscribers or devices. The X.509 ITU-T standard defined certificates carried identity attributes as two directory names: the certificate subject and the certificate issuer. X.509 certificates and PKI systems operate to prove the online "identity" of a subject. Therefore, in IT terms, one can consider identity management as the management of information (as held in a directory) that represents items identified in real life (e.g. users, organisations, devices, services, etc). The design of such systems requires explicit information and identity engineering tasks.

The evolution of identity management follows the progression of Internet technology closely. In the environment of static web pages and static portals of the early 1990s, corporations investigated the delivery of informative web content such as the "white pages" of employees. Subsequently, as the information changed (due to employee turnover, provisioning and de-provisioning), the ability to perform self-service and help-desk updates more efficiently morphed into what became known as Identity Management today[update].

Typical identity management functionality includes the following:

- User information self-service
- Password resetting
- Management of lost passwords
- Workflow
- Provisioning and de-provisioning of identities from resources

Identity management also addresses the age-old 'N+1' problem — where every new application may entail the setting up of new data stores of users. The ability to centrally manage the provisioning and de-provisioning of identities, and consolidate the proliferation of identity stores, all form part of the identity management process. The term identity engineering refers to putting engineering effort into managing large numbers of interrelated items that have identifiers or names.

5.9.2 Types of Identity Management Systems

We can distinguish three main types of IMS:

- **Type 1: IMS for account management**
  - Type 1 IMS are used within an organization especially for account and access administration for computers and network services (e.g. the Windows-NT-Domain-concept by Microsoft, NIS by SUN etc.).
- **Type 2: IMS for profiling of user data by an organization**
  - Is used for managing and exploiting large amount of statistical user information (for instance in Marketing).
- **Type 3: IMS for user-controlled context-dependent role and pseudonym management**
  - Type 3 IMS are characterised by the user control as basically decentralised, user and client-orientated (Management done by the user). The data managed are mainly personal data. This kind of IMS can for instance be found with the user profile in social network services.

5.9.3 Solutions

Solutions which fall under the category of identity management may include:

Management of identities

- Provisioning/De-provisioning of accounts
- Workflow automation
- Delegated administration
- Password synchronization
- Self-service password reset

Access control

- Policy-based access control
- Enterprise/Legacy single sign-on (SSO)
- Web single sign-on (SeoS)
- Reduced sign-on

Directory services

- Identity repository (directory services for the administration of user account attributes)
- Metadata replication/Synchronization
- Directory virtualization (Virtual directory)
- e-Business scale directory systems
- Next-generation systems - Composite Adaptive Directory Services (CADS) and CADS SDP

Other categories

- Role-based access control (RBAC)
- Federation of user access rights on web applications across otherwise untrusted networks
- Directory-enabled networking and 802.1X EAP
- Security Assertion Markup Language (SAML)
- Liberty Alliance — A consortium promoting federated identity management
- Shibboleth (Internet2) — Identity standards targeted towards educational environments
- Global Trust Center

5.10 ACCESS MANAGEMENT

An Access Management System is the process of creating, updating and deactivating accounts. This Process is responsible for allowing Users to make use of IT Services, data or other Assets.

Access Management helps to protect the Confidentiality, Integrity and Availability of Assets by ensuring that only authorized Users are able to access or modify the Assets. Access Management is sometimes referred to as Rights Management or Identity Management.

5.10.1 Extending Enterprise Security with Identity and Access Management

Banks, insurance companies, and capital markets institutions are faced with the monumental task of managing access to mission-critical systems. These organizations have large numbers of internal and external users accessing an increasing number of applications, with each user requiring a different level of security and control requirements. In addition, these organizations must also address identity management concerns that arise from compliance issues related to regulations like Sarbanes-Oxley, the Health Information Portability and Accountability Act, and the Gramm-Leach-Bliley Act.

High administrative costs due to account maintenance, password resets, inconsistent information, inflexible information technology (IT) environments, silos due to bank mergers and acquisitions, and, finally, aging IT infrastructures make this even more challenging for financial services organizations. Together, these factors are propelling the adoption of identity and access management solutions within the financial services sector.

5.10.2 What Is Identity and Access Management?

Identity and access management is far more than just a security technology. Ultimately, it will be the foundation for managing application services and will pave the way for smoother, Service-Oriented Architecture (SOA)–based business integration.

The commoditization of services, the automation of business processes, and the alignment of products and platforms are forcing many financial services organizations to re-evaluate their existing technology and move towards a shared services model. Organizations want to derive more business value from IT, and this is driving fundamental changes. Focus is shifting from individual applications and servers to services and automated business processes, which require a coherent shared-services model to deliver these functions.

Banks and insurance companies are no exception; they often have large user bases that require access to an increasing number of applications with different classes of users and different security and control requirements. The integration of identity and access management services provide individualized security and access rights based on a person's identity.

Leveraging identity management to automate provisioning and de-provisioning of user accounts and for centralized authentication logging and auditing capabilities can also play an important role in regulatory compliance. It provides a means to facilitate the audit reporting process by enabling institutions to track and manage user identities and security access while maintaining central control over security policies and security administration workflow.

Setting up an identity management environment can be a daunting task. The overall concept is complex and touches a tremendous number of applications and users. Companies deploying this type of solution need to align organizational processes and technology to allow consolidation and integration of identity and access management services. Moreover, they also need to provide individualized security and access rights based on a person's identity.

For example, a large insurance client was looking to establish an identity and integration management system for all its users and departments. The intent of this project was to decrease the amount of manual effort and time spent in the area of account and printer management. In addition, they were looking to implement an effective single point of administration portal.

Avanade evaluated the company's existing processes and identified the benefits of designing an identity management infrastructure. Microsoft Identity Integration Server was implemented and integrated with the company's intranet phonebook, Alcatel, USU Value wise, HP Service desk, and Windows Active Directory services for user and password management. The company also deployed an end-user portal to simplify password resets.

The insurance company was able to reduce the overall operational complexity for their help desk, while avoiding further resource costs with an automated user-provisioning process and centralized administration.

5.10.3 Build a Business Case

Given the complexity of identity and access management, it is often easy to underestimate the scope of a project. When it comes to planning, it is crucial to outline objectives and goals up front. In addition, it is important for financial institutions to focus on the following core drivers for identity management implementations:

Business

Reducing application maintenance costs, increasing productivity, and facilitating regulatory compliance.

Security

Enforcing the password policy, disabling user access privileges instantly, and maintaining effective control of the account life cycle.

Functional

Providing simplified sign-on, delegating security administration, and maintaining central control.

Before selecting partners or products, a plan must be in place that provides clear strategic direction and details the scope, end goals, and drivers for the project.

The return on investment from an identity and access management solution comes from the cost savings resulting from increased productivity, reduced administration time, improved profitability, and, most importantly, reduced security incidents.

In the longer term, SOA may be the driver of identity management as it dovetails with service orchestration into a single infrastructure solution. For now, identity management is still gaining momentum and provides a compelling solution for managing Webs of application services within financial services companies.

5.11 INTRUSION DETECTION

Intrusion detection is a type of security management system for computers and networks. An Intrusion detection system gathers and analyzes information from various areas within a computer or a network to identify possible security breaches, which include both intrusions (attacks from outside the organization) and misuse (attacks from within the organization). Intrusion detection uses vulnerability assessment (sometimes referred to as scanning), which is a technology developed to assess the security of a computer system or network. Intrusion detection functions include:

- Monitoring and analyzing both user and system activities
- Analyzing system configurations and vulnerabilities
- Assessing system and file integrity
- Ability to recognize patterns typical of attacks
- Analysis of abnormal activity patterns
- Tracking user policy violations

Intrusion detection systems are being developed in response to the increasing number of attacks on major sites and networks, including those of the Pentagon, the White House, NATO, and the U.S. Defense Department. The safeguarding of security is becoming increasingly difficult, because the possible technologies of attack are becoming ever more sophisticated; at the same time, less technical ability is required for the novice attacker, because proven past methods are easily accessed through the Web.

Typically, an Intrusion detection system follows a two-step process. The first procedures are host-based and are considered the passive component, these include: inspection of the system's configuration files to detect inadvisable settings; inspection of the password files to detect inadvisable passwords; and inspection of other system areas to detect policy violations. The second procedures are network-based and are considered the active component: mechanisms are set in place to reenact known methods of attack and to record system responses. In 1998, ICSA.net, a leading security assurance organization, formed the Intrusion Detection Systems Consortium (IDSC) as an open forum for Intrusion detection product developers with the aim of disseminating information to the end user and developing industry standards.

The major functions of intrusion detection are the following

- **Risk:** Accidental or unpredictable exposure of information, or violation of operations integrity due to the malfunction of hardware or incomplete or incorrect software design.
- **Vulnerability:** A known or suspected flaw in the hardware or software or operation of a system that exposes the system to penetration or its information to accidental disclosure.
- **Attack:** A specific formulation or execution of a plan to carry out a threat.
- **Penetration:** A successful attack — the ability to obtain unauthorized (undetected) access to files and programs or the control state of a computer system.

5.11.1 Introduction

In the last three years, the networking revolution has finally come of age. More than ever before, we see that the Internet is changing computing as we know it. The possibilities and opportunities are limitless; unfortunately, so too are the risks and chances of malicious intrusions. It is very important that the security mechanisms of a system are designed so as to prevent unauthorized access to system resources and data. However, completely preventing breaches of security appear, at present, unrealistic. Anderson, while introducing the concept of intrusion detection in 1980, defined an **intrusion attempt** or a **threat** to be the potential possibility of a deliberate unauthorized attempt to:

- Access information,
- Manipulate information, or
- Render a system unreliable or unusable.

5.11.2 The need for Intrusion Detection Systems

A computer system should provide confidentiality, integrity and assurance against denial of service. However, due to increased connectivity (especially on the Internet), and the vast spectrum of financial possibilities that are opening up, more and more systems are subject to attack by intruders. There are two ways to handle subversion attempts.

1. Prevent subversion itself by building a completely secure system

For this, we require all users to identify and authenticate themselves and we could protect data by various cryptographic methods and very tight access control mechanisms. However this is not really feasible because:

1. In practice, it is not possible to build a completely secure system. Miller gives a compelling report on bugs in popular programs and operating systems that seems to indicate that (a) bug free software is still a dream and (b) no-one seems to want to make the effort to try to develop such software. Apart from the fact that we do not seem to be getting our money's worth when we buy software, there are also security implications when our E-mail software, for example, can be attacked. Designing and implementing a totally secure system is thus an extremely difficult task.
2. The vast installed base of systems worldwide guarantees that any transition to a secure system, (if it is ever developed) will be long in coming.
3. Cryptographic methods have their own problems. Passwords can be cracked, users can lose their passwords, and entire crypto-systems can be broken.
4. Even a truly secure system is vulnerable to abuse by insiders who abuse their privileges.
5. It has been seen that that the relationship between the level of access control and user efficiency is an inverse one, which means that the stricter the mechanisms, the lower the efficiency becomes.

We thus see that we are stuck with systems that have vulnerabilities for a while to come. If there are attacks on a system, we would like to detect them as soon as possible (preferably in real-time) and take appropriate action. This is essentially what an Intrusion Detection System (IDS) does. An Intrusion Detection System does not usually take preventive measures when an attack is detected; it is a reactive rather than pro-active agent. It plays the role of an informant rather than a police officer.

2. Audit data generated by the operating system

The most popular way to detect intrusions has been by using the audit data generated by the operating system. An audit trail is a record of activities on a system that are logged to a file in chronologically sorted order. Since almost all activities are logged on a system, it is possible that a manual inspection of these logs would allow intrusions to be detected. However, the incredibly large sizes of audit data generated (on the order of 100 Megabytes a day) make manual analysis impossible. Audit data generated by the operating systems automate the drudgery of wading through the audit data jungle. Audit trails are particularly useful because they can be used to establish guilt of attackers, and they are often the only way to detect unauthorized but subversive user activity.

Many times, even after an attack has occurred, it is important to analyze the audit data so that the extent of damage can be determined, the tracking down of the attackers is facilitated, and steps may be taken to prevent such attacks in future. An audit data generated by the operating system can also be used to analyze audit data for such insights. This makes IDSs valuable as real-time as well as post-mortem analysis tools.

Anderson also classified intruders into two types, the external intruders who are unauthorized users of the machines they attack, and internal intruders, who have permission to access the system, but not some portions of it. He further divided internal intruders into intruders who masquerade as another user, those with legitimate access to sensitive data, and the most dangerous type, the clandestine intruders who have the power to turn off audit control for them selves.

5.12 CLASSIFICATION OF INTRUSION DETECTION SYSTEMS

Intrusions can be divided into 6 main types

1. Attempted break-ins, which are detected by atypical behavior profiles or violations of security constraints.
2. Masquerade attacks, which are detected by atypical behavior profiles or violations of security constraints.
3. Penetration of the security control system, which are detected by monitoring for specific patterns of activity.
4. Leakage, which is detected by atypical use of system resources.
5. Denial of service, which is detected by atypical use of system resources.
6. Malicious use, which is detected by atypical behavior profiles, violations of security constraints, or use of special privileges.

However, we can divide the techniques of intrusion detection into two main types.

5.12.1 Anomaly Detection

Anomaly detection techniques assume that all intrusive activities are necessarily anomalous. This means that if we could establish a "normal activity profile" for a system, we could, in theory, flag all system states varying from the established profile by statistically significant amounts as intrusion attempts. However, if we consider that the set of intrusive activities only intersects the set of anomalous activities instead of being exactly the same, we find a couple of interesting possibilities:

1. Anomalous activities that are not intrusive are flagged as intrusive.
2. Intrusive activities that are not anomalous result in false negatives (events are not flagged intrusive, though they actually are). This is a dangerous problem, and is far more serious than the problem of false positives.

The main issues in anomaly detection systems thus become the selection of threshold levels so that neither of the above 2 problems is unreasonably magnified, and the selection of features to monitor. Anomaly detection systems are also computationally expensive because of the overhead of keeping track of, and possibly updating several system profile metrics.

5.12.2 Anomaly Detection Systems

There have been a few major approaches to anomaly intrusion detection systems, some of which are described below.

5.12.2.1 Statistical Approaches

In this method, initially, behavior profiles for subjects are generated. As the system continues running, the anomaly detector constantly generates the variance of the present profile from the original one. We note that, in this case, there may be several measures that affect the behavior profile, like activity measures, CPU time used, number of network connections in a time period, etc. In some systems, the current profile and the previous profile are merged at intervals, but in some other systems profile generation is a one time activity.

The main advantage to statistical systems is that they adaptively learn the behavior of users; they are thus potentially more sensitive than human experts. However there are a few problems with statistical approaches: they can gradually be trained by intruders so that eventually, intrusive events are considered normal, false positives and false negatives are generated depending on whether the threshold is set too low or too high, and relationships between events are missed because of the insensitivity of statistical measures to the order of events.

An open issue with statistical approaches in particular and anomaly detection systems in general, is the selection of measures to monitor. It is not known exactly what the subset of all possible measures that accurately predicts intrusive activities is. Static methods of determining these measures are sometimes misleading because of the unique features of a particular system. Thus, it seems that a combination of static and dynamic determination of the set of measures should be done. Some problems associated with this technique have been remedied by other methods, including the method involving Predictive Pattern Generation, which takes past events into account when analyzing the data.

5.12.2.2 Predictive pattern generation

This method of intrusion detection tries to predict future events based on the events that have already occurred. Therefore, we could have a rule

E1 – E2 ⟶ (E3 = 80%, E4 = 15%, E5 = 5%)

This would mean that given that events E1 and E2 have occurred, with E2 occurring after E1, there is an 80% probability that event E3 will follow, a 15% chance that event E4 will follow and a 5% probability that event E5 will follow. The problem with this is that some intrusion scenarios that are not described by the rules will not be flagged intrusive. Thus, if an event sequence A - B - C exists that is intrusive, but not listed in the rule base, it will be classified as unrecognized. This problem can be partially solved by flagging any unknown events as intrusions (increasing the probability of false positives), or by flagging them as non-intrusive (thus increasing the probability of false negatives). In the normal case, however, an event is flagged intrusive if the left hand side of a rule is matched, but the right hand side is statistically very deviant from the prediction.

There are several advantages to this approach. First, rule based sequential patterns can detect anomalous activities that were difficult with traditional methods. Second, systems built using this model are highly adaptive to changes. This is because low quality patterns are continuously eliminated, finally leaving the higher quality patterns behind. Third, it is easier to detect users who try to train the system during its learning period. And fourth, anomalous activities can be detected and reported within seconds of receiving audit events.

Another approach taken in intrusion detection systems is the use of **neural networks**. The idea here is to train the neural network to predict a user's next action or command, given the window of n previous actions or commands. The network is trained on a set of representative user commands. After the training period, the network tries to match actual commands with the actual user profile already present in the net. Any incorrectly predicted events (events and commands are used interchangeably in this discussion) actually measure the deviation of the user from the established profile.

Some advantages of using neural networks are:

- They cope well with noisy data; their success does not depend on any statistical assumption about the nature of the underlying data.
- They are easier to modify for new user communities. However, they have some problems. First, a small window will result in false positives while a large window will result in irrelevant data as well as increase the chance of false negatives. Second, the net topology is only determined after considerable trial and error. And third, the intruder can train the net during its learning phase.

5.12.3 Misuse Detection

The misuse detection scheme is that there are ways to represent attacks in the form of a pattern or a signature so that even variations of the same attack can be detected. This means that these systems are not unlike virus detection systems — they can detect many or all known attack patterns, but they are of little use for as yet unknown attack methods. An interesting point to note is that anomaly detection systems try to detect the complement of "bad" behavior. Misuse detection systems try to recognize known "bad" behavior. The main issues in misuse detection systems are how to write a signature that encompasses all possible variations of the pertinent attack, and how to write signatures that do not also match non-intrusive activity.

5.12.4 Misuse Detection Systems

Some of Misuse Detection Systems are explained below

5.12.4.1 Expert Systems

Are modeled in such a way as to separate the rule matching phase from the action phase. The matching is done according to audit trail events. The Next Generation Intrusion Detection Expert System is an interesting case study for the expert system approach. NIDES follows a hybrid intrusion detection technique consisting of a misuse detection component as well as an anomaly detection component. The anomaly detector is based on the statistical approach, and it flags events as intrusive if they are largely deviant from the expected behavior. To do this, it builds user profiles based on many different criteria (more than 30 criteria, including CPU and I/O usage, commands used, local network activity, system errors etc.). These profiles are updated at periodic intervals.

The expert system misuse detection component encodes known intrusion scenarios and attack patterns. The rule database can be changed for different systems. One advantage of the NIDES approach is that it has a statistical component as well as an expert system component. This means that the chances of one system catching intrusions missed by the other increase. Another advantage is the problem's control reasoning is cleanly separated from the formulation of the solution.

There are some draw backs to the expert system approach too. For example, the expert system has to be formulated by a security professional and thus the system is only as strong as the security personnel who program it. This means that there is a real chance that expert systems can fail to flag intrusions. It is for this reason that NIDES has an anomaly as well as a misuse detection component. These two components are loosely coupled in the sense that they perform their operations independently for the most part. The NIDES system runs on a machine different from the machine(s) to be monitored, which could be unreasonable overhead. Furthermore, additions and deletions of rules from the rule-base must take into account the inter-dependencies between different rules in the rule-base. And there is no recognition of the sequential ordering of data, because the various conditions that make up a rule are not recognized to be ordered.

5.12.4.2 Keystroke Monitoring

Is a very simple technique that monitors keystrokes for attack patterns. Unfortunately the system has several defects; the method does not analyze the running of a program, only the keystrokes. This means that a malicious program cannot be flagged for intrusive activities. Operating systems do not offer much support for keystroke capturing, so the keystroke monitor should have a hook that analyses keystrokes before sending them on to their intended receiver. An improvement to this would be to monitor system calls by application programs as well, so that an analysis of the program's execution is possible.

5.12.4.3 Model Based Intrusion Detection

States that certain scenarios are inferred by certain other observable activities. If these activities are monitored, it is possible to find intrusion attempts by looking at activities that infer a certain intrusion scenario. The model based scheme consists of three important modules. The anticipator uses the active models and the scenario models to try to predict the next step in the scenario that is expected to occur. A scenario model is a knowledge base with specifications of intrusion scenarios. The planner then translates this hypothesis into a format that shows the behavior as it would occur in the audit trail. It uses the predicted information to plan what to search for next. The interpreter then searches for this data in the audit trail. The system proceeds this way, accumulating more and more evidence for an intrusion attempt until a threshold is crossed; at this point, it signals an intrusion attempt.

This is a very clean approach. Because the planner and the interpreter know what they are searching for at each step, the large amounts of noise present in audit data can be filtered, leading to excellent performance improvements. In addition, the system can predict the attacker's next move based on the intrusion model. These predictions can be used to verify an intrusion hypothesis, to take preventive measures, or to determine what data to look for next.

However, there are some critical issues related to this system. First, patterns for intrusion scenarios must be easily recognized. Second, patterns must always occur in the behavior being looked for. And finally, patterns must be distinguishing; they must *not* be associated with any other normal behavior.

5.12.4.4 A Misuse Detection System

Based on Pattern Matching, encodes known intrusion signatures as patterns that are then matched against the audit data. Like the state transition analysis model, this model attempts to match incoming events to the patterns representing intrusion scenarios. The implementation makes transitions on certain events, called labels, and Boolean variables called guards can be placed at each transition. The difference between this and the state transition model is that the state transition model associates these guards with states, rather than transitions. The important advantages of this model are:

1. **Declarative Specification:** It only needs to be specified what patterns need to be matched, not how to match them.
2. **Multiple event streams can be used together to match against patterns** for each stream without the need to combine streams. This means that streams can be processed independently, and their results can be analyzed together to give evidence of intrusive activity.
3. **Portability:** Since intrusion signatures are written in a system independent script, they need not be rewritten for different audit trails. The patterns' declarative specifications enable them to be exchanged across different Operating Systems and different audit trails.

4. **It has excellent real-time capabilities.** It reports a CPU overhead of 5-6% when scanning for 100 different patterns, which is excellent.
5. **It can detect some attack signatures** like the failed logins signature that the state transition model cannot do.

One problem with this model it can only detect attacks based on known vulnerabilities. In addition, pattern matching is not very useful for representing ill-defined patterns and it is not an easy task to translate known attack scenarios into patterns that can be used by the model. Also, it cannot detect passive wire-tapping intrusions, nor can in detect spoofing attacks where a machine pretends to be another machine by using its IP address. An interesting fact about this Intrusion Detection System is that, it is called IDIOT (Intrusion Detection in Our Time), and we leave it to the reader to ponder the appropriateness of the name for the state of the art in intrusion detection.

5.12.4.5 Generic Intrusion Detection Model

A set of profiles for subjects (usually, but not necessarily users of a system) is maintained. When an audit record is generated, the model matches it with the appropriate profile and then makes decisions on updating the profile, checking for abnormal behavior and reporting anomalies detected. To do this, it monitors system services such as file accesses, executable programs, and logins. It has no specific knowledge of the target system's vulnerabilities, although this knowledge would be extremely useful in making the model more valuable. In fact, the Intrusion Detection Expert System (IDES) developed based on this model. However, there are some systems that do not fit easily into this model.

5.12.4.6 Network Security Monitor

Is an intrusion detection system developed at the University of California-Davis. NSM is a network-based Intrusion Detection System that differs from all of the Intrusion Detection Systems discussed earlier because it does not use or analyze the host machine(s) audit trails. Rather, it monitors network traffic in order to detect intrusions. Since network based attacks are expected to be prevalent in the future due to the mushrooming of the Internet, NSM could prove to be a valuable tool to detect intrusive activity.

NSM has several perceived advantages. First, the Intrusion Detection System gets instantaneous access to network data. Second, the Intrusion Detection System is hidden from the intruder because it is passively listening to network traffic. Therefore, it cannot be shut off or its data compromised. Finally, the Intrusion Detection System can be used with any system, because it is monitoring network traffic, protocols for which (TCP, UDP etc.) are standardized. There is no problem with different audit files.

5.13 SECURITY INFORMATION MANAGEMENT

Security Information Management (SIM)

Is the industry-specific term in computer security referring to the collection of data (typically log files; e.g. eventlogs) into a central repository for trend analysis. Security Information Management products generally comprise software agents running on the computers that are to be monitored, communicating with a centralized server acting as a "security console", sending it information about security-related events, which displays reports, charts, and graphs of that information, often in real time. The software agents can incorporate local filters, to reduce and manipulate the data that they send to the server. The security console is monitored by a human being, who reviews the consolidated information, and takes action in response to any alerts issued.

The data that are sent to the server, to be correlated and analyzed, are normalized by the software agents into a common form, usually XML. Those data are then aggregated, in order to reduce their overall size. The terminology can easily be mistaken as a reference to the whole aspect of protecting one's infrastructure from any computer security breach. Due to historic reasons of terminology evolution; SIM refers to just the part of information security which consists of discovery of 'bad behavior' by using data collection techniques. The term commonly used to represent an entire security infrastructure that protects an environment is commonly called information security management. Security information management is also referred to as SEM (security event management) and SIEM (security information and event management). Commercial SIEM products include EventTracker by Prism Microsystems, Trigeo, ArcSight, SenSage, Cisco Security MARS, Snare and others. Open Source SIEM products include OSSIM, and Prelude.

5.14 SUMMARY

- **Security Management** is a broad field of management related to asset management, physical security and human resource safety functions. It entails the identification of an organization's information assets and the development, documentation and implementation of policies, standards, procedures and guidelines.
- **Security** is the degree of protection against danger, loss, and criminals. Security has to be compared and contrasted with other related concepts: Safety, continuity, reliability.
- The key difference between security and reliability is that security must take into account the actions of people attempting to cause destruction.
- **Computer security** is a branch of technology known as information security as applied to computers and networks.
- The objective of computer security includes protection of information and property from theft, corruption, or natural disaster, while allowing the information and property to remain accessible and productive to its intended users.
- When a computer connects to a network and begins communicating with others, it is taking a risk.
- **Internet security** involves the protection of a computer's internet account and files from intrusion of an unknown user.Basic security measures involve protection by well selected passwords, change of file permissions and back up of computer's data.
- **Information security** means protecting information and information systems from unauthorized access, use, disclosure, disruption, modification or destruction.

- **Physical security** describes both measures that prevent or deter attackers from accessing a facility, resource, or information stored on physical media and guidance on how to design structures to resist various hostile acts. It can be as simple as a locked door or as elaborate as multiple layers of armed Security guards and Guardhouse placement.
- A security threat is defined as a circumstance, condition or event with the potential to cause economic hardship to data or network resources in the form of destruction, disclosure, and modification of data, denial of service and fraud waste and abuse.
- The most commonly accepted network protection is a barrier – a firewall between the corporate network and the outside world. The term firewall can mean many things to many people, but basically it is a method of placing a device – a computer or a router between the network and the internet to control and monitor all traffic between the outside world and the local network.
- Identity management (ID management) is a broad administrative area that deals with identifying individuals in a system (such as a country, a network, or an enterprise) and controlling their access to resources within that system by associating user rights and restrictions with the established identity.
- An **identity management system** refers to an information system, or to a set of technologies that can be used to support the management of identities.
- An Access Management System is the process of creating, updating and deactivating accounts. This Process is responsible for allowing Users to make use of IT Services, data or other Assets.
- Access Management helps to protect the Confidentiality, Integrity and Availability of Assets by ensuring that only authorized Users are able to access or modify the Assets. Access Management is sometimes referred to as Rights Management or Identity Management.
- Intrusion detection is a type of security management system for computers and networks. An Intrusion detection system gathers and analyzes information from various areas within a computer or a network to identify possible security breaches, which include both intrusions (attacks from outside the organization) and misuse (attacks from within the organization).
- **Security information management (SIM)** is the industry-specific term in computer security referring to the collection of data (typically log files; e.g. eventlogs) into a central repository for trend analysis.

5.15 REVIEW QUESTIONS

1. What lets us access the shared network folders quickly without having to browse the entire network?
2. What is Pix Firewall Security? How does it differ from a firewall?
3. Explain what routing protocol is and its working of this?

4. What is the difference between RIPv1 vs. RIPv? State advantages and disadvantages in detailed. Which is better to use?
5. A software company owns four branches and Internet connection is available at every branch what will be required to build a Virtual Private Network between them and how it will be done.
6. Suppose in a LAN, if one host does not get connection, what problem could have occurred?
7. What is domain controller and how it manages a network security.
8. How to create trust relationship between two different forests.

CHAPTER 6

Legal Issues for E-Business

The legal aspect of e-business is all about managing risks. It is important to ensure that the content of website is accurate and complies with current law. It is also important to regularly review the website once it is up and running to ensure that it continues to comply. Some of the important general legal issues affecting e-business are listed below

- Privacy laws
- Defamation
- Taxation and GST
- Contracts
- Terms and conditions
- Trade practices
- Intellectual property
- Copyright
- Trade marks
- Confidential information
- Digital signatures
- Security
- Jurisdiction
- Disability discrimination

6.1 E-BUSINESS

Broadly speaking, the term "e-business" refers to using the Internet for doing business.

6.1.1 Are you doing e-business?

Is your business doing e-business? Here's a checklist to find out. If you can say yes to any of these, then you are doing e-business.

- We communicate with customers, clients or suppliers via email.
- We send emails to other businesses to order products and services.
- We sell our products or services via our website.
- We use the Web to find information, such as prices, phone numbers, reviews of products.
- We use the Web for research, such as the latest industry trends.
- We use our website to provide information about our products and services.
- We use our website as a means of managing the information in our business.
- We use the Internet for online banking and paying our bills using BPAY.

No level of e-business is necessarily better than any other level. Some businesses don't need a website but deal all day with other businesses and customers online via email and an e-marketplace. Other businesses have a website that helps them sell their products all around the world. It's up to each business to determine what level of e-business is right for them.

6.1.2 The Difference Between e-Business and e-Commerce

The term e-commerce has a narrower meaning than e-business. It refers to using the Internet to order and pay for products or services. So e-commerce is a sub-set of e-business. E-commerce happens when a consumer orders a product from a business and pays for it either when they receive the product or directly online at the time of ordering. It happens when a business pays another business via its website for supplies.

E-commerce refers specifically to the paying for goods and services, whereas e-business covers the full range of business activities that can happen or be assisted via email or the Web.

6.2 BENEFITS OF E-BUSINESS

6.2.1 Create Cost-savings and Operational Efficiencies

Some businesses make a great deal of money from their websites through greatly increased sales and uptake of services. Many more benefit from the ability of an e-business plan, properly thought out and implemented, to minimize day-to-day costs and save staff time. Many companies still rely on purchasing and back-office systems that revolve around the fax machine, telephone, or even handwritten forms. Companies that have adopted e-business are reaping the advantages that come from replacing manual processes with automated, digital systems that provide fast, accurate, customer-centric experiences. This can lead to a range of efficiencies such as getting paid faster.

6.2.2 Cost saving Checklist

Use this checklist to identify the cost-saving centres and areas of efficiency gains that effective use of email and a carefully planned website can offer:

- *Providing information* – reduce staff time on the telephone with customers and suppliers by referring them to the website – also some telephone enquirers will be better informed as a result of referring to the site and therefore will take less time.
- *Bookings and orders* – data entered into an online form with appropriate links into the organisation's database accounting system bypasses staff, freeing them to market and sell more tickets, memberships etc.
- *Publishing/printing* – reduce cost of outsourcing to printers and graphic designers for brochures, research, concert programmes.
- *Photocopying* – reduce through-put and need for more and/or larger photocopiers.
- *Faxing* – reduce cost and time involved in re-keying data and reduce errors in interpretation of poor quality originals, e.g. handwritten forms and poor quality faxes.
- *Postage and handling* – reduce expense and time.
- *Paper* – reduce the overall paper consumption and therefore cost.
- *Processing time* – streamline processing of forms, e.g. online membership applications and orders.
- *Account management* – an e-commerce solution reduces processing of accounts, reconciliation, banking and can improve cash-flow.
- *Communication and meeting costs* – using email groups can reduce phone calls, time consumed in arranging meetings, number of face-to-face meetings, cost of getting people to meetings

6.2.3 Create Additional Revenue

In the early days of the Web, some people sold websites to businesses promising they would generate large revenues from online sales. That kind of over-sell back-fired, sometimes leading to extreme scepticism and unwillingness to use the Internet for business at all. Of course, the reality of the potential of websites to provide another source of revenue lies somewhere in the middle. For some, their website will not generate income directly; rather it supports their offline activities and contributes to meeting business goals and financial targets. Others reap considerable additional revenue from their website via selling information, products or services online.

Some businesses are fortunate because they provide information, goods and services that users seem very willing to purchase online, such as travel, financial services, books, CDs, entertainment, and many items traditionally bought through mail-order catalogues. The Internet has provided many businesses with a whole new revenue stream at relatively low cost.

6.2.4 Reach More Customers and Markets

One of the great benefits of the Web is that it can help broaden your customer base at a relatively low cost. As more and more people get access to the Internet and become confident Web users, the potential to expand customer-bases will increase proportionally.

Effective use of email and an appropriately designed and promoted website can attract new customers and open new markets for products and services by providing:

- Affordable access to customers over the world.
- A means by which to communicate with people for whom English is not their native language.
- Access to your products and services for people with a disability who may not have had access to them when distributed by traditional means – e.g. a shop-front.

A number of online market places have been created in Australia and elsewhere that match up suppliers and buyers. They work by creating a website featuring a common catalogue to which suppliers add their products, and from which buyers can search and select the best product. Joining an appropriate market place (often called e-marketplaces) as a supplier can provide cheap access to many more buyers than an average small business could hope to reach on its own.

6.2.5 Improve Marketing and Promotions

A well-designed and maintained website can be a highly effective promotional tool. This is not to say that promoting a business on the Web is better or more effective than traditional forms of promotion. It is simply another promotional tool that should complement other forms of promotion.

A website provides some unique promotional potential because:

- It is visible to potential customers and suppliers 24 hours a day, seven days a week.
- It does not know about borders and oceans so it is visible to potential customers wherever they are in the world.
- A great deal more information can be provided on a website than on a brochure.
- Products can be illustrated from multiple angles and animations can be used, allowing the user to turn an image of the product around, up and down, giving a better understanding of its advantages.
- It is very easy to collate and analyze information about those visiting and buying from the site and equally easy to change the promotional aspects to maximize their impact on sales.

6.2.6 Meet the Needs and Expectations of Customers and Suppliers

Increasingly today, the terms "available" and "accessible" to a business mean twenty-four hours a day, seven days a week access to information, products and services. Customers, suppliers and interested parties are less and less satisfied with being restricted to the traditional opening hours of business and will not be impressed if they cannot do such things as order items, book tickets or discover information for themselves in the comfort of their own homes and offices when it suits them.

The expectations of online audiences will not diminish over time – they will only increase. For example, the increasing ability to provide video and sound online at premium quality and speed is likely to force many businesses into presenting information in multimedia format on their websites. This will raise the bar in terms of delivery methodology, content, structure and quality of online material. To fail to be online or to fail to provide a website that is user-friendly, informative, and up-to-date in every respect is to risk alienating web-enabled customers and suppliers and thereby lose their confidence and business.

6.2.7 Concentrate on the Things that Matter

One of the most important consequences of using the Internet in your business is that it can reduce the time staff spend doing administrative tasks, freeing them up to concentrate on the things that really matter – servicing customers and increasing sales. Whether the things that matter to you are promoting the business, generating repeat business, managing customers and suppliers, chasing leads, or undertaking professional development, your e-business plan should minimise wasted time doing unproductive tasks.

By shifting the emphasis of the role of staff from processing data and undertaking routine administrative work, to providing quality of service, seeking new customers and selling more products, a business is likely to make a fundamental improvement in staff satisfaction and sales figures.

6.2.8 Make it Easier for People to do Business with You

Your website is an additional and unique tool for facilitating business. An effective use of email and a website can make it easier for customers, visitors, suppliers, distributors or associates to do business with you. It will be easier for people to do business with you if you have a website that:

- Is quick and easy to navigate
- Is customer-focused
- Offers abundant relevant information – eg contact details
- Provides numerous opportunities for two-way communication
- Provides a variety of convenient ways of ordering and paying for information, products and services.

Your website and email address form another shop-front, helpdesk, outlet, channel, advertisement and contact point, through which you make your information, products and services available twenty four hours a day, seven days a week to the whole world. The success of the website as a business tool will ultimately depend on the appropriateness of its design, promotion and on-going maintenance and the extent to which the business embraces it. It will also rely on the imagination of staff in providing content and features on the site that will entice users and make it easy for them to do business with you.

6.2.9 The Cost of Not Being There

The "cost" of **not** having a credible website or using email effectively can be measured in terms of lost opportunities to create more revenue and cut costs. Some of the costs of not being there (online) include:

- Loss of customers to competitors who do have a good website and email contact with customers.
- Loss of potential revenue from online sales or uptake of services.
- Mounting costs associated with existing inefficient office practices that an effective e-business plan could minimise.
- Mounting costs associated with existing inefficient supply-chain management.
- Loss of credibility as an innovative, forward-thinking business.

6.2.10 Play on a Level Playing Field

The street location of a business, or the size and design of the building it is in, gives the physical visitor an immediate impression of the stature of the business. For some customers and clients, this first impression of company size is an important factor in determining whether they will even walk in the front door. However, the Web is a great leveler because there is no main shopping street or business address or hierarchy of web addresses on the Internet.

Even when the Web visitor has entered a company's website, they cannot easily tell how big the business is at first glance. Without being deceptive, a small business can appear to be as large as any of its larger competitors, and large companies can appear to be as small as the corner shop.

Website front doors are all on the same street and are the same size on the Web. This leveling effect can help neutralize any prejudices potential customers, clients or suppliers might have about the size of the company they prefer to deal with.

6.2.11 Help Meet Business Goals

Businesses the world over develop business plans to provide direction for their business activities. Business plans generally cover areas such as: sales targets, marketing plans, staffing, competitor analysis, research and development and budgets.

The Internet can be used to help businesses research their business plans and as a tool for achieving the aims of the plan. The Web provides a relatively cheap means of investigating competitors, testing out the market, entering new markets and seeking new strategic partners. A company's website can contribute to achieving increased sales and can be used to improve the management of relations with customers.

There are numerous ways in which a website and clever use of email can help a company meet its business goals.

6.3 PLANNING TO MEET BUSINESS GOALS

Most businesses would not adopt a new business strategy, such as opening up a new office or shop, without first doing some very careful planning. Planning helps to ensure that the precious time, money and energy invested in any new strategy are not wasted. Without good plans new ventures can easily go wrong, due to such things as poor timing, unreasonable expectations or even adopting the wrong approach in the first place. Good planning maximizes the benefits to a business of a new or expanded business venture and reduces the risk of things going wrong.

6.3.1 How to plan

The planning process needs to be managed well and involve the people who hold important roles in the business – or who provide important business advice to the business. For some very small businesses, the owner/operator may be the sole person to develop the e-business plan. But whether it is developed by one person or a team, the goal is to produce an e-business plan document and to implement a practical schedule for reviewing and updating it.

Managing the planning process is not difficult, but it does require a disciplined approach.

6.3.2 What to do

The person responsible for delivering the plan should establish:

- Who should be involved in the process, e.g. micro-businesses might have the owner and the accountant; larger organizations may have people from management, accounts, marketing, sales, technical, operations and possibly external advisors.
- The responsibilities of the planning team.
- What the plan is to include.
- What background research is required in order to produce the plan?
- The time-frame for delivering the plan.
- An internal communications plan to keep everyone informed about the plan.
- When and how the plan will be reviewed and updated.

The other sections in Planning will help you identify what you need to know d provide important information and resources on which to base your e-business plan.

6.3.3 Researching the Opportunities

There are many ways the Internet can be used to help a business conduct its day-to-day business. When developing an e-business plan is sure you know what the possibilities are for your business so they can be incorporated into your planning.

Below are a number of day-to-day business activities that can be improved by using the Internet. It is suggested you explore each one to see whether it has possibilities for your business, whether it should be incorporated into your e-business plan, and if so, to what extent.

6.3.4 Key Planning Issues to Consider

The key issues need to be considered by whoever is developing the e-business plan in parallel because decisions made on one issue will often impact on other issues. Read through these issues and determine which ones are relevant to your business. The issues of planning are the followings

- Innovation and imagination

- Integration with existing office systems
- Developing a healthy e-business culture
- Security
- Knowledge management
- Estimating the budget

6.3.5 What level of e-business is right for you?

Businesses should ask themselves in the planning stage, what is the optimum level of e-business for us? For one business there maybe nothing to be gained by doing anything more than simply using email and banking online. Whereas, for another business, the optimum level of e-business may be having a website with e-commerce facilities.

- Identify the aims of your e-business
- Identify your target audience
- Select the appropriate level of e-business

6.4 WRITING YOUR E-BUSINESS PLAN

The e-business plan is a document that states the type and level of e-business that a business will engage in. Refer to the beginning of the planning section if you are unsure about whether adequate preparation has been undertaken to write the e-business plan. This section assumes you have worked through the topics in this Planning section of the e-business guide or you are familiar with the ideas and have thought about the issues. Before you begin the plan you might want to contact a local e-business advisor who can help you with it.

6.4.1 Building

This section explains how an organisation might approach the building of a website that meets its needs. This is not a technical manual that will turn someone into a Web technical expert. It raises and explains key technical, content and design issues so that business owners, their staff and advisors can confidently brief technical experts about their e-business needs and manage those experts.

The main areas of this section are:

- Technical issues
- Choosing and preparing contents
- What do you want users to do?
- Marketing and your website
- Designing your website
- E-commerce – selling via your website
- Maintenance considerations
- Developing the website

6.4.2 Protecting

As the Internet becomes an increasingly important tool for businesses, electronic security (e-security) has emerged as a major issue. Many businesses want to expand their use of the Internet but are not sure how to do so in a secure way. The e-business guide will help you decide which strategies and processes are appropriate for your business e-security needs.

If your business is connected to the Internet, it is essential to ensure that your business data, including customer information, is safe and that your transactions are carried out securely. Otherwise, there is a risk of transactions being intercepted, privacy codes being breached, confidential information being taken or money being stolen. It focuses on one of these topics:

- Why be secure?
- Where do I start?
- What can I do?
- Key issues
- Top Ten E-security Tips

6.4.3 Managing

Like any key aspect of your business, e-business requires good management if it is to be benefit the organisation. Just as people require managing, systems need to be maintained and budgets have to be monitored, any strategic use of the Internet by a business needs to be closely controlled. The major aspects of managing are the following

- Who does the managing?
- Maintaining e-business systems
- Internal policies and guidelines
- Promoting your website
- Budgeting for maintenance
- Controlling the risks
- Legal issues
- Spam and ethical e-marketing

6.4.5 Improving

Most businesses using the Internet as a business tool know that the technology and use of email, e-commerce and just about everything to do with the Internet is always changing. So looking for ways to improve current uses of the Internet is necessary and makes sense.

This section provides suggestions for ways in which a business that already has a website and uses email, can make even better use of the Internet. It contains:

- Information and resources on how to identify improvements in the way the Internet is used in a business.
- Information about some advanced uses of the Internet.

The major aspects of improving are the following

- Evaluating your e-business
- Doing business with government online
- Procurement over the Internet
- Managing the supply-chain and logistics
- Putting your catalogue online
- E-marketplaces
- Exporting

6.5 LEGAL ISSUES FOR E-BUSINESS

The legal problems reported affect all parts of electronic transactions for e-commerce, main importance was given to the issues related with electronic signature, security of payments and the validity of a contract concluded by electronic means. With less importance also the issues related with e-invoices, Taxation/Customs and the obligation to register /authorisation to provide cross-border on-line services were considered with a significant level of importance.

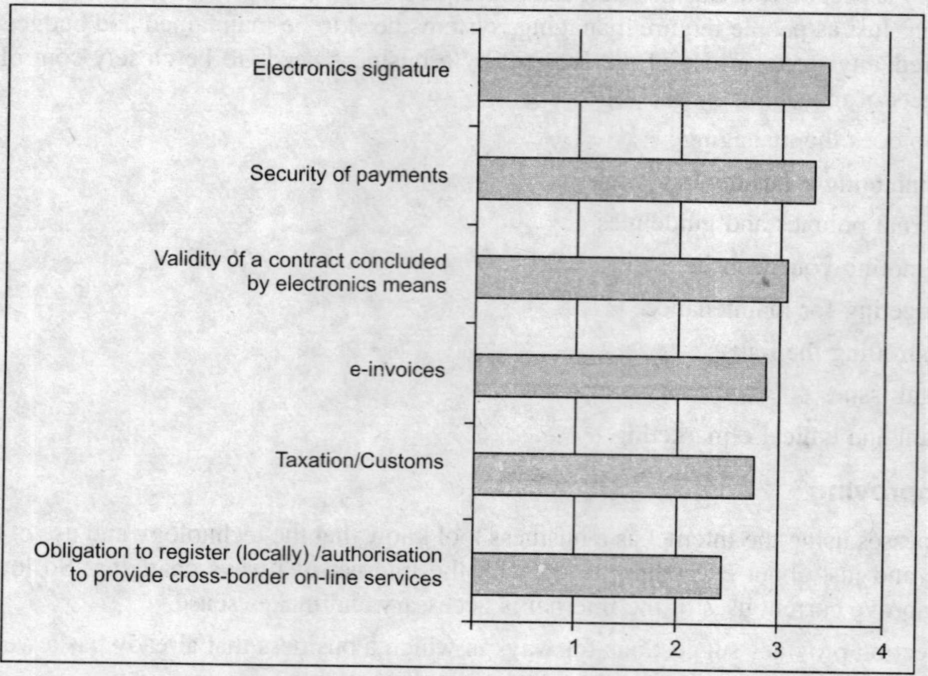

Fig. 6.1: Legal issues reported regarding e-commerce transactions

As main important issues relate to new e-commerce initiatives (electronic signature, security of payments, and validity of contracts), companies might have to modify their commercial policy in order to comply with legal provisions. As we can see this issues relate to the fact that enterprises admit that they might not be familiar with online payment systems and contracts or that consumers do not trust the use of electronic payments over the Internet. Also, companies complain about the lack of common standards for the implementation of e-signatures and e-invoices.

6.5.1 Ethical Issues in e-Business and Challenges for Implementing e-Commerce

There are many legal and web site regulatory issues involved. Electronic copyright, e-commerce, credit/cash policies, international trade, tariffs, privacy, digital media offers, and security are a few of the items to be considered.

Trust, Importance of Ethics

- The Ethics of Internet Marketing
- E-business legal, ethical, and regulatory issues with B2B and B2C
- Marketing on B2B Web site
- Ethics B2B Copyright Law
- Ethical B2B Practices
- Marketing Ethics Issues
- B2B vs. B2C legal
- E-commerce Ethical Facts site
- Ethics In Advertising site
- Advertising And Marketing On The Internet – Honesty

In a society where legal and ethical limits are pushed to the max and how the attitude pervades those around us that if there are no rules against something then it is ok to do, why even ask about ethics and values on the Web? Because, it affects you and your business.

6.5.2 Business Ethics

The Internet is a growing and a continually evolving creature that will live on in perpetuity. As such, it would be wise to ponder the e business legal and Internet marketing ethical issues of B2B & B2C.. Whatever is written and published online will be there forever. Imagine the billions upon billions of text information pages that are and will be stored for a long time. There is even a site where you can go Way Back to check out archives of other websites and view pages that were created at the beginning of their infancy. Additionally, video, films, movies, and audio in various applications formats are also viewable.

Now, with the new wireless web mail from cell phones and other PDA communication devices, the Internet will be affecting more lives than ever before. Security and privacy concerns along with e-business regulatory issues will become more prevalent. It will become more difficult to figure out who you can trust online; with all the unethical, illegal, and Internet marketing and online advertising frauds and E-business email scams.

6.5.3 Important Ethical E-Business Legal Issues

If you are writing copy and maintaining a client's e-business or e-commerce website consider the following consumer privacy and legal matters:

What you say when copywriting and publishing for a client is a reflection of how they are viewed to the rest of the world. Negative or defamatory articles published about various people and companies on other websites, if not properly researched, could possibly have legal consequences of libel that can stretch across countries. Additionally, consider carefully what is published on Web logs or Blogs for short. A blog is simply a website where daily, weekly, or monthly personal or corporate thoughts, ideas, and happenings can be published and shared with others. Interaction with readers can be set up in the form of comments from visitors.

If webmasters perform unethical optimization of a client's website, it could have long lasting negative business consequences for that client that can not be easily repaired. Consequences that at first glance may seem insignificant. People are getting savvier online. They are starting to see the e business false advertising that is upon us. Beware; it's just a matter of time until we hear more stories and legal action taken.

6.5.3.1 Intellectual Property

When dealing with ethics in a B2B company and B2C clients there is a major degree of trust and responsibility that is imparted to a person or group that maintains the Web site. It is very important from both an ethical values based e-business and legal B2B and B2C perspective to make sure that the written words and what is portrayed about a company are factual. Because issues arise involving marketing ethics and the importance of understanding a business for Internet marketing issues and advertising purposes, there are potential areas for revealing trade secrets or intellectual property if proper B2B ethical behavior is not followed.

Email correspondence should be private and confidential. While certain individuals might not see any harm quoting it on the Web from an email sent, it is always advisable to get a person's consent prior to publishing anything. While the person might give consent, they might not realize the full implications, online privacy issues, or impact of having it published online. Therefore, it would be wise to consider it very carefully before even asking for their approval.

6.5.3.2 Email Marketing

Email has a number of regulations implemented by the government. Email marketing View IAB, Interactive Advertising Bureau Standards and Guidelines – e-Mail Guidelines. Share your comments at unsolicited b2b and b2c emails "The Email Junk Mail Trash Heap" Pop up ads, email, instant messengers, consumer privacy information, and online security threats. Ads that make you double click at a wrong location and the very click installs some sort of ad ware, spy ware, or mal ware on your computer.

6.5.3.3 Consumers Survey Scams and Hoaxes

This is one to watch out for closely! Beware Phone "Survey" Scams, "Charity" Appeals for Chain mail, online security, and spam. Another area that can be a real pain is "The Never-Ending Hoax Viruses".

6.5.3.4 Copyright Infringement

Watch out for this particular crime of sites that copy your website text (legal issues) or name while trying to pawn off some other item they are selling.

6.5.3.5 Website Issues

Unethical redirects to other pages with completely different information than what was shown in the search results. For an example site may no longer be available, of this type of spamming ethical issues in B2C website. One of the top results is/was an example of Internet ethics cheating, involving ethics in B2B and B2C online, from an online group that promotes cheating.

6.5.3.6 Advertising and Keywords Scams

Unethical spyware/adware companies are promoting themselves as: "get to the top of Goggle, Yahoo, and MSN search guaranteed for your keywords." These companies are using the term "Search Engine Data Merging." Spy ware and ad ware is installed on some users computers then they sell keywords to professionals for thousands of dollars a year. This is a huge money making scam. The company is using various names: Search Elevators, Link Positions, Window Billboards Network, Win speed Network, Real Positions Network, Keywords Guru, and even a new search engine labeled Red Zee Search.

6.5.3.7 Identity Theft & Internet Fraud

Identity theft is a major problem; this issue is related to online B2C ethical business issues and legal issues.

6.5.3.8 Domain Name Registration Issues and Scams

Domain name registration is another area online where ethics have been thrown out. Certainly there are some gray areas for someone to be registering a domain name that is close to some other corporate identity's name. But, many of these individuals and corporations that register domain names in the same country and other countries that are near to, or similar to the spellings of others, are registering the names to infringe upon the trademarks and brands of other corporations and organizations.

6.5.3.9 Domain Name Disputes

Briefly, I'd like to point out that use of a name can be legal for many parties whether they have a trademark or not. Two or more parties may have the same trademark in different jurisdictions, may have the same trademark in the same jurisdiction but in different industries, or may legally use a name without owning a trademark to it. It is not necessary to own a trademark, to use a particular name. This being the case, domain name registration on a first-come, first-serve basis is the most logical. If two (or more) parties have the right to use a name (even if one has a trademark and the other doesn't), neither party should be given preference in using a domain name with that name.

With the proliferation of world wide domain name registrars from all countries around the globe, in which many of these countries, such as China do not even maintain the same social/ethical value systems, makes it even more difficult to protect corporate trademarks, copyrights, and intellectual property rights. Additionally, because many of these countries have their own rules and regulations for bringing domain disputes in which the complainant bears the legal burden of proof for their own claims in the native language of the country (as opposed to English), and differs greatly from that of the ICANN, Internet Corporation for Assigned Names and Numbers, registration and domain dispute resolution policies, it will become increasingly difficult to protect corporate identities on the Internet.

6.5.4 Definition of Ethical Issues in B2B

Ethics in B2B and B2C is defined as "A set of principles of right conduct" and "The rules or standards governing the conduct of a person or the conduct of the members of a profession"

6.5.4.1 Honesty, Integrity, and Trustworthy

"Honesty the best policy" When dealing with customers and clients, not following this policy comes back to bite people time and time again.

Do not be swayed by shortsightedness. If you see a potential for a quick buck, ask yourself if this really is a proper way to go about doing something. Businesses have been guilty of shortsightedness themselves. They have extracted a quick buck at the expensive of their integrity and consumers' wallets.

Remember, when working with clients, he or she is placing web site trust in you. Hold onto that trust dearly and don't do anything that would harm it. They are trusting you to help them out on the Net. Remember this saying: Tell it like it is and do it with style! Customers will appreciate it.

6.5.4.2 Personal and Consumer Rights

Companies consider data protection a very important issue, followed by privacy and data retention. It is important that personal and consumer rights are consistent, with better and harmonized information on the regulatory framework for these issues in e-business. Legal information for commercial and technological advice is needed.

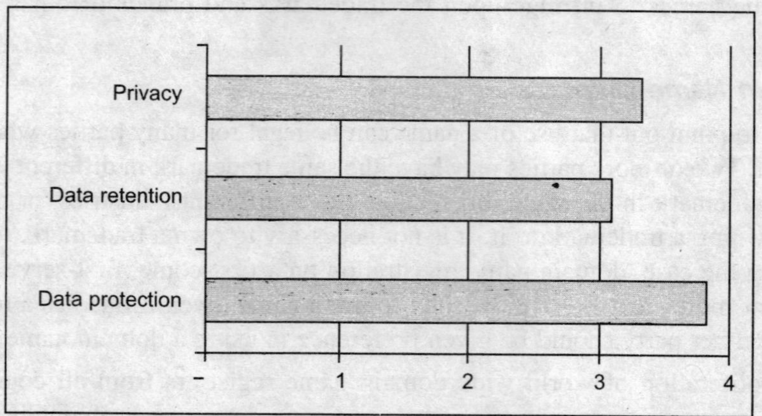

Fig. 6.2: Legal issues reported regarding personal and consumer rights

6.5.4.3 *Liabilities*

In this regard, differences in the legal validity of electronic contracts, registration requirements, appropriate action towards conflict resolution and appropriate actions towards consumer protection and complaints. On average, all issues were scored with a very similar importance. Although, for a few decimals the highest importance was given to liability.

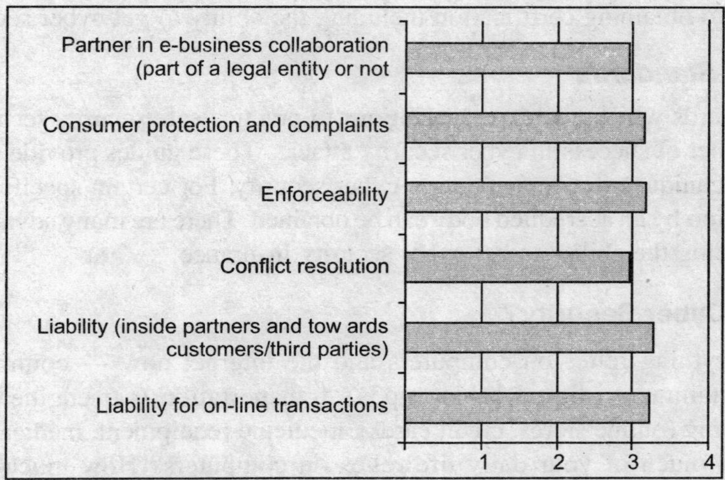

Fig. 6.3: Legal issues reported regarding liabilities

6.5.4.4 *IPR*

In this area, main importance is given to issues related to the protection of copyrights and the usage of licenses. In order to exploit the potential of e-business and market opportunities, they need to count on a long term strategy, which currently they cannot.

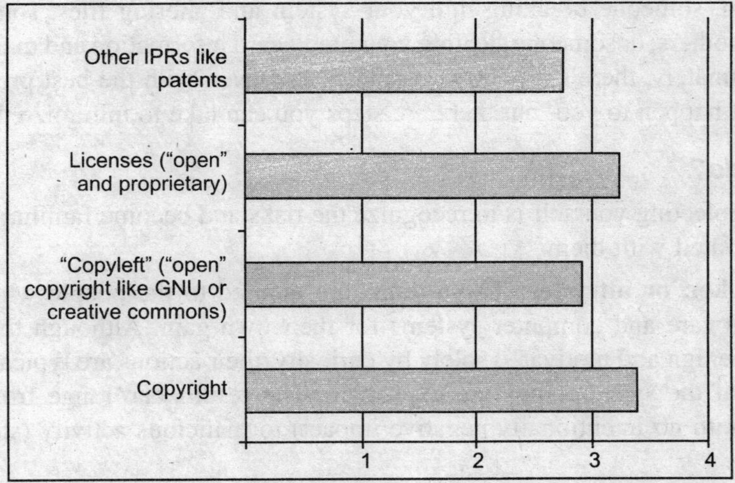

Fig. 6.4: Legal issues reported regarding IPR

6.6 CYBER SECURITY

ber security standards are security standards which enable organizations to practice safe security techniques in order to minimize the number of successful cyber security attacks. These guides provide general outlines as well as specific techniques for implementing cyber security. For certain specific standards, **cyber security certification** by an accredited body can be obtained. There are many advantages to obtaining certification including the ability to get cyber security insurance.

Cyber Security Standards

Are security standards which enable organizations to practice safe security techniques in order to minimize the number of successful cyber security attacks. These guides provide general outlines as well as specific techniques for implementing cyber security. For certain specific standards, **cyber security certification** by an accredited body can be obtained. There are many advantages to obtaining certification including the ability to get cyber security insurance.

6.6.1 What is Cyber Security?

It seems that everything relies on computers and the internet now — communication (email, cellphones), entertainment (digital cable, mp3s), transportation (car engine systems, airplane navigation), shopping (online stores, credit cards), medicine (equipment, medical records), and the list goes on. How much of your daily life relies on computers? How much of your personal information is stored either on your own computer or on someone else's system?

Cyber security involves protecting that information by preventing, detecting, and responding to attacks.

6.6.2 What are the Risks?

There are many risks, some more serious than others. Among these dangers are viruses erasing your entire system, someone breaking into your system and altering files, someone using your computer to attack others, or someone stealing your credit card information and making unauthorized purchases. Unfortunately, there's no 100% guarantee that even with the best precautions some of these things won't happen to you, but there are steps you can take to minimize the chances.

What can you do?

The first step in protecting yourself is to recognize the risks and become familiar with some of the terminology associated with them.

Hacker, attacker, or intruder: These terms are applied to the people who seek to exploit weaknesses in software and computer systems for their own gain. Although their intentions are sometimes fairly benign and motivated solely by curiosity, their actions are typically in violation of the intended use of the systems they are exploiting. The results can range from mere mischief (creating a virus with no intentionally negative impact) to malicious activity (stealing or altering information).

Malicious code: Malicious code, sometimes called malware, is a broad category that includes any code that could be used to attack your computer. Malicious code can have the following characteristics:

- It might require you to actually do something before it infects your computer. This action could be opening an email attachment or going to a particular web page.
- Some forms propagate without user intervention and typically start by exploiting software vulnerability. Once the victim computer has been infected, the malicious code will attempt to find and infect other computers. This code can also propagate via email, websites, or network-based software.
- Some malicious code claims to be one thing while in fact doing something different behind the scenes. For example, a program that claims it will speed up your computer may actually be sending confidential information to a remote intruder.

Viruses and worms are examples of malicious code.

Vulnerability: In most cases, vulnerabilities are caused by programming errors in software. Attackers might be able to take advantage of these errors to infect your computer, so it is important to apply updates or patches that address known vulnerabilities.

6.6.3 Cyber Crime

A main issue is to build trust for consumers so that there are better e-market perspectives and wider opportunities. The importance of showing and ensuring to consumers a high level of consumer protection. However, constant threats, such as unsolicited commercial e-mails, do not reassure customers. The issue of fighting cyber crime also constrains the practical aspects for advertising and commercial practices in e-commerce. The need to balance between consumer rights and practical lawful advertisement for companies.

6.6.4 Conventional Crime

Crime is a social and economic phenomenon and is as old as the human society. Crime is a legal concept and has the sanction of the law. Crime or an offence is "a legal wrong that can be followed

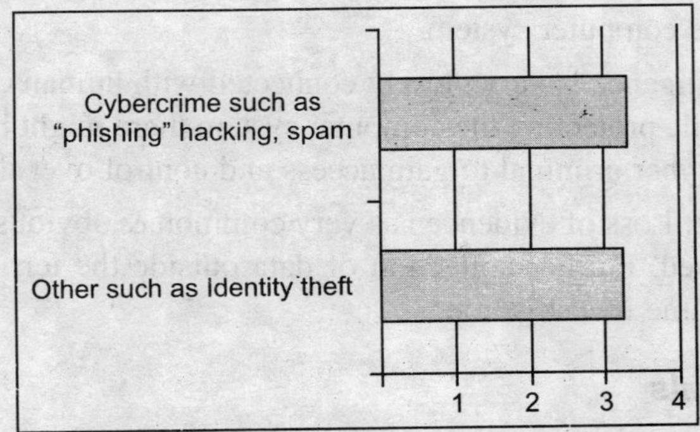

Fig. 6.5: Legal issues reported regarding Cybercrime

by criminal proceedings which may result into punishment." The hallmark of criminality is that, it is breach of the criminal law. Per Lord Atkin "the criminal quality of an act cannot be discovered by reference to any standard but one: is the act prohibited with penal consequences".

A crime may be said to be any conduct accompanied by act or omission prohibited by law and consequential breach of which is visited by penal consequences

6.6.5 Distinction between Conventional and Cyber Crime

There is apparently no distinction between cyber and conventional crime. However on a deep introspection we may say that there exists a fine line of demarcation between the conventional and cyber crime, which is appreciable. The demarcation lies in the involvement of the medium in cases of cyber crime. The *sine qua non* for cyber crime is that there should be an involvement, at any stage, of the virtual cyber medium.

6.6.6 Reasons for Cyber Crime

The Concept of Law has said 'human beings are vulnerable so rule of law is required to protect them'. Applying this to the cyberspace we may say that computers are vulnerable so rule of law is required to protect and safeguard them against cyber crime. The reasons for the vulnerability of computers may be said to be:

1. **Capacity to store data in comparatively small space:** The computer has unique characteristic of storing data in a very small space. This affords to remove or derive information either through physical or virtual medium makes it much easier.
2. **Easy to access:** The problem encountered in guarding a computer system from unauthorised access is that there is every possibility of breach not due to human error but due to the complex technology. By secretly implanted logic bomb, key loggers that can steal access codes, advanced voice recorders; retina imagers etc. that can fool biometric systems and bypass firewalls can be utilized to get past many a security system.
3. **Complex**: The computers work on operating systems and these operating systems in turn are composed of millions of codes. Human mind is fallible and it is not possible that there might not be a lapse at any stage. The cyber criminals take advantage of these lacunas and penetrate into the computer system.
4. **Negligence:** Negligence is very closely connected with human conduct. It is therefore very probable that while protecting the computer system there might be any negligence, which in turn provides a cyber criminal to gain access and control over the computer system.
5. **Loss of evidence:** Loss of evidence is a very common & obvious problem as all the data are routinely destroyed. Further collection of data outside the territorial extent also paralyses this system of crime investigation.

6.6.7 Cyber Criminals

The cyber criminals constitute of various groups/category. This division may be justified on the basis of the object that they have in their mind. The following are the category of cyber criminals-

1. ***Children and adolescents between the age group of 6–18 years:*** The simple reason for this type of delinquent behaviour pattern in children is seen mostly due to the inquisitiveness to know and explore the things. Other cognate reason may be to prove them to be outstanding amongst other children in their group. Further the reasons may be psychological even. E.g. the Bal Bharati (Delhi) case was the outcome of harassment of the delinquent by his friends.
2. ***Organised hackers:*** These kinds of hackers are mostly organised together to fulfil certain objective. The reason may be to fulfil their political bias, fundamentalism, etc. The Pakistanis are said to be one of the best quality hackers in the world. They mainly target the Indian government sites with the purpose to fulfil their political objectives.
3. ***Professional hackers / crackers:*** Their work is motivated by the colour of money. These kinds of hackers are mostly employed to hack the site of the rivals and get credible, reliable and valuable information. Further they are ven employed to crack the system of the employer basically as a measure to make it safer by detecting the loopholes.
4. ***Discontented employees:*** This group include those people who have been either sacked by their employer or are dissatisfied with their employer. To avenge they normally hack the system of their employee.

6.6.8 Mode and Manner of Commiting Cyber Crime

1. ***Unauthorized access to computer systems or networks / Hacking:*** This kind of offence is normally referred as hacking in the generic sense. However the framers of the information technology act 2000 have no where used this term so to avoid any confusion we would not interchangeably use the word hacking for 'unauthorized access' as the latter has wide connotation.
2. ***Theft of information contained in electronic form:*** This includes information stored in computer hard disks, removable storage media etc. Theft may be either by appropriating the data physically or by tampering them through the virtual medium.
3. ***Email bombing:***This kind of activity refers to sending large numbers of mail to the victim, which may be an individual or a company or even mail servers there by ultimately resulting into crashing.
4. ***Data diddling*** : This kind of an attack involves altering raw data just before a computer processes it and then changing it back after the processing is completed. The *electricity board* faced similar problem of data diddling while the department was being computerised.
5. ***Salami attacks:*** This kind of crime is normally prevalent in the financial institutions or for the purpose of committing financial crimes. An important feature of this type of offence is that the alteration is so small that it would normally go unnoticed. E.g. the *Ziegler case* wherein a logic bomb was introduced in the bank's system, which deducted 10 cents from every account and deposited it in a particular account.
6. ***Denial of Service attack:*** The computer of the victim is flooded with more requests than it can handle which cause it to crash. Distributed Denial of Service (DDoS) attack is also

a type of denial of service attack, in which the offenders are wide in number and widespread. E.g. *Amazon. Yahoo*.

7. ***Virus / worm attacks:*** Viruses are programs that attach themselves to a computer or a file and then circulate themselves to other files and to other computers on a network. They usually affect the data on a computer, either by altering or deleting it. Worms, unlike viruses do not need the host to attach themselves to. They merely make functional copies of themselves and do this repeatedly till they eat up all the available space on a computer's memory. E.g. *love bug virus*, which affected at least 5 % of the computers of the globe. The losses were accounted to be $ 10 million. The world's most famous worm was the Internet worm let loose on the Internet by *Robert Morris* sometime in 1988. Almost brought development of Internet to a complete halt.
8. ***Logic bombs:*** These are event dependent programs. This implies that these programs are created to do something only when a certain event (known as a trigger event) occurs, E.g. even some viruses may be termed logic bombs because they lie dormant all through the year and become active only on a particular date (like the *Chernobyl virus*).
9. ***Trojan attacks:*** This term has its origin in the word 'Trojan horse'. In software field this means an unauthorized programme, which passively gains control over another's system by representing itself as an authorised programme. The most common form of installing a Trojan is through e-mail. E.g. a Trojan was installed in the computer of a *lady film director* in the U.S. while chatting. The cyber criminal through the web cam installed in the computer obtained her nude photographs. He further harassed this lady.
10. ***Internet time thefts:*** Normally in these kinds of thefts the Internet surfing hours of the victim are used up by another person. This is done by gaining access to the login ID and the password. E.g. *Colonel Bajwa's case*- the Internet hours were used up by any other person. This was perhaps one of the first reported cases related to cyber crime in India. However this case made the police infamous as to their lack of understanding of the nature of cyber crime.
11. ***Web jacking:*** This term is derived from the term hi jacking. In these kinds of offences the hacker gains access and control over the web site of another. He may even mutilate or change the information on the site. This may be done for fulfilling political objectives or for money. E.g. recently the site of MIT (Ministry of Information Technology) was hacked by the Pakistani hackers and some obscene matter was placed therein. Further the site of Bombay crime branch was also web jacked. Another case of web jacking is that of the *'gold fish'* case. In this case the site was hacked and the information pertaining to gold fish was changed. Further a ransom of US $ 1 million was demanded as ransom. Thus web jacking is a process where by control over the site of another is made backed by some consideration for it.

Classification

The subject of cyber crime may be broadly classified under the following three groups. They are

1. Against Individuals

(a) their person and

(b) their property of an individual

2. Against Organization

(a) Government

(c) Firm, Company, Group of individuals

3. Against Society at large

The following are the crimes, which can be committed against the followings group :

Against Individuals:

(i) Harassment via emails

(ii) Cyber-stalking

(iii) Dissemination of obscene material

(iv) Defamation.

(v) Unauthorizedcontrol /access over computer system

(vi) Indecent exposure

(vii) Email spoofing

(viii) Cheating and Fraud

Against Individual Property:

(i) Computervandalism

(ii) Transmitting vircus

(iii) Netrespass

(iv) Unauthorized control/access over computer system

(v) Intellectual property crimes

(vi) Internet time thefts

Against Organization:

(i) Unauthorized control/access over computer system

(ii) Possession of unauthorized information

(iii) Cyber terrorism against the government organization

(iv) Distribution of pirated software etc.

Against Society at large:

(i) Pornography (basically child pornography)

(ii) Polluting the youth through indecent exposure

(iii) Trafficking

(iv) Financial crimes

(v) Sale of illegal articles

(vi) Online gambling

(vii) Forgery

The above mentioned offences may discuss in brief as follows:

1. **Harassment via e-mails:** Harassment through e-mails is not a new concept. It is very similar to harassing through letters. Recently I had received a mail from a *lady wherein she complained* about the same. Her former boy friend was sending her mails constantly sometimes emotionally blackmailing her and also threatening her. This is a very common type of harassment via e-mails.
2. **Cyber-stalking:** The Oxford dictionary defines stalking as "pursuing stealthily". Cyber stalking involves following a person's movements across the Internet by posting messages (sometimes threatening) on the bulletin boards frequented by the victim, entering the chat-rooms frequented by the victim, constantly bombarding the victim with emails etc.
3. **Dissemination of obscene material/ Indecent exposure/ Pornography (basically child pornography) / Polluting through indecent exposure:** Pornography on the net may take various forms. It may include the hosting of web site containing these prohibited materials. Use of computers for producing these obscene materials. Downloading through the Internet, obscene materials. These obscene matters may cause harm to the mind of the adolescent and tend to deprave or corrupt their mind. Two known cases of pornography are the *Delhi Bal Bharati case* and the *Bombay case* wherein two Swiss couple used to force the slum children for obscene photographs. The Mumbai police later arrested them.
4. **Defamation :** It is an act of imputing any person with intent to lower the person in the estimation of the right-thinking members of society generally or to cause him to be shunned or avoided or to expose him to hatred, contempt or ridicule. Cyber defamation is not different from conventional defamation except the involvement of a virtual medium. E.g. the mail account of Rohit was hacked and some mails were sent from his account to some of his batch mates regarding his affair with a girl with intent to defame him.
5. **Unauthorized control/access over computer system:** This activity is commonly referred to as hacking. The Indian law has however given a different connotation to the term hacking, so we will not use the term "unauthorized access" interchangeably with the term "hacking" to prevent confusion as the term used in the Act of 2000 is much wider than hacking.
6. **E mail spoofing:** A spoofed e-mail may be said to be one, which misrepresents its origin. It shows it's origin to be different from which actually it originates. Recently spoofed mails were sent on the name of Mr. *Na. Vijayashankar* (naavi.org), which contained virus.

   Rajesh Manyar, a graduate student at Purdue University in Indiana, was arrested for threatening to detonate a nuclear device in the college campus. The alleged e- mail was sent from the account of another student to the vice president for student services. However the mail was traced to be sent from the account of Rajesh Manyar.
6. **Computer vandalism:** Vandalism means deliberately destroying or damaging property of another. Thus computer vandalism may include within its purview any kind of physical

harm done to the computer of any person. These acts may take the form of the theft of a computer, some part of a computer or a peripheral attached to the computer or by physically damaging a computer or its peripherals.

7. **Transmitting virus/worms:** This topic has been adequately dealt herein above.

8. **Intellectual Property crimes / Distribution of pirated software:** Intellectual property consists of a bundle of rights. Any unlawful act by which the owner is deprived completely or partially of his rights is an offence. The common form of IPR violation may be said to be software piracy, copyright infringement, trademark and service mark violation, theft of computer source code, etc.

   The Hyderabad Court has in a land mark judgement has convicted three people and sentenced them to six months imprisonment and fine of 50,000 each for unauthorized copying and sell of pirated software.

9. **Cyber terrorism against the government organization:** At this juncture a necessity may be felt that what is the need to distinguish between cyber terrorism and cyber crime. Both are criminal acts. However there is a compelling need to distinguish between both these crimes. A cyber crime is generally a domestic issue, which may have international consequences, however cyber terrorism is a global concern, which has domestic as well as international consequences. The common form of these terrorist attacks on the Internet is by distributed denial of service attacks, hate websites and hate emails, attacks on sensitive computer networks, etc. Technology savvy terrorists are using 512-bit encryption, which is next to impossible to decrypt. The recent example may be cited of – *Osama Bin Laden*, the *LTTE*, attack on *America's army deployment system* during Iraq war.

   Cyber terrorism may be defined to be " *the premeditated use of disruptive activities, or the threat thereof, in cyber space, with the intention to further social, ideological, religious, political or similar objectives, or to intimidate any person in furtherance of such objectives*"

   Another definition may be attempted to cover within its ambit every act of cyber terrorism.

   A terrorist means a person who indulges in wanton killing of persons or in violence or in disruption of services or means of communications essential to the community or in damaging property with the view to –

   1. *Putting the public or any section of the public in fear; or*
   2. *Affecting adversely the harmony between different religious, racial, language or regional groups or castes or communities; or*
   3. *Coercing or overawing the government established by law; or*
   4. *Endangering the sovereignty and integrity of the nation*

   and a cyber terrorist is the person who uses the computer system as a means or ends to achieve the above objectives. Every act done in pursuance thereof is an act of cyber terrorism.

10. **Trafficking:** Trafficking may assume different forms. It may be trafficking in drugs, human beings, arms weapons etc. These forms of trafficking are going unchecked because they

are carried on under pseudonyms. A racket was busted in Chennai where drugs were being sold under the pseudonym of honey.

11. **Fraud and Cheating:** Online fraud and cheating is one of the most lucrative businesses that are growing today in the cyber space. It may assume different forms. Some of the cases of online fraud and cheating that have come to light are those pertaining to credit card crimes, contractual crimes, offering jobs, etc.

Recently the *Court of Metropolitan Magistrate Delhi* found guilty a 24-year-old engineer working in a call centre, of fraudulently gaining the details of Campa's credit card and bought a television and a cordless phone from Sony website. Metropolitan magistrate Gulshan Kumar convicted Azim for cheating under IPC, but did not send him to jail. Instead, Azim was asked to furnish a personal bond of Rs 20,000, and was released on a year's probation.

Statutory Provisons

The Indian parliament considered it necessary to give effect to the resolution by which the General Assembly adopted Model Law on Electronic Commerce adopted by the United effective manner.

The Information Technology Act deals with the various cyber crimes in chapters IX & XI. The important sections are Ss. 43,65,66,67. Section 43 in particular deals with the unauthorised access, unauthorised downloading, virus attacks or any contaminant, causes damage, disruption, denial of access, interference with the service availed by a person. This section provide for a fine up to Rs. 1 Crore by way of remedy. Section 65 deals with '*tampering with computer source documents*' and provides for imprisonment up to 3 years or fine, which may extend up to 2 years or both. Section 66 deals with '*hacking with computer system*' and provides for imprisonment up to 3 years or fine, which may extend up to 2 years or both. Further section 67 deals with publication of obscene material and provides for imprisonment up to a term of 10 years and also with fine up to Rs. 2 lakhs.

6.6.9 Prevention of Cyber Crime

Prevention is always better than cure. It is always better to take certain precaution while operating the net. A should make them his part of cyber life. Sailesh kumar Zarkar, technical advisor and network security consultant to the Mumbai Police Cyber crime Cell advocates the 5P mantra for online security: *Precaution, Prevention, Protection, Preservation and Perseverance.* A netizen should keep in mind the following things-

1. To prevent cyber stalking avoid disclosing any information pertaining to one. This is as good as disclosing your identity to strangers in public place.
2. Always avoid sending any photograph online particularly to strangers and chat friends as there have been incidents of misuse of the photographs.
3. Always use latest and up date anti virus software to guard against virus attacks.
4. Always keep back up volumes so that one may not suffer data loss in case of virus contamination

5. Never send your credit card number to any site that is not secured, to guard against frauds.
6. Always keep a watch on the sites that your children are accessing to prevent any kind of harassment or depravation in children.
7. It is better to use a security programme that gives control over the cookies and send information back to the site as leaving the cookies unguarded might prove fatal.
8. Web site owners should watch traffic and check any irregularity on the site. Putting host-based intrusion detection devices on servers may do this.
9. Use of firewalls may be beneficial.
10. Web servers running public sites must be physically separate protected from internal corporate network.

Adjudication of a Cyber Crime – On the directions of the Bombay High Court the Central Government has by a notification dated 25.03.03 has decided that the Secretary to the Information Technology Department in each state by designation would be appointed as the AO for each state.

6.7 LEGAL PROBLEMS OR LEGAL INSECURITIES DRIVERS

The majority of respondents mentioned at least one driver for their legal problems or insecurities when doing e-business. Also, most of the respondents did not know how to solve these problems and had to go for specialized legal services. This happened in many cases, at least partially, due to the fact of lack of awareness of the legal framework. Basically, legal problems and legal insecurities result from:

- **Not enough legal advising in many contracts**: No legal practices have been established, such of the kind of administrative or court practices. Also, lack of legal information for legal aspects related to workers. To overcome this barrier some companies contracted a professional legal advisor. They also stated that there is a lack of professionals specialized in e-business/e-commerce law.
- **Fear due to ignorance, and fear to spread the prices openly**: To overcome this kind of problem, some companies created a package of supply services, so consumers can choose between a selective set of options.
- **Lack of awareness of the legal framework is a recurrent problem**: This evolves into the fact that most of the mentioned legal issues are perceived as legal business barriers, although in reality those are "practical o logistics" e-business barriers. The lack of awareness of these legal practices, in addition to the lack of trust that consumers has created a wider perception of "un-trust", and in consequence raising a direct barrier on e-business. There are still many legal gaps and grey areas. Some concerns are related to taxes, VAT, domain registration, brands, copyright and data confidentiality abroad.

To overcome these gaps, prefer to compensate the client/consumer when something wrong happens and fix the problem once the customer is satisfied. They absorbed the costs when a problem occurs and they fix their logistics or sales management in order to fix the procedures and avoid further similar problems. To avoid further problems, contracting legal advisors or training an employee or the owner with reference to legal matters. In addition, the impact of consumer mismanagement is high, because having problems with consumers might evolve toward a big issue regarding image affecting future sales. This could create big damage. Information Over the Internet is spread very fast.

6.8 SOURCES CURRENTLY USED FOR BEING INFORMED ABOUT RELEVANT LEGAL ISSUES FOR THE E-BUSINESS

The majority of the respondents did perceive significant legal barriers for e-business and there are many uncertainties that related to the legal framework. However, in reality legal issues are mixed with factual not harmonized deployment of e-business legal policies and different technical IT issues among the EU countries. Due to the necessity of legal knowledge, at current stage, almost everyone want to keep themselves informed through contracted legal advisors (27,4%), on-line portals (22,6%), personal contacts (21,4%), news from Chambers of Commerce, industry associations etc. (17,9%) and through newsletters (9,5%).

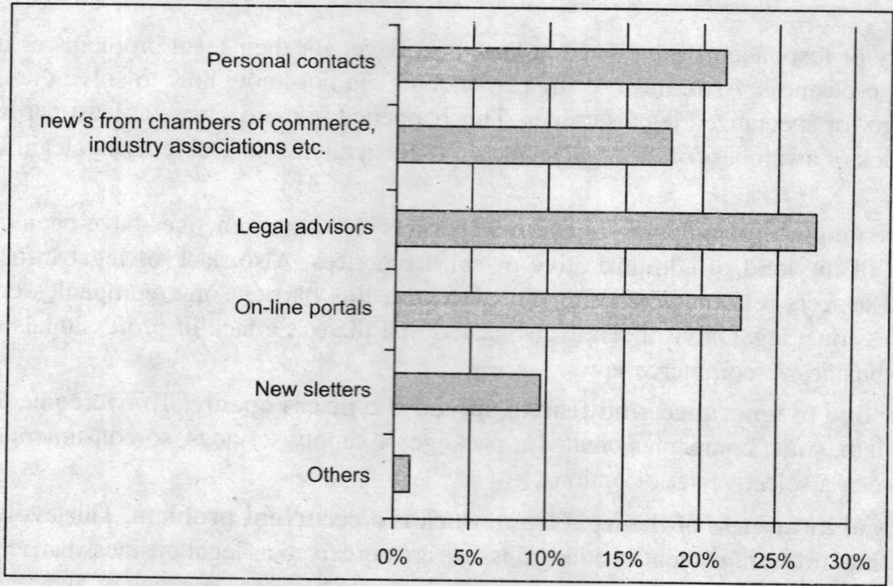

Fig. 6.6: Sources of information for Legal issues

About 84% of total interviewed might currently use on-line tools for being informed about relevant legal issues for the e-business, while a 16% wouldn't. Those who gave a negative answer said that legal issues have many shades of meaning so it would be better to contract a legal advisor. They reported to have a need of interpreted information from someone who is a professional in the field.

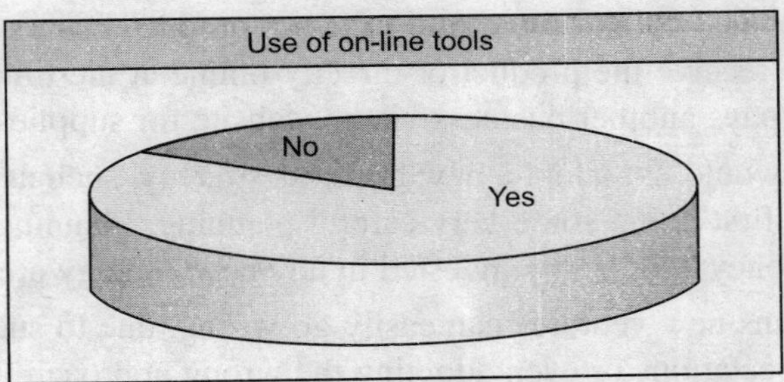

Fig. 6.7

To keep informed about legal aspects that could be important for the business, 27% of companies said that they would surf through websites (mainly using a search engine), 25% would use a wiki type of catalogue and 16% might purchase information (16%), preferably if the supplier is a Government source. Also they might get information from on-line forums (14%), blogs (13%) or P2P file sharing (5%).

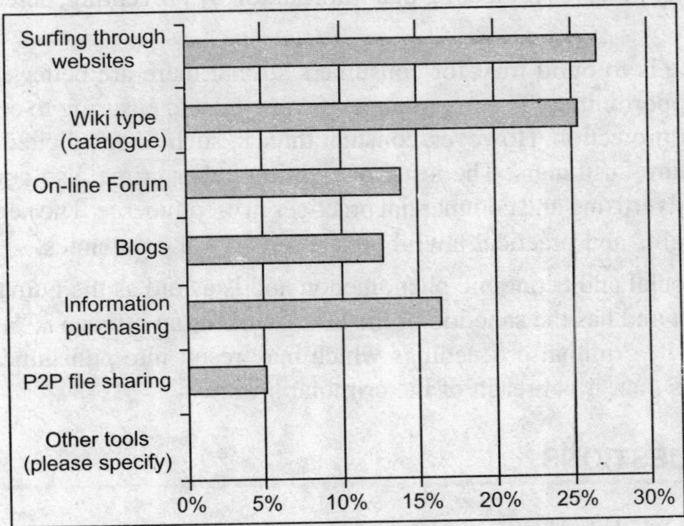

Fig. 6.8: Sources of information for Legal issues

6.9 SUMMARY

- The legal aspect of e-business is all about managing risks. It is important to ensure that the content of website is accurate and complies with current law. It is also important to regularly review the website once it is up and running to ensure that it continues to comply.
- Broadly speaking, the term "e-business" refers to using the Internet for doing business.
- The term e-commerce has a narrower meaning than e-business. It refers to using the Internet to order and pay for products or services. So e-commerce is a sub-set of e-business.

- E-commerce happens when a consumer orders a product from a business and pays for it either when they receive the product or directly online at the time of ordering. It happens when a business pays another business via its website for supplies.
- Most businesses would not adopt a new business strategy, such as opening up a new office or shop, without first doing some very careful planning. Planning helps to ensure that the precious time, money and energy invested in any new strategy are not wasted.
- Without good plans new ventures can easily go wrong, due to such things as poor timing, unreasonable expectations or even adopting the wrong approach in the first place.
- Good planning maximizes the benefits to a business of a new or expanded business venture and reduces the risk of things going wrong.
- Cyber security standards are security standards which enable organizations to practice safe security techniques in order to minimize the number of successful cyber security attacks. These guides provide general outlines as well as specific techniques for implementing cyber security.
- Cyber security involves protecting that information by preventing, detecting, and responding to attacks.
- A main issue is to build trust for consumers so that there are better e-market perspectives and wider opportunities. The importance of showing and ensuring to consumers a high level of consumer protection. However, constant threats, such as unsolicited commercial e-mails, do not reassure customers. The issue of fighting cyber crime also constrains the practical aspects for advertising and commercial practices in e-commerce. The need to balance between consumer rights and practical lawful advertisement for companies.
- Crime is a social and economic phenomenon and is as old as the human society. Crime is a legal concept and has the sanction of the law. Crime or an offence is "a legal wrong that can be followed by criminal proceedings which may result into punishment." The hallmark of criminality is that, it is breach of the criminal law.

6.10 REVIEW QUESTIONS

1. Discuss the term E-business and how planning for e- business is done.
2. Discuss the business ethics and explain the importance of business ethics in an organization.
3. Explain the various legal issues related to e- business.
4. Define cyber crime and differentiate it with conventional crime.
5. Explain the cyber security and its various methods.

CHAPTER 7

Emerging Trends in I.T.

Introducing technologies and services where opportunities exist for corporations and individuals to make an impact, including emerging technical trends in retail, mobile application development, and business intelligence software.

7.1 ELECTRONICS COMMERCE

Electronic Commerce is a modern business methodology that addresses the needs of organizations, merchants and consumers to cut costs while improving the quality of goods and services and increasing the speed of service delivery.

The term also applies to the use of computer network to search and retrieve information in support of human and corporate decision-making. E-Commerce is associated with the buying and selling of information, products and services via computer networks today and in the future via any one of the myriad of networks that make up the information superhighway (I-Way).

The effects of E-Commerce are already appearing in all areas of business, from customer service to new product design. It facilitates new types of information based business processes for reaching and interacting with customers – on line advertising and marketing on line order taking and on line customer service, to name a few. Finally, e-commerce enables the information of new types of information based products such as interactive game, electronic books and information on demand that can be very profitable for content providers and useful for consumers clearly a key element of e-commerce is information processing. The information processing activity is usually in the form of business transactions for which several broad categories can be observed –

(i) Transaction between a company and the consumer over public networks for the purpose of home shopping or home banking using encryption for security and electronic cash, credit or debit tokens for payment.

(ii) Transactions with trading pattern using EDI.

(iii) Transactions for information gathering such as market search using bar code scanners, information processing for managerial decision making or organizational problem solving and information manipulation for operations and supply chain management.

(iv) Transactions for information distribution with prospective customers, including interactive advertising sales & Marketing.

7.1.1 Electronic Commerce – Technology and Prospects

Commerce (the trading of goods) has been a major impetus for human survival since the beginning of recorded history and beyond. The mass adoption of the Internet has created a paradigm shift in the way businesses are conducted today. The past decade has seen the emergence of a new kind of commerce: e-commerce, the buying and selling of goods through human-computer interaction over the Internet. Traditional physical trading of goods and currency is becoming increasingly unpopular and more businesses are jumping on the e-commerce bandwagon. Today, the line between e-commerce and traditional commerce is becoming more blurred as more businesses start and continue to integrate the Internet and e-commerce technologies into their business processes.

7.1.2 Definition of e-Commerce

The e-commerce can be defined as a modern business methodology that addresses the needs of organizations, merchants, and consumers to cut costs while improving the quality of goods and services and increasing the speed of service delivery, by using Internet. It differs from the traditional electronic commerce (e-commerce) in the way that it enables the trading of goods, money and information electronically from computer to computer. Business is done electronically and there is no longer a need for physical currency or goods to conduct business.

7.1.3 Evolution of e-Commerce

Evolution of e-commerce can be attributed to a combination of regulatory reform and technological innovation. Though Internet (which played an important role in evolution) appeared in the late 1960s, e-commerce of today took off with the arrival of World Wide Web and browsers in early 1990s. The liberalization of the telecommunications sector and innovations such as optic fiber, DSL etc. (which has helped to expand the volume and capacity of communications) have helped in the process of that rapid growth. As a result the barriers to entry and engage in e-commerce have fallen rapidly. A brief timeline of evolution is as follows:

- 1969 Internet/Arpanet
- 1989 WWW HTML invented at CERN
- 1991 NSF lifts restrictions on commercial use of Internet
- 1993 Mosaic browser invented at University of Illinois, Urbana Champagne, is released to public
- 1994 Netscape releases Navigator browser
- 1995 Dell, Cisco, Amazon etc. began aggressively to use Internet for commercial transactions
- The growth of Internet has a special significance in the growth of e-commerce.

It has the potential to involve general people into the process thereby increasing its reach far beyond large companies.

7.1.4 Conducting Business Online (e-Commerce)

Doing business online is electronic commerce, and there are four main areas in which companies conduct business online today:

1. Direct marketing, selling, and services.
2. Online banking and billing.
3. Secure distribution of information.
4. Value-chain trading and corporate purchasing.

7.1.4.1 Direct Marketing, Selling, and Services

Today, more websites focus on direct marketing, selling, and services than on any other type of electronic commerce. Direct selling was the earliest type of electronic commerce, and has proven to be a stepping-stone to more complex commerce operations for many companies. Successes such as Amazon.com, Barnes and Noble, Dell Computer, and the introduction of e-tickets by major airlines, have catalyzed the growth of this segment, proving the reach and customer acceptance of the Internet.

7.1.4.2 Financial and Information Services

A broad range of financial and information services are performed over the Internet today and sites that offer them are enjoying rapid growth. These sites are popular because they help consumers, businesses of all sizes, and financial institutions distribute some of their most important information over the Internet with greater convenience and richness that is available using other channels. For example, you have:

- Online banking
- Online billing
- Secure information distribution

Online Banking

Consumers and small businesses can save time and money by doing their banking on the Internet. Paying bills, making transfers between accounts, and trading stocks, bonds, and mutual funds can all be performed electronically by using the Internet to connect consumers and small businesses with their financial institutions.

Online Billing

Companies whose bill can achieve significant cost savings and marketing benefits through the use of Internet-based bill-delivery and receiving systems. Today, consumers receive an average of 23 bills per month by mail from retailers, credit card companies, and utilities.

Secure Information Distribution

To many businesses, information is their most valuable asset. Although the Internet can enable businesses to reach huge new markets for that information, businesses must also safeguard that information to protect their assets. Digital Rights Management provides protection for intellectual and information property, and is a key technology to secure information distribution.

7.1.4.3 Maintenance, Repair, and Operations (MRO)

The Internet also offers tremendous time and cost savings for corporate purchasing of low-cost, high-volume goods for maintenance, repair, and operations (MRO) activities. Typical MRO goods include office supplies (such as pens and paper), office equipment and furniture, computers, and replacement parts. The Internet can transform corporate purchasing from a labor and paperwork-intensive process into a self-service application. Company employees can order equipment on websites, company officials can automatically enforce purchase approval and policies through automated business rules, and suppliers can keep their catalog information centralized and up-to-date. Purchase order applications can then use the Internet to transfer the order to suppliers.

In response, suppliers can ship the requested goods and invoice the company over the Internet. In addition to reduced administrative costs, Internet-based corporate purchasing can improve order-tracking accuracy, better enforce purchasing policies, provide better customer and supplier service, reduce inventories, and give companies more power in negotiating exclusive or volume discount contracts. In other words, the Internet and e-business have changed the way enterprises serve customers and compete with each other, and have heightened awareness for competing supply chains.

7.1.4.4 Value-Chain Integration

No other business model highlights the need for tight integration across suppliers, manufacturers, and distributors quite like the value chain. Delays in inventory tracking and management can ripple from the cash register all the way back to raw material production, creating inventory shortages at any stage of the value chain. The resulting out-of-stock events can mean lost business. The Internet promises to increase business efficiency by reducing reporting delays and increasing reporting accuracy. Speed is clearly the business imperative for the value chain.

7.2 IMPACT OF E-COMMERCE ON BUSINESS

E-commerce will change the way the businesses are being carried on. It will lead to the emergence of new businesses as well as business practices and also a new role for intermediaries. Indeed, all the functional areas of business will undergo change as follows:

- The new technology will transform business processes, the way products and services are created and marketed, dynamics of competitions, the organization structure of the enterprise and the nature of the enterprise itself. This will include marketing, supply management, customer and sales management, product development etc.

- Local proximity may no longer be a significant factor in retaining customer. Local markets will be replaced by global markets. Indeed it may bring to reality the goal of making the whole world as one family.
- Transparency and openness continue and will continue, to be effective business strategy. Already many businesses have started recognizing key customers, employees and suppliers more like a partner in the business. E-commerce will lead to better customer service, more personalized products, reduced costs, supply chain efficiency and faster time to market. The most significant aspect of e-commerce is new market development. The e-commerce links and the infrastructure, initially set up, can be successfully used in other sectors.
- The change in the business functions will lead to new business models and create new set of facts and circumstances that can materially change the incidence of taxation.
- The Internet will emerge as a new platform for marketing of products and services that will displace and rebuild existing economy. It will affect organizational structure; require different skills for negotiation, new regulatory and legal framework, electronic money, taxation and many other things. The evolution of e-commerce will have profound impact on competition, mobility of enterprises, effect on consumer behavior, changes in the way the work is defined and managed. The net will enable businesses to save time on product design, design according to the individual customer specification, order and delivery of components, tracking sales and getting feedback from customers.
- The businesses can have virtual project team, virtual learning space so that the employees who are dispersed over various countries can work together as if they are together in one physical room. Business can be connected to the retail points in order to ascertain market trends, demand of the products and with the suppliers upstream to order the desired requirements. Better demand forecasting and stock replenishment can lead to significant reduction in the cost. Selling through websites is the fastest growing method of trading worldwide. There are two main forms of e-commerce:
  - Business to business (B2B) trading where companies trade and exchange information using the World Wide Web.
  - Business to consumer (B2C) trading where companies deal directly with customers through web pages, and ordering is carried out online.

There are many different types of products and services that are traded on line including books, CDs, cars, holidays, and insurance. In response to e tailing and e trading, most businesses have now set up their own websites.

Trading online enables businesses to reach much wider audiences while cutting the costs of traditional retailing methods. For example, an e-tailer does not have to spend so much on an expensive High Street presence. Until recently The Times 100 was a paper-based resource that was used by every school in the United Kingdom. Now the resource appears in two formats - in a photocopiable folder of materials, and online. The online presence has opened up viewing of The Times 100 to a global market and a large number of hits are recorded from students in almost every country in the world. Existing users are able to benefit from the convenience of quickly accessing case studies online and a range of additional online features have been added such as a theory section, and a range of tests and questions for students

Although the outlay on developing a good website is substantial the potential benefits are enormous in providing most types of business with a competitive advantage. One group of businesses that have been particularly successful as a result of the development of the web are specialist suppliers of items such as paintings, photographs, confectionery, and other items. An individual working from home can now advertise and sell their produce worldwide. A web page is a single document. A website is a collection of related documents. The World Wide Web consists of graphic and text documents that can be connected together through clickable 'hypertext' links.

7.3 ISSUES IN IMPLEMENTING ELECTRONIC COMMERCE

Although it is simple to describe their benefits, it is not nearly as easy to develop and deploy commerce systems. Companies can face significant implementation issues:

- Cost
- Value
- Security
- Leveraging existing systems
- Interoperability

7.3.1 Cost

Electronic commerce requires significant investments in new technologies that can touch many of a company's core business processes. As with all major business systems, electronic commerce systems require significant investments in hardware, software, staffing, and training. Businesses need comprehensive solutions with greater ease-of-use to help foster cost-effective deployment.

7.3.2 Value

Businesses want to know that their investments in electronic commerce systems will produce a return. Business objectives such as lead generation, business-process automation, and cost reduction must be met. Systems used to reach these goals need to be flexible enough to change when the business changes.

7.3.3 Security

The Internet provides universal access, but companies must protect their assets against accidental or malicious misuse. System security, however, must not create prohibitive complexity or reduce flexibility. Customer information also needs to be protected from internal and external misuse. Privacy systems should safeguard the personal information critical to building sites that satisfy customer and business needs.

7.3.4 Leveraging Existing Systems

Most companies already use information technology (IT) to conduct business in non- Internet environments, such as marketing, order management, billing, inventory, distribution, and customer service. The Internet represents an alternative and complementary way to do business, but it is imperative that electronic commerce systems integrate existing systems in a manner that avoids duplicating functionality and maintains usability, performance, and reliability.

7.3.5 Interoperability

When systems from two or more businesses are able to exchange documents without manual intervention, businesses achieve cost reduction, improved performance, and more dynamic value chains. Failing to address any of these issues can spell failure for a system's implementation effort. Therefore, your company's commerce strategy should be designed to address all these issues to help customers achieve the benefits of electronic commerce. Your company's vision for electronic commerce should also be to help businesses establish stronger relationships with customers and industry partners. For example, a successful strategy for delivering this vision is described by three work-flow elements (platform, portal, and industry partners), each backed by comprehensive technology, product, and service offerings. From self-service portals to transaction processing, a successful work-flow strategy can be the underlying engine delivering state-based, processed-focused control services for e-business applications. Human labor is expensive, and work-flow technology allows e-businesses to supplement, and in some cases eliminate, reliance on human supervision and intervention.

7.4 HOW DO YOU WORK WITH E-COMMERCE?

E-commerce is about setting your business on the Internet, allowing visitors to access your website, and go through a virtual catalog of your products/services online. When a visitor wants to buy something he/she likes, they merely "add" it to their virtual shopping basket. Items in the virtual shopping basket can be added or deleted, and when you're all set to checkout, you head to the virtual checkout counter, which has your complete total, and that will ask you for your name, address etc. and method of payment (usually via credit card). Once you have entered all this information (which by the way is being transmitted securely) you can then just wait for delivery.

7.5 COMPARISON BETWEEN TRADITIONAL COMMERCE AND E-COMMERCE

In many cases business processes use traditional commerce activities very effectively, and these processes cannot be improved upon through technology. Products that buyers prefer to touch, smell, or examine closely are difficult to sell using electronic commerce. For example, customers might be reluctant to buy high-fashion clothing and perishable food products, such as meat or produce, if they cannot examine the products closely before agreeing to purchase them. In the case of traditional commerce retail merchants have years of experience in creating store environments that help convince a customer to buy. This combination of store design, layout and product display knowledge is called merchandising. Sales people in course of time develop skills that allow them to identify customer needs and find products and services that meet those needs. The arts of merchandising and personal selling can be difficult to practice over an electronic link. Through ecommerce branded products such as books or CDs can be easily sold. As one copy of a new book is identical to other copies and because a customer would not be concerned about freshness he would willingly order a title without examining the specific copy they would receive. The advantage of electronic commerce, namely the ability of one site to offer a wider selection of titles than even the largest physical bookstore, can outweigh the advantage of a traditional bookstore, namely the facility to browse. Some examples of business processes are listed in the following table that suit to the e-commerce and traditional commerce respectively.

Business processes well-suited to

Electronic commerce	Traditional commerce
• Sale/purchase of books and CDs	• Sale/purhcase of high-fashion clothing
• Online delivery of software	• Sale/purchase of perishable food products
• Advertising and promotion of travel services	• Small denomination transactions
• Online tracking of shipments	• Sale of expensive jewellery and antiques

7.6 E-COMMERCE TECHNOLOGIES

What technologies are necessary for e-commerce? The short answer is that most information technologies and Internet technologies that we discuss throughout the book are involved in e-commerce systems, viz.–

- The Internet, intranets, and extranets are the network infrastructure or foundation of e-commerce.
- Customers must be provided with a range of secure information, marketing, transaction, processing, and payment services.
- Trading and business partners rely on Internet and extranets to exchange information and accomplish secure transactions; including electronic data interchange (EDI) and other supply chain and financial systems and databases.
- Company employees depend on a variety of Internet and intranet resources to communicate and collaborate in support of their EC work activities.
- Information system professionals and end users can use a variety of software tools to develop and manage the content and operations of the websites and other EC resources of a company.

7.7 ECONOMIC POTENTIAL OF E-COMMERCE

Consumers are pushing retailers to the wall, demanding lower process, better quality, a large selection of in-season goods. Retailers are scrambling to fill the order. They are slashing back-office costs, reducing profit margins, reducing cycle times, buying more wisely, and making huge investments in technology. They are revamping distribution channels to make sure that warehouse costs are down by reducing their average inventory levels and coordinating the consumer demand and supply patterns. In the push to reduce prices, more and more retailers are turning to overseas suppliers, in part because of cheaper labor costs. The effect of e-commerce can also be seen over the retail industry and marketing.

7.7.1 e-Commerce and Retail Industry

Retailers are in the immediate line of fire and are first to bear the brunt of cost cutting. They are putting that pressure on the manufacturing and supplier end of the pipeline. At the same time, the quest for efficiencies has led to turmoil and consolidation within the retail industry. The pressure experienced by retailers and suppliers can be seen in the disappearance of jobs, in mergers, and in the increase in business failures in the manufacturing sector. The problems are indeed serious. Electronic markets could provide a partial solution by promising customers more convenience and merchants greater efficiency and interactivity with suppliers to revitalize the troubled retailing sector.

7.7.2 e-Commerce and Marketing

Electronic commerce is forcing companies to rethink the existing ways of doing target marketing (isolating and focusing on a segment of the population), relationship marketing (building and sustaining a long-term relationship with existing and potential customers), and even event marketing (setting up a virtual booth where interested people come and visit). Consider the case of conventional direct marketers, who devote some 25 percent of their revenues to such costs as printing and postages for catalogs. Interactive marketing could help cut such expenses and may even deliver better results. Interactive marketing is accomplished in electronic markets via interactive multimedia catalogs that give the same look and feel as a shopping channel. Users find moving images more appealing than still images and listening more appealing than reading text on screen. Those are two powerful reasons why every text-based and still-picture-based interactive experimental-based service has ever generated anywhere near the volume of retail merchandise orders that televised shopping channels have achieved. Maximum public acceptance will require that interactive catalog services have a more entertaining visual appearance than traditional text-intensive catalogs have had. Ideally, an interactive shopping program should produce full-motion demonstrations of selected products, but such a practical and economical technology has yet to be developed.

7.8 INCENTIVES FOR ENGAGING IN E-COMMERCE

A basic fact of Internet retailing is that all retail websites are created equal as far as the "location, location, location" imperative of success in retailing is concerned. No site is any closer to its web customers and competitors offering similar goods and services may be only a mouse click away. This makes it vital that businesses find ways to build customer satisfaction, loyalty, and relationships, so customers keep coming back to their web stores. Thus, the key to e-commerce success is to optimize several key factors such as selection and value, performance and service efficiency, the look and feel of the site, advertising and incentives to purchase, personal attention, community relationships, and security and reliability. The incentives for engaging in e-commerce are listed as follows:

1. **Selection and Value:** Attractive product selections, competitive prices, satisfaction guarantees, and customer support after the sale.
2. **Performance and Service:** Fast, easy navigation, shopping, and purchasing, and prompt shipping and delivery.
3. **Look and Feel:** Attractive web storefront, website shopping areas, multimedia product catalog pages, and shopping features.
4. **Advertising and Incentives:** Targeted web-page advertising and e-mail promotions, discounts and special offers, including advertising at affiliate sites.
5. **Personal Attention:** Personal web pages, personalized product recommendations, web advertising, and e-mail notices, and interactive support for all customers.
6. **Community Relationships:** Virtual communities of customers, suppliers, company representatives, and others via newsgroups, chat rooms, and links to related sites.
7. **Security and Reliability:** Security of customer information and website transactions, trustworthy product information, and reliable order fulfillment.

7.9 DRIVING FORCES BEHIND E-COMMERCE

The various driving forces behind e-commerce can be listed as below:

1. **Global Customers:** Customers are people who may travel anywhere or companies with global operations. Global IT can help provide fast, convenient service.
2. **Global Products:** Products are the same throughout the world or are assembled by subsidiaries throughout the world. Global IT can help manage worldwide marketing and quality control.
3. **Global Operations:** Parts of a production or assembly process are assigned to subsidiaries based on changing economic or other conditions. Only global IT can support such geographic flexibilities.
4. **Global Resources:** The use and cost of common equipment, facilities, and people are shared by subsidiaries of a global company. Global IT can keep track of such shared resources.
5. **Global Collaborations:** The knowledge and expertise of colleagues in a global company can be quickly accessed, shared, and organized to support individual or group efforts. Only global IT can support such enterprise collaboration.

7.10 ADVANTAGES OF E-COMMERCE

7.10.1 Primary Benefits of E-Commerce

Apart from innumerable missives on the subject, it is an attempt to explore the potential of e-Commerce in a way to transform your business surpassing all geographical boundaries and trade barriers. Understandably, the tremendous potential of information technology for purposes of communication and information storage and retrieval has impacted the Commercial world like nothing before. The quality of communication on the web has progressed in quantum leaps and has bridged more effectively, unlike traditional methods of commerce, the distance between the markets and the customers.

Getting your business online in the first place increases your visibility; a vital effect for any business. In the second, it opens your customer base beyond border, simply because it makes it easy to do business with you. And in the third place it slashes your costs, enhances your productivity, steam lines your entire business process.

Global Accessibility and Sales Reach: An e-Business can receive orders from any country in the world. The global reach of local companies that have become e-Businesses has posed a major threat to many established firms, thus enhancing competition in the market.

Increased Profit: With e-Business, companies reach more and different customers and gain exposure in new markets not covered by existing physical channels, thus increasing the profits.

Improved customer service and loyalty: e-Commerce enables a company to be open for business whenever a customer needs it. Up-to-date information about product can be offered on the web, making it easier and more convenient for customers to serve themselves. Combining the interactive nature of the web with a proper understanding of a customers needs helps a merchant to provide products and services built to order for each customer, and thus to build a long term relationships, increase loyalty and sustain a competitive edge.

Shorter time-to-market: e-Commerce makes for fast and flexible execution and response to market opportunities. The web enables a company to introduce a new product into the market, get immediate customer reaction to it, and refine and perfect it.

Supply chain integration: e-Commerce enables the full integration of the business, making the entire supply chain more efficient from the point of customer contact all the way back through physical distribution, ware housing, manufacturing, resource management and purchasing.

Capturing valuable market information from customers: e-Commerce enables you to get your potential customers details and buying habits, facilitating an easy marketing strategy and building a direct customer relationship.

Release from working hour restrictions: e-Commerce removes the restrictions enforced on your business operating hours. An online business provides 24x7 access to customers taking orders and selling goods to your valuable customers worldwide. There is no barrier on time.

7.10.2 Customer Benefits and Services

The proposed solution is bound to bring about a fully functional Information Infrastructure. The advantages of the solution include

- Uniqueness in approach to Internet Commerce.
- Scalability of solution to match diverse business needs of clients.
- Adaptability to present day global Internet based Commerce.
- Full support to customers in developing sales channels through e-Commerce services.
- Handling of diverse merchant business models.
- Ensures secure purchasing.
- Ensures future Internet payment vehicles such as debit cards and electronic checks to Internet customers.

7.10.3 Major Advantages of E-Commerce

With the astonishing growth of the Internet, many companies are finding new and exciting ways to expand upon their business opportunities. There are very few successful companies that do not use computers in their everyday business activities, which also mean there are few companies that do not use e-commerce. These are the advantages of Internet and e-commerce in general:

1. **Speed:** The Internet and World Wide Web give businesses opportunities to exchange messages or complete transactions almost instantaneously. Even with the slowest connections, doing business electronically is much faster than traditional modes. With increased speeds of communication, the delivery time is expedited and that makes the whole transaction from start to finish more efficient. Even more significant is the fact that information appearing on the Internet can be changed extremely rapidly. This gives business owners the ability to inform customers of any changes to the service that you are offering. This also allows for you to update marketing and promotional materials as often and as frequently as you would like.
2. **Cost Saving**: By using the Internet, marketing, distribution, personnel, phone, postage and printing costs, among many others, can be reduced. You can start doing business in cyberspace for as little as thousand of rupees. Most businesses will spend more than this but compared to the cost of opening a physical store, the savings are tremendous. These funds can then be diverted to marketing and advertising of your product or service.
3. **No Boundaries:** Cyberspace does not know any national boundary. That means you can do business all over the world as easily as you can in your own neighborhood. Since the Internet connects everyone in cyberspace, information is transmitted at the speed of sound or the speed of light, depending on your connection. Either way, distance becomes meaningless, which makes you able to link to anyone on the globe and anyone on the globe can link to you. The ability to provide links makes doing business on the Internet attractive to customers in any part of the world.

4. One advantage of the Internet is that is allows people to easily meet, gather data/information and stay in touch with others at a very low cost. Now almost everyone can automatically expose his/her business to the international market. The web will enable firms to build on the assets that they already possess, like brand name recognition, operational infrastructure, information, and customer relationships in order to develop new markets and distribution channels. Meeting with new network locally and from other countries can be done anytime and anywhere now.

7.10.4 Advantages to Customers

1. **Reduced Prices:** Costs of products are reduced since stages along the value chain are decreased. For instance, intermediaries can be eliminated by the company directly selling to the consumer instead of distributing through a retail store.
2. **Global Marketplace:** Consumers can shop anywhere in the world. Currently, according to the World Trade Organization (WTO) there are no custom duties put on products bought and traded globally electronically. This also provides wide selection of products and services to consumers.
3. **24-Hour Access:** Online businesses never sleep as opposed to brick and mortar businesses. E-commerce allows people to carry out businesses without the barriers of time or distance. One can log on to the Internet at any point of time, be it day or night and purchase or sell anything one desires at a single click of the mouse.
4. **More Choices:** Provides consumers with more choices. For example, before making any purchase, customer can study about all the major brands and features of any item. It also provides consumers with less expensive products and services by allowing them to shop in many places and conduct quick comparisons.
5. **Quicker Delivery :** Allows quick delivery of products and services (in some cases) especially with digitized products.
6. Consumers can receive relevant and detailed information in seconds, rather than in days or weeks.
7. Makes it possible to participate in virtual auctions.
8. Allows consumers to interact with other consumers and electronic communities and exchange ideas as well as compare experiences.

7.10.5 Advantages to Businesses

1. **Increased Potential Market Share:** The Internet enables businesses to have access to international markets thereby increasing their market share. Companies can also achieve greater economies of scale.
2. **Low-cost Advertising:** Advertising on the Internet costs less than advertising on print or television depending on the intricacies and extent of the advertisement. A company can still spend a lot on advertising on the Internet if the company hires an external party to create

their advertisements but advertising on the Internet itself is less costly since there is less cost associated with it in terms of printing and limited television spots.

3. **Low Barriers to Entries:** Anyone can start up a company on the Internet. Start-up costs are a lot lower for companies since there is less need for money for capital.
4. **Strategic Benefit**—The strategic benefit of making a business 'e-commerce enabled' is that it helps reduce the delivery time, labour cost and the cost incurred in the following areas:
   - Document preparation
   - Error detection and correction
   - Reconciliation
   - Mail preparation
   - Telephone calling
   - Data entry
   - Overtime
   - Supervision expenses

7.10.6 Advantages to Society

1. Enables people in Third world countries and rural areas to enjoy products and services which otherwise are not available to them.
2. Facilitates delivery of public services at a reduced cost, increases effectiveness, and/or improves quality.
3. Enables more individuals to work at home, and to do less traveling for shopping, resulting in less traffic on the roads, and lower air pollution.
4. Allows some merchandise to be sold at lower prices since organization may not need a physical place and full inventory.

7.10.7 Advantages to Women

People in general think that women unlike men are reluctant to purchase online. On the contrary, NPD research found that women tend to shop online more than men in most product categories. The study asserts that women were more likely to shop toys, clothing, and games and make up online more than men.

In short all the major advantages of e-commerce can be summarized as follows:

1. Cost reduction due to competitiveness in the procurement of products. Many suppliers of the product compete for customer patronage in open electronic markets. This competition brings down the product price.
2. Cost reduction due to reducing the paper work. The cost effective electronic documents will be delivered almost instantly and safely. This enables both parties to take quick decisions.

3. Information dissemination at a wider level is possible. Information about the product, cost, size, specification etc. may be made available to the customer located at widely distant geographical boundaries.
4. Improved customer relationship may be achieved by fast dissipation of the information to the potential customers.
5. Because all orders and inquiries are processed online, the product is directly supplied to the customer. This eliminates the need for wholesalers and retailers and brings down the product prices.
6. Total time reduction in the order processing, as e-commerce minimizes the time taken from order to delivery.
7. Provides better, fast and effective linkage with the clients. Since all information has to be processed in the electronic medium, that is online, it is possible to identify the customers' requirements that lead to quick product design.
8. Opens new vistas for the organization and generates better business avenues because of easy and cheap reach to the potential customer base.
9. Enhances the organization's product and market analysis as the organization gets faster feedback from the customer. These feedbacks may be processed online.

7.11 E-COMMERCE DISADVANTAGES

Although the list of e-commerce advantages is long, yet the e-commerce environment is far from perfection. In fact, some of the e-commerce disadvantages cause both consumers and businesses to suffer considerable misfortune. Although cost savings are usually mentioned, there are hidden costs that can quickly turn a credit into a debit. In addition, the technology is not perfect, for example, the network unreliability is a continuing concern. Moreover, some other concerns involve security, the loss of privacy, low and remote service levels, and complex legal issues. Let us discuss these disadvantages one by one.

7.11.1 Hidden Costs

Although buying on-line is convenient, the cost of this convenience is not always clear at he front end. For example, on-line purchases are often accompanied by high shipping and re-stocking fees, a lack of warranty coverage, and unacceptable delivery times. The online purchases must be shipped and the shipping charges may be considerable. In fact, too many e-commerce companies have developed a reputation of overcharging for

Shipping and handling.

7.11.2 Network Unreliability

With a user population of well over 100 million in North America alone, the Internet is a very busy information highway. Although the Internet is designed to overcome the single point of failure problem, there have been several well-publicized incidents of network failures during the past few years. An e-commerce website that cannot serve its customers loses sales, credibility, and even customers. In effect, a network failure can be compared to having a location at an exclusive mall that is in middle of nowhere and has no access roads that lead to it. Network reliability problems may be generated by such factors as:

- Equipment failure in the network connection provider or ISP.
- Long response time due to increased network traffic or inadequate bandwidth.
- Accidental problems caused by nature—such as lightning, floods, earthquakes that affect communication lines—or by human error—such as a road construction worker severing a network line by accident.

7.11.3 The Cost of Staying in Business

We included operational cost savings and lower barriers of entry in the list of ecommerce advantages. That is, getting into business is relatively easier in an e-commerce environment. Unfortunately, the flip side of the coin is that staying in business may be more difficult. Remember that the easy access means increased competition, thus causing businesses to operate with very thin profit margins. To be profitable, e-businesses must maintain high sales volumes, which in turn means developing and maintaining a big and loyal customer base. Attracting customers and transforming them into repeat buyers is the key to profitability. To survive and remain competitive, businesses must invest heavily in often-costly technology. The introduction of computer technology within a business not only automates the business process but it also changes the way the company does business internally and externally. Such synergy between technology and business operations makes the company more dependent on technology, therefore making it more vulnerable to the pace and network failures.

7.11.4 Lack of Security

One of the main roadblocks to the wide acceptance of e-commerce by businesses and consumers alike is the perceived lack of adequate security for on-line transactions. For example, consumers are growing increasingly weary about providing credit card information over the Internet. During the past few years, the press has been filled with reports about hackers breaking into e-business websites and stealing credit card information. In many cases, the break-ins passed inadvertently for several months before either the seller or the buyer discovered the problem. Securing on-line transaction data during its generation and then safeguarding it after it has been stored in the database are critical issues to be faced. For example, in June of 2001, a small computer retailer exposed credit card information through its website. The problem, caused by a coding error in a web page, allowed unauthorized access to stored order and credit card information for thousand of customers, dating as far back as one year.

7.11.5 Lack of Privacy

Ensuring the security of the data is of paramount importance to customers and to the credibility of the business. Customers also worry about the privacy implications of data gathered by organizations of all types and sizes. The incredible data collection process is a mixed blessing to customers. Even at the simplest data level, sales information is stored in databases connected to web servers, thus exposing the information to cyber criminals. Because data gathering on the web is so easy, databases routinely contain information about customer purchasing habits, demographic data, credit information, and so on. In many cases, companies sell customer database information to marketing companies.

In turn, the marketing companies engage in massive e-mail campaigns to attract new customers. It doesn't take long for the customer's e-mail box to be filled with unwanted and unsolicited e-mail (also known as "spam"). The growing sales of personal firewalls and the large number of "hits" on websites that deal with privacy issues are testimony to the fact that customers are growing increasingly worried about their online privacy, and that they are seeking ways to protect themselves from cyber attackers.

7.11.6 Low Service Levels

Another common complaint about doing business online is the low level of customer service that online companies tend to provide. Although technology has automated business transactions to a large extent, there remains a real need for the human touch. Therefore, customer service has become a major differentiating factor. Because the web buying experience is much more impersonal than the traditional one, providing good customer service is critical to the survival of any e-business. Therefore, e-commerce websites must provide

- A pleasant and problem-free pre-ordering and ordering experience. The website design is an important interface.
- Readily available easily used feedback options. Major customer complaints include the lack of contact information on websites and the difficulty of contacting a customer service representative.
- Quick and courteous complaint resolution.
- Timely and low-cost shipping and prompt delivery of merchandise to customers.

7.11.7 Legal Issues

Legal problems encountered in the e-commerce environment include

- Software and copyright infringements. The amount of illegal content flowing freely on the Internet is illustrated by the so-called Napster case. Napster, a popular music website, was sued by the Recording Industry Association because it hosted millions of illegal digital copies of copyrighted songs that were freely downloaded by millions of users worldwide. After court action, Napster was forced to change its business model and to eliminate all illegal material from its website.
- Credit card fraud and stolen identities. The lack of security we mentioned earlier has put credit card fraud on the proverbial front burner. In addition, lack of security makes it relatively easy to assume another person's identity in order to make fraudulent transactions. Loss of confidence in the security of online transactions is a brake on the e-business train.

- Business fraud. Online fraud also takes the form of companies that fail to deliver products and/or services to the customers who paid for them.

7.12 REASONS FOR THE E-COMMERCE NOT BEING VERY SUCCESSFUL

Although vast amounts of money have been invested into making e-commerce work, and although it causes vast amounts of money and large numbers of goods to change hands every day, it has so far failed to deliver the goods for a broad audience. The answer to why e-commerce has not been an overwhelming success for the masses can roughly be answered as follows:

1. Not everybody has access to a computer.
2. Buying goods over the internet is not 'natural':
   - One cannot feel or see the products in real life
   - The interaction is unnatural, there is no salesperson present.
3. People are concerned that it is unsafe to buy over the internet.

1. Limited Access to Computers

The computer is very essential to access e-commerce sites on Internet. Using a computer screen, people have visual access to a large amount of information, i.e., large number of goods to choose from. They can browse, select, get in-depth information, get overviews and so on, all at the click of a mouse button. But still in India or abroad, a large number of people do not have access on computers and therefore they are not able to take the advantage of the era of e-commerce.

2. Lack of Natural Quality

There are two issues to be addressed with respect to lack of natural quality in ecommerce. The first pertains to the fact that people are not able to touch and feel products with their own hands before buying something. Buying something from just the picture is essentially different from buying it in a shop. People probably only tend to buy things over the internet from which they already know what they look/feel/sound like from real life, and which have little between-product variation (examples are books, CDs and videotapes) or products that they can assess from behind their computer (an example is software). This seems to be a problem for e-commerce, which can be labeled as the 'Seeing is believing' problem.

The second natural quality problem has to do with natural interaction during a purchase. People are used to talking to a salesperson when they purchase something. Asking questions like: "Is this product really waterproof?" or "Do I get a money back guarantee on this item?" and thousands of questions like these seem to sooth people in their purchase. It guarantees them that they get what they want.

3. Unsafe Buying

A third problem of e-commerce is that of unsafe connections to the vendor. When sending credit card information over the internet, hackers could seize this information and use it for illegal transactions.

7.13 ELECTRONIC DATA INTERCHANGE

Electronic data interchange (EDI) technology enables unrelated organizations to conduct their business computer to computer without the need to use the same computer applications or technology in all locations. Combining *just in time* (JIT) manufacturing with EDI truly transforms the process:

1. A salesperson accepts an order through a laptop computer system.
2. Using the electronic mail facilities of the organization, the order is shipped to the order entry system.
3. The component parts are determined, and electronic purchase orders are generated to each supplier.
4. The EDI link routes the order, which is processed by the supplier's order system.
5. An EDI link is used to validate the purchaser's credit worthiness.
6. The paperless invoice is sent by way of EDI back to the purchaser.
7. When it is time for payment, an EDI link is used to generate the electronic funds transfer (EFT) to pay.

With EDI, a single entry by the person closest to the customer causes the facilities of the manufacturer and its suppliers to schedule appropriate production, shipping, and billing. The maximum possible time is allowed for all parties to process the order, thus reducing their need to carry inventory. A further advantage comes when production is driven by orders, because only those products that will actually be sold are manufactured. Manufacturers are able to offer more flexibility in product configuration, because they are manufacturing to order. The use of EDI standards allows organizations to participate in this electronic dialog regardless of differences among their individual technologies or application systems.

6.13.1 Overview of EDI benefits and drawbacks vides many benefits.

Computer-to-computer exchange of information is much less expensive than handling paper documents. Studies have shown that manually processing a paper-based order can cost $70 or more while processing an EDI order costs a dollar or less. Much less labor time is required. Fewer errors occur because computer systems process the documents rather than processing by hand.

EDI transactions between companies flow faster and more reliably than paper documents. Faster transactions support reduction in inventory levels, better use of warehouse space, fewer out-of-stock occurrences and lower freight costs through fewer emergency expedites.

Paper purchase orders can take up to 10 days from the time the buyer prepares the order to when the supplier ships it. EDI orders can take as little as one day. Drawbacks are few, but there are some. For example, companies choosing to implement both paper and EDI processes must manage both of these processes. However, as stated before, using EDI is much more efficient than using paper, lending strength to the argument against paper documents. Also, companies must ensure that they have the resources in place to make an EDI program work; however, the need for these resources (or their hiring) may be offset by the increased efficiency that EDI provides.

7.13.2 EDI example

Here is an example of how the electronic data interchange process works. A buyer prepares an order in his purchasing system and has it approved. Next, the EDI order is translated into an EDI document format called an 850 purchase order.

The EDI 850 purchase order is then securely transmitted to the supplier either via the internet or through a VAN (Value Added Network). The buyer's VAN is a like an electronic post office that interconnects with the supplier's VAN. The VANs make sure that EDI transactions are sent and received. The supplier's VAN ensures that the supplier receives the order. The supplier's computer system then processes the order. In the case of Covalent Works' clients, we provide VAN transportation and our servers provide all of the software and hardware required to process EDI documents. Only internet access and email are needed.

Data security and control are maintained through out the transmission process using passwords, user identification and encryption. Both the buyer's and the supplier's EDI applications edit and check the documents for accuracy.

7.13.3 EDI Requirements

Each trading partner has unique EDI requirements. These will include the specific kinds of EDI documents to be processed, such as the 850 purchase order used in the example above, 856 advance ship notices and 810 invoices. The fact is that most any business document that one company would exchange with another company can be sent via EDI. However each EDI document must be exchanged with the partner in exactly the format they specify.

Many partners will have an EDI implementation guide or kit that explains their specific requirements. Maps are required to translate the EDI documents from the trading partner's format into the format that is useable by the receiving party. Covalent Works handles all of the mapping and translation requirements for our clients.

EDI capability involves either buying or outsourcing the following components:

- Software for communications
- VAN service for EDI transmission
- Mail boxing of EDI transactions
- Mapping
- Translation

VAN, ASYNC, BISYNC, FTP and AS/2 Internet communications will be required by various partners. A server or PC, communication devices and peripherals will be needed as well as secured office space, monitored security, backups and redundant power. Additional software will be needed if integration of the EDI transactions with back office systems is desired. A VAN will need to be contracted for transmissions. Personnel must be trained in how to use the software and communication devices. Maps will then need to be developed.

7.13.4 Advantages vs. Disadvantages of using EDI

Advantages

There are several advantages of using EDI all of which provide distinct benefits to the user. One of the most notable benefits to using EDI is the time-saving capability it provides. By eliminating the process of distributing hard copies of information throughout the company, easy access to electronic data simplifies inter-department communication. Also, another time-savings advantage is the ability to track the origin of all information therefore significantly reducing time spent on corresponding with the source of the information.

Another benefit for the user of this information system is the ultimate savings in costs for the company. Although the initial set-up costs may seem high, the overall savings received in the long run ensures its value. For any business, regardless of its size, hard-copy print outs and document shipping costs add up. EDI allows for a paper-less exchange of information reducing handling costs and worker productivity that is involved with the organization of paper documents.

Electronic data interchange has another strong advantage over paper-based information exchange which has to do with accuracy of information. When the information is already stored electronically, it speeds up an organization's ability to check for accuracy and make any necessary corrections as the data is already inputted in the system. Also, unlike paper-based methods, EDI allows for the ability to send and receive information at any time thereby tremendously improving an organization's ability to communicate quickly and efficiently.

Disadvantages

There are a few barriers to using electronic data interchange. One of the most significant barriers is the accompanying process change. Existing processes built around slow paper handling may not be suited for EDI. For example, a business may receive the bulk of their goods by 1 or 2 day shipping and all of their invoices by mail. The existing process may therefore assume that goods are typically received before the invoice. With EDI, the invoice will typically be sent when the goods ship and will therefore require a process that handles large numbers of invoices whose corresponding goods have not yet been received.

Another significant barrier is the initial set-up. The preliminary expenses and time that arise from the implementation, customization and training can be costly and therefore may discourage some users.

Note: EDI is defined as the inter-process communication (computer application to computer application) of business information in standardized electronic forms. The primary benefits of EDI to business is a considerable reduction is transaction costs by improving the speed and efficiency of filling orders. EDI is not widely used.

Electronic commerce is often equated with EDI, so it is important to clarify that electronic commerce embraces EDI and much more. EDI is one well known example of structured document inter change, which enables data in the form of document content to be exchanged between software applications that are working together to process a business transaction.

- EDI is the paperless exchange electronic transfer from one computer to another of computer from one computer to another of computer process able data using an agreed standard to structure the data.

7.13.5 EDI Layered Architecture

EDI Semantic Layer	Application level Services	
EDI Standard Layer	EDI Business from Standard	
	ANSI x 12 Business from Standard	
EDI Transport Layer	Electronic mail	X.435, NIME
	Point to Point	FTP, TELNET
	World Wide Web	HTTP
Physical Layer	Dial up lines, Internet, I-way	

Fig 7.1: Layered Architecture of EDI

EDI architecture specifies four layers, the semantic layer (application layer), the standard translation layer, the packing (or transport) layer and the physical network infrastructure layer.

Semantic Layer

The EDI semantic layer describes the business application that is driving EDI. This laye specific to a company and the software it uses. In other words, the user interface and content visible on the screen are tailored or customized to local environments.

When a company receives the document, their EDI translation software automatically changes the standard format into the proprietary format of their document processing software so that the company can manipulate the information in what ever way it chooses to.

EDI Standard Layer

EDI standards specify business form structure and to some extent influence content seen at the application layer. For instance, a purchase order name field in an X12 standard might be specified to hold a maximum of 50 characters. An application using 75 character field lengths will produce name truncation during the translation from the application layer to standard layer.

In short, the EDI standards and application level, although separate are closely intertwined.

Transport Layer

The EDI transport layer corresponds closely with the non-electronic activity of sending a business form from one company A to company B. The business form could be sent via regular postal service, registered mail, certified mail or private carrier such as united parcel service (UPS) or simply faxed between the companies.

In other words, the content and structure of the form are separated from the transport carrier. EDI document are exchanged rapidly over electronic networks using the existing email programs and infrastructure.EDI document transport is far more complex than simply sending email messages or sharing files through a network. These EDI documents are more structured than email.

EDI vs E-mail

- EDI is a structured document where email is an unstructured document there is no fixed structure in email.
- In EDI, the interchange is composed by one software for interpretation by another software. If a reply is involved it is composed by a software to be interpreted by another software ie. EDI is a S/W to S/W interface.
- In E-mail, the message is composed by a human and or interpreted by a human and/or a reply is composed by a human and interpreted by a human. ie. S/W can not understand E mail document.
- In EDI, there is typically no human involvement in the processing of the information. Whereas in E0mail, the human involvement is necessary. A Human-to-Software interface is involved at minimum of one end of the interchange.

Note : EDI – Structured doc, S/W to S/W interface

E-mail – unstructured doc, human to S/W interface

EDI in Action

The idea behind EDI is very simple. EDI seeks to take what has been a manually prepared form or a form from a business application, translates that data into a standard electronic format and transmit it. At the receiving end, the standard format is "un-translated" into a format that can be read by the recipient applications.Hence output from one application becomes input to another through the computer to computer exchange of information.

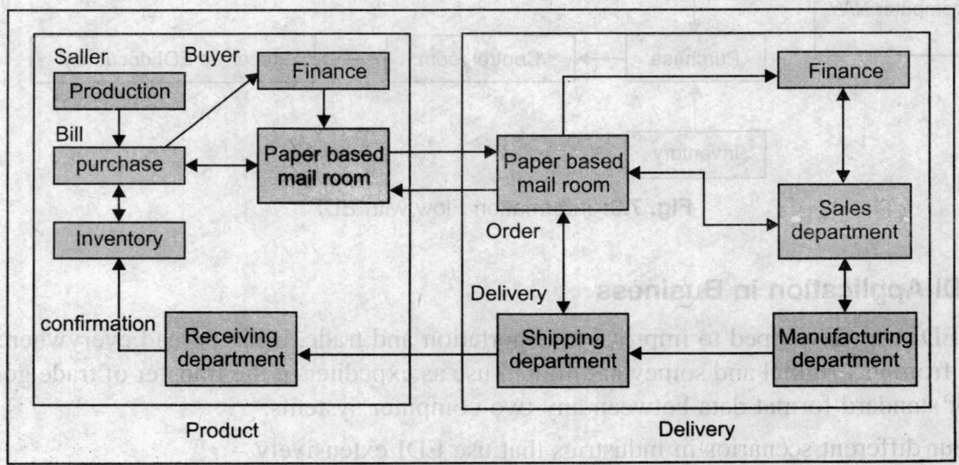

Fig 7.2: Information Flow without EDI

When the buyer sends a purchase order to a seller, the relevant data must be extracted from the internal database and recorded on hard copy. This hard copy is then forwarded to the seller after passing through several intermediate steps. Sellers receive information in the form of letters and in some cases a vast number of facsimiles. This information is manually entered into the internal information systems of the recipient by data entry operators. This process generates a considerable amount of overhead in labour costs and time delays.

Disadvantage

- Overhead in labor costs
- Time delays
- Increase the risk of error

7.13.6 Benefits of EDI

- Paperless Exchange
- Improved problem resolution and services.
- Less time in comparison of manual.
- Reduce costs
- Decrease the risk of error
- Transmission error: 1299–1929
- Transcription error: 1299–12992
- Expanded customer base/supplier

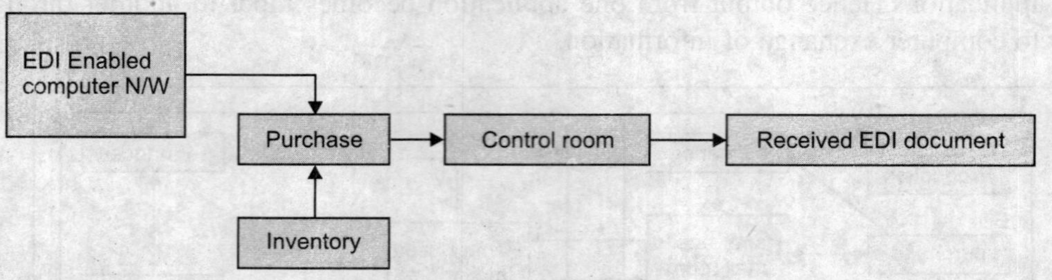

Fig. 7.3: Information Flow with EDI

7.13.7 EDI Application in Business

Although EDI was developed to improve transportation and trade, it has spread everywhere. EDI has grown from its original and somewhat limitėd use as expediter of the transfer of trade goods to Facilitor of standard format data between any two-computer systems.

The four different scenarios in industries that use EDI extensively –

(i) International or cross border trade.

(ii) Electronic funds transfer (EFT).

(iii) Health care EDI for insurance claim processing.

(iv) Manufacturing and retail procurement.

Companies have applied a number of EDI – based solutions to improve business processes for both strategic and competitive advantages. EDI has shaped a company's marketing and distribution efforts by helping to create new distribution channels, introduce new market research method and introduce better customer services.

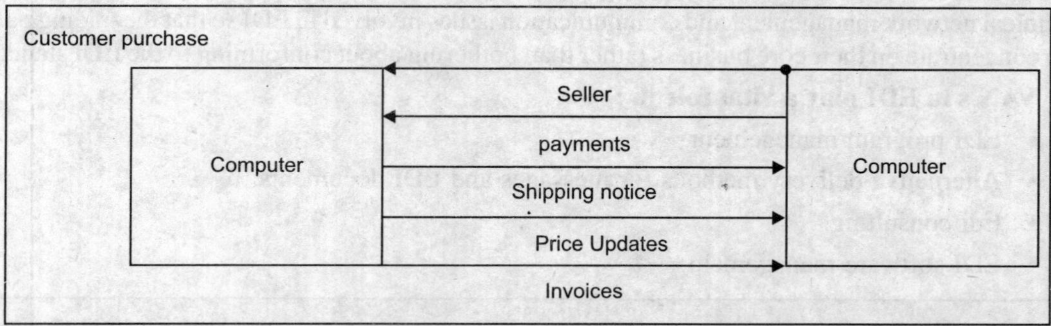

Fig. 7.4: Electronic Data Interchange

Companies can use EDI to automate electronic commerce applications. Purchase orders and payments can be transmitted directly from the customer's computers to the seller computer. The seller can transmit shipping notices, price changes and invoices electronically back to the customer.

7.13.8 EDI and VAN (Value Added Network):

Electronic Data Interchange (EDI) is the computer-to-computer exchange of business data in standard formats. In EDI, information is organized according to a specified format set by both parties, allowing a "hands-off" computer transaction that requires no human intervention or re-keying on either end. All information contained in an EDI transaction set is, for the most part, the same as on a conventionally printed document. Organizations have adopted EDI for the same reasons they have embraced much of today's modern technology-enhanced efficiency and increased profits. Benefits of EDI include: reduced cycle time, better inventory management, increased productivity, reduced costs, improved accuracy, improved business relationships, enhanced customer service, increased sales, minimized paper use and storage & increased cash flow.

Industries currently using EDI include retail, insurance, education, entertainment, mortgage banking, and numerous departments of the U.S. Government. Note, however, that this list is far from complete! As more and more businesses turn to EDI, several standards committees - including the Accredited Standards Committee X12 (ASC X12) and EDIFACT - are working to include appropriate transactions in its body of standards.

A Value-Added Network (VAN) is a private network provider (sometimes called a turnkey communications line) that is hired by a company to facilitate electronic data interchange (EDI) or provide other network services. Before the arrival of the World Wide Web, some companies hired value-added networks to move data from their company to other companies. With the arrival of the World Wide Web, many companies found it more cost-efficient to move their data over the Internet instead of paying the minimum monthly fees and per-character charges found in typical VAN contracts. In response, contemporary value-added network providers now focus on offering EDI translation, encryption, secure e-mail, management reporting, and other extra services for their customers.

Value added networks are essential part of B2B e-commerce as they provide a common EDI platform connecting various participating organizations of trade partners and take care of various technical network management and communication issues involved in EDI so that the trading partners can concentrate on their core business rather than bothering about conforming to the EDI standards:-

VAN's in EDI play a vital role in :

- EDI program management
- Alternative delivery methods for messages and EDI documents.
- Edi consulting.
- EDI software management.

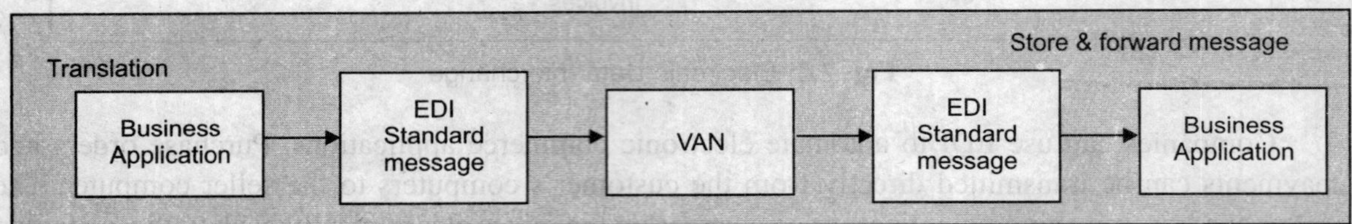

Fig. 7.5

VAN's are mostly provided by third party service providers like ISP's. the advantages by VAN's to EDI are –

- Flexibility and Scalability.
- Adherence to local rules and regulations governing communication and transactions.
- Infra-structure allocation, development and sharing.

There are three basic components of VAN's.

Technical - Message formatting / communication protocols.

Mail - Maintaining email boxes and buffering to support EDI transactions.

Links - Between various VAN Networks.

VAN's in EDI business offer additional peripheral services other than just direct connections. For example

- Direct communication links between trading partners.
- Maintenance of the EDI standards and technologies by the VAN service provider.
- VAN support to multiple data format standards.
- Store and forward systems.
- Varied protocol / access support.

- Availability round the clock.
- VAN's dial up services to connect to companies which do not participate in VAN.

7.13.9 Financial EDI

Financial EDI (FEDI) is the computer-to-computer exchange of payment and payment-related information between companies using a standard format. Financial EDI works much like non-Financial EDI—which involves the electronic exchange of business data such as price quotes, purchase orders, and shipping information but is also significantly different in that, to move a payment, a bank must be involved. Because of this difference, the buyer and seller must work closely with their respective banks to effect a Financial EDI transaction. Today, it is estimated that 60,000 companies are doing EDI in the U.S. and a growing percentage is starting to adopt FEDI.

This is the sequence of events:

- The buyer, or originator, electronically extracts payment information from the company's accounts payable system.
- The buyer formats the data into an EDI ANSI standard, the ANSI 820 transaction set, or the ANSI 835 transaction set for health care. (This is usually done by sending the file through an EDI translation software package.)
- The buyer then transmits an ANSI 820 format to its bank for processing.

  The bank then takes the 820 data and puts it into a format so that it can be sent through the Automated Clearinghouse network as an ACH transaction.
- The ACH network then delivers the payment data to the seller's, or receiver's, bank.
- The receiving bank credits the seller's account with the proceeds and delivers the remittance information to the seller for automatic accounts receivable posting. The remittance data can be delivered electronically in a variety of formats: ANSI 820, 835 or 823 format (true EDI formats), and in a BAI format. (Information can also be sent in other ways that cannot generally result in automatic cash application for the seller: through a bank's on-line balance reporting system, or in a paper report via fax or mail.)

The Benefits of Financial EDI

To be successful in any business practice usually means that all the participants affected by the process share in the benefits. In Financial EDI, there are ample advantages for both the buyer and the seller.

The buyer enjoys a number of benefits: increased productivity, the ability to use a less expensive payment method (electronic vs. paper check) that does not require reconciliation, a reduction in the risk of fraud, and the ability to invoice electronically. The seller benefits because it can reduce the average age of its receivables, lower processing costs by automatic A/R posting, improve quality by minimizing errors, and generate predictable cash flows. The result of these benefits is that both buyer and seller become more valued trading partners to one another.

Expanding the Use of Financial EDI

Financial EDI has been actively used by corporations for the last five or six years and has increasingly become the payment method of choice as more and more trading partners have seen the benefits provided to their competitors and have consequently adopted an EDI platform for their own company.

As corporations reengineer their current business practices, many are looking to outsource their payments processing, which results in a single file of all payment instructions being sent to the bank in an EDI format. The bank will then execute all payment orders, including ACH and wire transfers, and will also print and mail the payable checks. In this way, a company can deal electronically with all of its payments even though some are being converted to paper checks by the bank for those trading partners who still want the paper.

On the collection side, companies are also streamlining the receivables process by having remittance information collected by their bank - whether through the ACH, lockbox, or wire transfer payments - and then sent electronically to the companies' accounts receivable system for automatic cash application. Here again, the company is deriving the benefit of streamlined, automated posting for all of its collections, even though some or perhaps most of its payments received are paper based.

Another Kind of Receivables Application

Several financial institutions are going one step beyond this and are beginning to provide true matching of accounts receivable. In this scenario, a company has outsourced a good portion of its A/R processing to its bank.

It works in the following manner:

- The company electronically sends its receivables file to the bank on either a daily or weekly basis.
- The bank stores this data in a data base.
- As lockbox receipts or ACH collections are received, the database is queried to determine if there is a match between an open receivable item and a remittance.
- If there is a match, then the database is appended with the remittance information and a file of the matched items is created.
- Unmatched items are separately batched.
- Optionally, a bank might display the unmatched remittance information on its balance reporting systems.

Also optionally, the company can then view this data and, based on information it has, now match the previously unmatched items.

- Matched items and the remaining unmatched items are electronically sent to the customer in any desired format, EDI or proprietary.
- The customer automatically updates its accounts receivable system.

7.14 FINANCIAL EDI FOR CONSUMER PAYMENTS

Although Financial EDI has been confined to business-to-business transactions, it can also be successfully deployed in the handling of consumer payments and associated remittance data. As an example, consumer payments initiated through a bill payment service or a home banking system can be directed through Visa's ePay network by having this data handled by a bank's Financial EDI system. The bank can reformat the remittance data and deliver it electronically to the biller (for example, a utility company) for automated posting. This new way of using Financial EDI benefits large billers by eliminating the expense and operating inefficiency of receiving a check and a list and having the billet manually key in the remittance data for cash application.

Financial EDI comprises the electronic transmission of payments and remittance information between a payer, payee and their respective banks. Financial EDI allows businesses to replace the labour – intensive activities associated with issuing, mailing and collecting cheques through the banking system with automated initiation, transmission and processing of payment systems. Thus it eliminates the delays inherent in processing cheques.

Types of financial EDI

Business to business payment is accomplished using cheques, EFT and automated clearing houses (ACH) for domestic and international funds transfer.

Bank Cheques: Cheques are instruments for debit transfers, where payees collects funds from payers. Businesses use cheques to make payments for two reasons –

- They are a familiar and readily accepted form of payment despite some uncertainly about receiving final payments.
- Businesses benefit from the float created by the delays in the check collection processes.

Businesses find float valuable because they continue to use or invest funds for several days after they have issued a cheque. Float is created when a delay between the initiation of a payment and the availability of the funds to the recipient.

- Electronic funds transfers are credit transfers between banks where funds flow directly from the payer's bank to the payee's bank.
- EFT is one of the earliest examples of payment systems that use on-line transactions although these transactions are carried out on private networks.

Automated Clearing House

Two types of ACH transfers are used:

Credit transfers.

Debit transfers.

Credit transfers are similar to large dollar funds transfers in that funds flow directly from the payer's bank to the payee's where as ACH debit transfers are used when the payee's bank initiates the transfer and receives funds immediately from payers.

An ACH provides the following services

- Preauthorized debits – such as repetitive bill payments and consumer initiated payments.
- Preauthorized credits – such as the direct deposit of payrolls.

To provide these and other services, banks not only have set up their own systems but also have shared ACH systems with other banks.

Note : CHIPS – Clearing house inter-bank payments systems.
SWIFT – Society for world wide inter-bank financial telecommunications.

7.15 MOBILE COMMUNICATION DEVELOPMENT

7.15.1 Mobile Service Typology

A variety of mobile services have already been developed and these types of services are likely to expand through the introduction of alleged "third generation" (3G) services that emerge as new wireless technologies such as GRPS and UMTS are implemented provide a taxonomy of wireless services, distinguishing four major categories: communication, information, transaction, and entertainment services.

Mobile Communication	Communication services form the most elementary and well-known type of mobile services. Voice-to-voice application is the primary service in wireless technology.
Mobile Information	Information is developing into an essential service of m-commerce. According to PCIA, presently there exists a substantial amount of interest in mobile information regarding daily news, soccer, traveling, and weather reports for instance.
Mobile Transaction	Transaction services encompass m-shopping, m-finance and m-payment. Mobile shopping services provide customers the opportunity to purchase anything at any point in time. 'One-click-purchasing' possibilities will create convenient shopping experiences for mobile customers. Mobile banking and brokerage are part of M-finance. According to Data monitor (2000), a significant portion of European consumers will be banking via mobile phones by 2003. Moreover, by 2004 there will be over 2.9 million online stock traders using m-broking services.
Mobile Entertainment	According to the Mobile Entertainment Forum (2001) entertainment will be the 'backbone' of wireless value-adding services for a substantial time period. Moreover, m-entertainment applications are recognized as a way of exploring new technology. For this reason, Ericsson, Motorola, Nokia, and Siemens launched the Mobile Games Interoperability (MGI) Forum, which aims to specify a global standard and to develop certification procedures to encourage a wide adoption of the standard, simultaneously enhancing adoption of wireless technology itself.

7.15.2 Mobile and Wireless Computing Fundamentals

Mobile computing means different things to different people. The key feature of the mobile computing environment is that the user need not maintain a fixed position in the network. The terms wireless and mobile are not synonymous. Wireless is a transmission or information transport method that enables mobile computing. It covers many approaches to communications without wires. The goal of wireless is to enable distributed and mobile computing, thus bringing an end to the tyranny of geography.

Growth in several market segments of wireless communications has been explosive and has stimulated activity in all the related areas including technical, regulatory, security, legal and business. Mobile computing on the other hand, focuses on the application side. It builds on the concepts of being able to compute no matter where the user is. The goal of mobile computing is to work toward true computing freedom.

7.15.3 Mobile Computing Framework

Mobile Computing is expanding in four dimensions –

(i) Wireless delivery technology and switching methods

(ii) Mobile information access devices

(iii) Mobile data internetworking standards and equipment.

(iv) Mobile Computing based business applications.

7.15.3.1 Wireless Delivery Technology and Switching Methods

Wireless communications are evolving in several directions. The many approaches seen in wireless industry evolution are aimed at different consumer need, yet a number of underlying technical concepts are common to the different activities.

The wireless industry has become very complicated to understand as it splits into a number of subsets.

- Radio based (Land based wireless systems and satellite based wireless system)
- Light based wireless systems

  Radio based wireless systems

  Radio based services can be grouped into main categories
- Land based – cellular communications, packet data networks and specialized mobile radio (SMR)
- Satellite based – paging systems and very small aperture terminal (VSAT).

7.15.3.2 Mobile Information Access Devices

Information can be sent over a coaxial cable or a telephone line in many forms – email, data files, video and other information. For utilizing this information, there are a wide variety of information access devices

- Portable computers.

- Hybrid Pen computers.
- Personal digital Assistants.
- Data communication Equipment.

Portable Computers: -

A Portable computer is a computer that is designed to be moved from one place to another (in other words, it is a computer that is portable). Portable computers, by their nature, are microcomputers. Early portables were unkindly referred to as "luggables," referring to their great size and weight (owing partly to the need to include a full-blown CRT monitor, as LCD technology was not yet mature). The term "luggable" is today used mainly when speaking of 17" and larger widescreen laptops.

Fig. 7.6: Portable computer

The Compaq Portable; the first portable IBM PC compatible. The term portable computer is now almost exclusively used to refer to portable computers that are larger than a laptop, often use conventional parts and usually do not run on batteries. Smaller portable computers are referred to by their more specific terms:

- The laptop (or notebook) with a flat panel display and keyboard, requiring a seated position and both hands. A relatively recently introduced modification has been the Tablet PC, which essentially is a laptop operated with a stylus on a touch-sensitive screen. See also desktop replacement computer, a large laptop designed to perform all of the functions of a desktop computer.
- The palmtop which is something between a laptop and a PDA (q.v.).
- The pocket computer, which was mostly a phenomenon of the 1980s, and combined the features of an alphanumeric calculator, a small home computer (usually programmable in BASIC), and a PDA (q.v.). Manufacturers of these included Tandy/Radio Shack, Hewlett-Packard, Casio, and Sharp Corporation.
- The personal digital assistant (PDA), usually held in one hand and operated with the other.
- The wearable computer with handsfree interface, and usually some voice capability (speech recognition and speech synthesis).

Portable computers have been increasing in popularity over the past decade, as they do not restrict the user in terms of mobility as a desktop computer would. Wireless Internet, extended battery life and more comfortable ergonomics have been factors driving this increase in popularity.

Portable computers are divided into three distinct types:

- Laptops
- Note Books
- Hand Helds.

These varies broadly by their method of entering, storing playing and processing data.

- **Laptops:** are useful for running applications that demand very powerful hardware, such as computer aided design (CAD) and video presentations.
- **Notebooks:** serve the more traditional general purpose, user who wants to do a large amount of word processing and manipulate sizable spreadsheets.
- **Hand held:** have less powerful versions of these capabilities combined with more intuitive functions such as phone lists and messaging.

Note: The Sub-note Books have become the mainstream of mobile computing, and they provide a close approximation of desktop computing experience.

Among eh more novel approaches to sub-notebook design are those that include windows software and applications in ROM.

Hybrid pen Computers

One of the initial applications envisioned for pen computer was that of insurance adjusters creating charts of an accident or pointing out which parts of a car were damaged. Pen Computers are often equipped with wireless communications.

One of the recent developments in pen based computing systems is the addition of a keyboard, which seeks to harness the best of both worlds. It is provided in two ways, when open, it reveals a full size keyboard and the pen can be used as a mouse. When the display is closed, the user is presented with a tablet – size-writing pad.

Personal Digital Assistants (PDA's)

Personal Digital Assistants (PDAs) are handheld devices that were originally designed as personal organisers, but became much more versatile over the years. PDAs have many uses: calculating, use as a clock and calendar, playing computer games, accessing the Internet, sending and receiving E-mails, use as a radio or stereo, video recording, recording notes, use as an address book, and use as a spreadsheet. Newer PDAs also have both color screens and audio capabilities, enabling them to be used as mobile phones (smartphone), web browsers or media players. Many PDAs can access the Internet, intranets or extranets via Wi-Fi, or Wireless Wide-Area Networks (WWANs). One of the most significant PDA characteristic is the presence of a touch screen.

Touch Screen

Many original PDAs, such as the Palm Pilot, featured touch screens for user interaction, having only a few buttons usually reserved for shortcuts to often used programs. Touch screen PDAs, including Windows Pocket PC devices, usually have a detachable stylus that can be used on the touch screen. Interaction is then done by tapping the screen to activate buttons or menu choices, and dragging the stylus to, for example, highlight text.

Text input is usually done in one of two ways:

- Using a virtual keyboard, where a keyboard is shown on the touch screen. Input is done by tapping the letters.
- Using letter or word recognition, where letters or words are written on the touch screen, and then "translated" to letters in the currently activated text field. Despite rigorous research and development projects, this data input method still requires much patience from the user since it tends to be rather inaccurate.

PDAs for business use, including the BlackBerry and Treo, have a full keyboards and scroll wheels or thumb wheels to facilitate data entry and navigation, in addition to supporting touch-screen input. There are also full-size foldable keyboards available that plug directly into the PDA and allow for normal typing

Synchronization

An important functionality for PDAs is the possibility of synchronizing data with a contact database, such as Microsoft Outlook or ACT!, hosted on a Personal Computer (PC) or a corporate server or servers. The data synchronized ensures that the PDA has an accurate list of contacts, appointments and e-mail, allowing users to access the same information on the PDA as the host computer.

The synchronizing also prevents the loss of information stored on the device in case it is lost, stolen, or destroyed. Another advantage is that data input is usually a lot quicker on a PC, since text input via a touch screen is still not quite optimal. Transferring data to a PDA via the computer is therefore a lot quicker than having to manually input all data on the handheld device.

Most PDAs come with the ability to synchronize to a PC. This is done through synchronization software provided with the handheld, such as HotSync Manager, which comes with Palm OS handhelds, or Microsoft ActiveSync, which comes with Windows Mobile handhelds.

These programs allow the PDA to be synchronized with a Personal information manager. This personal information manager may be an outside program or a proprietary program. For example, the BlackBerry PDA comes with the Desktop Manager program which can synchronize to both Microsoft Outlook and ACT!. Other PDAs come only with their own proprietary software. For example, some early Palm OS PDAs came only with Palm Desktop while later Palms such as the Treo 650 has the built-in ability to sync to Palm Desktop and/or Microsoft Outlook. Third-party synchronization software is also available for many PDAs from companies like Intellisync and CompanionLink. This software synchronizes these handhelds to other personal information managers which are not supported by the PDA manufacturers, such as GoldMine and Lotus Notes.

Customization

As with personal computers, it is possible to install additional software on most PDAs. Software can be bought or downloaded from the Internet, allowing users to personalize their PDAs to their liking. Some PDAs also allow for adding hardware. The most common is a memory card slot, which allows the users to get additional and exchangeable storage space on their handheld devices. There are also miniature keyboards that can be connected to some PDAs for quicker text input. PDAs with Bluetooth can also use Bluetooth devices like headsets, mouse and foldable keyboards with their PDAs.

Ruggedized PDAs

For many years businesses and government organizations have relied upon rugged PDAs for mobile data applications. Typical applications include supply chain management in warehouses, package delivery, route accounting, medical treatment and record keeping in hospitals, facilities maintenance and management, parking enforcement, access control and security, capital asset maintenance, meter reading by utilities, and "wireless waitress" applications in restaurants and hospitality venues. There are even PDAs designed to take significant amounts of punishment, probably meant for military use. Unfortunately, these devices come with a steep price tag.

Medical and Scientific Uses

In medicine, PDAs have been proven to aid diagnosis and drug selection and some studies have concluded that their use by patients to record symptoms improves the effectiveness of communication with hospitals during follow-up. The first landmark study in testing the effectiveness of PDAs in a medical setting was conducted at the Brigham & Women's Hospital and Massachusetts General Hospitals in affiliation with Harvard Medical School. Led by the team of Sandeep Shah & Steven Labkoff, MD, the Constellation project used Apple's Newton (first PDA in the market) to cater to the demands of the medical professionals. Today, the company evolved from the effort Skyscape offers a wide range of resources including drug information, treatment options, guidelines, evidence based information and journal summaries including the drug & safety alerts. Other entrants include epocrates and ABX guide, which supply drug databases, treatment information and relevant news in formats specific to mobile devices and services such as Avantgo translate medical journals into readable formats and provide updates from journals. WardWatch organizes medical records to remind doctors making ward rounds of information such as the treatment regimens of patients and programs. Finally, Pendragon provides tools for conducting research on mobile devices, with a connection back to a central server allowing the user to enter data into a centralized database using their PDA. Recently the development of [sensor web] technology has led to discussion of using wearable bodily sensors to monitor ongoing conditions like diabetes and epilepsy and alerting medical staff or the patient themselves to the treatment required via communication between the web and PDAs.

Educational Uses

As mobile technology has become almost a necessity, it is no surprise that personal computing has become a vital learning tool by this time. Educational institutes have commenced a trend of integrating PDAs into their teaching practices (mobile learning). With the capabilities of PDAs, teachers are now able to provide a collaborative learning experience for their students. They are also preparing their students for possible practical uses of mobile computing upon their graduation.

PDAs and handheld devices have recently allowed for digital note taking. This has increased student's productivity by allowing individuals to quickly spell-check, modify, and amend their class notes or e-notes. Educators are currently able to distribute course material through the use of the internet connectivity or infrared file sharing functions of the PDA. With concerns to class material, textbook publishers have begun to release e-books, electronic textbooks, which can be uploaded directly to your PDA. This eliminates the exhausting effort of carrying multiple textbooks at one time.

To meet the instructive needs sought by educational institutes, software companies have developed programs with the learning aspects in mind. Simple programs such as dictionaries, thesauri, and word processing software are important to the digital note taking process. In addition to these simple programs, encyclopedias and digital planning lessons have created added functionality for users.

With the increase in mobility of PDAs, school boards and educational institutes have now encountered issues with these devices. School boards are now concerned with students utilizing the internet connectivity to share test answers or to gossip during class time, which creates disruptions. Many school boards have modernized their computer policies to address these new concerns. Software companies such as Scantron Corp. have now created a program for distributing digital quizzes. The quiz software disables the infrared function on PDAs, which eliminates the element of information sharing among individuals during the examination.

Sporting Uses

PDAs are used by glider pilots for pre-flight planning and to assist navigation in cross-country competions. They are linked to a GPS to produce moving-map displays showing the tracks to turn-points, airspace hazards and other tactical information. The currently major PDA operating systems are:

- Palm OS - owned by PalmSource
- Windows Mobile (Pocket PC), (based on the Windows CE kernel) - owned by Microsoft
- RIM for the BlackBerry - owned by Research In Motion
- Many operating systems based on the Linux kernel - free (not owned by any company) These include:
- GPE - Based on GTK+/X11
- OPIE/Qtopia - based on Qt/E Qtopia is developed by Trolltech, OPIE is a fork of Qtopia developed by volunteers
- Symbian OS (formerly EPOC) owned by Ericsson, Motorola, Panasonic, Nokia, Samsung, Siemens and Sony Ericsson

Architecture

Many PDAs run using a variation of the ARM architecture (usually denoted by the Intel XScale trademark). This encompasses a class of RISC microprocessors that are widely used in mobile devices and embedded systems, and its design was influenced strongly by a popular 1970s/1980s CPU, the MOS Technology 6502.

Popular Consumer PDAs

- Psion
- Amida
- Apple Newton
- BlackBerry
- hp iPAQ Pocket PC (originally Compaq iPAQ until HP merged in 2002)
- hp Jornada Pocket PC (phased out/merged with iPAQ line in 2002)
- Palm Pilot, Tungsten E2, LifeDrive, Treo and Zire
- Sharp Wizard and Zaurus

Fig. 7.7: Palm IIIxe PDA

A PC reduced in size to lit inside the coat pocket. PDA's reflect the never-ending quest to build the smallest possible useful computer. The PDA market is dividing up into three functional segments:

Digital Assistant – Market segment where the hand held device captures data and digitizes it.

Personal Communications – Cellular telephone with an LCD screen integrated into it.

Palmtops – Large storage segment for the user who wants to carry a lot of data and be able to retrieve it easily.

Cellular modems and PCMCIA Adapters

Like most computer and communications products, wireless modems have undergone extensive solution. Originally designed for vehicle installation, the wireless modem has evolved into an integrated transceiver receiver and data modem in a portable compact format.

- Capable of sending or receiving data
- The cost of using cellular system for data can be high
- The speed and reliability of Cellular's circuit – switched voice channels can vary widely.

There are two major market sectors for cellular modems –

- Industry Oriented Applications – include areas such as retailing, warehousing, manufacturing and health care in which products are used for the collection of data. They tend to be slow speed and typically connect hand-held devices to a corporate system.
- General Purpose applications – requires LAN connectivity white they move from location to location within a given environment and applications are typically used to send and receive electronic mail, access databases and transmit files. They tend to have higher transmission speed.

7.15.3.3 Mobile Data Internet Working Standards

The phenomenal growth in the cellular industry presents a significant challenge – overcoming the inherent capacity and quality limitations of the current analog systems. The specific reasons for the analog to digital transition follow:

(i) Limited available Bandwidth

(ii) Over crowding.

Many feel that digital technology provides the key to spectrum efficiency. The efficient spectrum use is also seen as the key to the creation of the next generation personal communication services. The current analog system divides the available spectrum into 3-KHz wide channels. This method of channelization (division of the spectrum into multiple channels) is commonly called FDMA (Frequency Division Multiple Access).

Alternative means of channelization are being developed to allow more users in the same region of the spectrum. Two dominant methods are

- **TDMA** (Time Division Multiple Access)
- **CDMA** (Code Division Multiple Access)

Code Division Multiple Access (CDMA)

Code division multiple access (CDMA) is a form of multiplexing (not a modulation scheme) and a method of multiple access that does not divide up the channel by time (as in TDMA), or frequency (as in FDMA), but instead encodes data with a special code associated with each channel and uses the constructive interference properties of the special codes to perform the multiplexing. **CDMA** also refers to digital cellular telephony systems that make use of this multiple access scheme, such as those pioneered by Qualcomm, and W-CDMA by the International Telecommunication Union or ITU.

CDMA has since been used in many communications systems, including the Global Positioning System (GPS) and in the OmniTRACS satellite system for transportation logistics.

Usage in Mobile Telephony

A number of different terms are used to refer to CDMA implementations. The original U.S. standard defined by QUALCOMM was known as IS-95, the IS referring to an Interim Standard of the

Telecommunications Industry Association (TIA). IS-95 is often referred to as 2G or second generation cellular. The QUALCOMM brand name cdmaOne may also be used to refer to the 2G CDMA standard. The CDMA has been submitted for approval as a mobile air interface standard to the ITU International Telecommunication Union.

Whereas the Global System for Mobile Communications (GSM) standard is a specification of an entire network infrastructure, the CDMA interface relates only to the air interface—the radio part of the technology. For example GSM specifies an infrastructure based on internationally approved standard while CDMA allows each operator to provide the network features as it finds suited. On the air interface, the signalling suite work has been progressing to harmonise these.

After a couple of revisions, IS-95 was superseded by the IS-2000 standard. This standard was introduced to meet some of the criteria laid out in the IMT-2000 specification for 3G, or third generation, cellular. It is also referred to as 1xRTT which simply means "1 times Radio Transmission Technology" and indicates that IS-2000 uses the same 1.25 MHz shared channel as the original IS-95 standard. A related scheme called 3xRTT uses three 1.25 MHz carriers for a 3.75 MHz bandwidth that would allow higher data burst rates for an individual user, but the 3xRTT scheme has not been commercially deployed. More recently, QUALCOMM has led the creation of a new CDMA-based technology called 1xEV-DO, or IS-856, which provides the higher packet data transmission rates required by IMT-2000 and desired by wireless network operators.

The QUALCOMM CDMA system includes highly accurate time signals (usually referenced to a GPS receiver in the cell base station), so cell phone CDMA-based clocks are an increasingly popular type of radio clock for use in computer networks. The main advantage of using CDMA cell phone signals for reference clock purposes is that they work better inside buildings, thus often eliminating the need to mount a GPS antenna on the outside of a building.

This CDMA system is frequently confused with a similar but incompatible technology called Wideband Code Division Multiple Access (W-CDMA) which forms the basis of the W-CDMA air interface. The W-CDMA air interface is used in the global 3G standard UMTS and the Japanese 3G standard FOMA, by NTT DoCoMo and Vodafone; however, the CDMA family of US national standards (including cdmaOne and CDMA2000) are not compatible with the W-CDMA family of International Telecommunication Union (ITU) standards. Another important application of CDMA — predating and entirely distinct from CDMA cellular — is the Global Positioning System, GPS.

Coverage and Applications

The size of a given cell depends on the power of the signal transmitted by the handset, the terrain, and the radio frequency being used. Various algorithms can reduce the noise introduced by variations in terrain, but require extra information be sent to validate the transfer. Hence, the radio frequency and power of the handset effectively determine the cell size. Long wavelengths need less energy to travel a given distance vs. short wavelengths, so lower frequencies generally result in greater coverage while higher frequencies result in shorter coverage. These characteristics are used by mobile network planners in determining the size and placement of the cells in the network. In cities, many small cells are needed; the use of high frequencies allows sites to be placed more-closely together, with more subscribers provided service. In rural areas with a lower density of subscribers, use of lower frequencies allows each site to provide broader coverage.

Various companies use different variants of CDMA to provide fixed-line networks using Wireless local loop (WLL) technology. Since they can plan with a specific number of subscribers per cell in mind, and these are all stationary, this application of CDMA can be found in most parts of the world. CDMA is suited for data transfer with bursty behaviour and where delays can be accepted. It is therefore used in Wireless LAN applications; the cell size here is 500 feet because of the high frequency (2.4 GHz) and low power. The suitability for data transfer is the reason for why W-CDMA seems to be "winning technology" for the data portion of third-generation (3G) mobile cellular networks.

Code Division Multiplexing (Synchronous CDMA)

Synchronous CDMA, also known as Code Division Multiplexing (CDM), exploits at its core mathematical properties of orthogonality. Suppose we represent data signals as vectors. For example, the binary string "1011" would be represented by the vector (1, 0, 1, 1). We may wish to give a vector a name, we may do so by using boldface letters, e.g. **a**. We also use an operation on vectors, known as the dot product, to "multiply" vectors, by summing the product of the components. The operation is denoted with a dot between the vectors. For example, the dot product of

a = (1, 0, 1, 1) and b = (1, –1, –1, 0), written as a.b. would be

$$(1) \times (1) + (0) \times (-1) + (1) \times (-1) + (1) \times (0) = 1 + (-1) = 0.$$

For the special case when the dot product of two vectors is identically 0, the two vectors are said to be orthogonal to each other.

The dot product has a number of properties, which will aid in understanding how CDM works. For vectors **a, b, c:**:

$$a.\,(b + c) = a\,.b + a\,.\,c, \text{ and}$$

$$a.\,kb = k\,(a.\,b).,$$

where k is an arbitrary constant, and not a vector.

The square root of $a\,.\,a$ is a real number, and is called the magnitude of the vector a.. It is denoted as

$$\|a\| = \sqrt{a \cdot a}\,.$$

Suppose vectors a and b are orthogonal. Then:

$$a.\,(a + b) = \|a\|^2 \quad \text{since } a.a + a.\,b = \|a\|^2 + 0,$$

$$a.\,(-a + b) = -\,\|a\|^2 \quad \text{since } -a.a + a.b = -\,\|a\|^2 + 0,$$

$$b.\,(a + b) = \|b\|^2 \quad \text{since } b.\,a + b.b = 0 + \|b\|^2,$$

$$b.\,(a - b) = -\,\|b\|^2 \quad \text{since } b\,.\,a - b\,.\,b = 0 - \|b\|^2.$$

Example

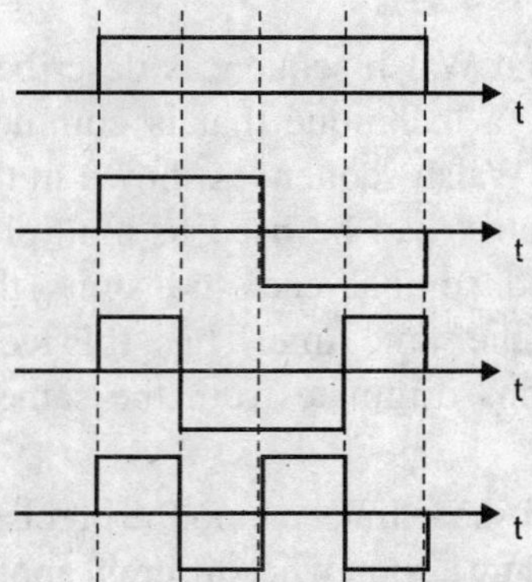

Fig. 7.8: An example of 4 orthogonal digital signals.

Suppose now we have a set of vectors that are mutually orthogonal to each other. Usually these vectors are specially constructed for ease of decoding — they are columns or rows from Walsh matrices that are constructed from Walsh functions—but strictly mathematically the only restriction on these vectors is that they are orthogonal. An example of orthogonal functions is shown in the picture on the right. Now, associate with one sender a vector from this set, say **v**, which is called the chip code. Associate a zero digit with the vector -**v**, and a one digit with the vector **v**. For example, if $v = (1,-1)$, then the binary vector (1, 0, 1, 1) would correspond to (1,–1,–1,1,1,–1,1,–1). For the purposes of this article, we call this constructed vector the transmitted vector.

Each sender has a different, unique vector chosen from that set, but the construction of the transmitted vector is identical. Now, the physical properties of interference say that if two signals at a point are in phase, they will "add up" to give twice the amplitude of each signal, but if they are out of phase, they will "subtract" and give a signal that is the difference of the amplitudes. Digitally, this behaviour can be modelled simply by the addition of the transmission vectors, component by component. So, if we have two senders, both sending simultaneously, one with the chip code (1, -1) and data vector (1, 0, 1, 1), and another with the chip code (1, 1), and data vector (0,0,1,1), the raw signal received would be the sum of the transmission vectors (1,-1,-1,1,1,-1,1,-1)+(-1,-1,-1,-1.1,1,1,1)=(0,-2,-2,0,2,0,2,0).

Suppose a receiver gets such a signal, and wants to detect what the transmitter with chip code (1, -1) is sending. The receiver will make use of the property described in the above foundation section, and take the dot product to the received vector in parts. Take the first two components of the received vector, that is, (0, -2). Now, (0, -2).(1, -1) = (0)(1)+(-2)(-1) = 2. Since this is positive, we can deduce that a one digit was sent. Taking the next two components, (-2, 0), (-2, 0).(1,-1)=(-2)(1)+(0)(-1)=-2. Since this is negative, we can deduce that a zero digit was sent. Continuing in this fashion, we can successfully decode what the transmitter with chip code (1, -1) was sending: (1, 0, 1, 1).

Likewise, applying the same process with chip code (1, 1): (1, 1).(0,-2) = -2 gives digit 0, (1, 1).(-2,0)=(1)(-2)+(1)(0)=-2 gives digit 0, and so on, to give us the data vector sent by the transmitter with chip code (1, 1): (0, 0, 1, 1).

Asynchronous CDMA

The previous example of orthogonal Walsh sequences describes how 2 users can be multiplexed together in a synchronous system, a technique that is commonly referred to as Code Division Multiplexing (CDM). The set of 4 Walsh sequences shown in the figure will afford up to 4 users, and in general, an NxN Walsh matrix can be used to multiplex N users. Multiplexing requires all of the users to be coordinated so that each transmits their assigned sequence *v* (or the complement, -**v**) starting at exactly the same time. Thus, this technique finds use in base-to-mobile links, where all of the transmissions originate from the same transmitter and can be perfectly coordinated.

On the other hand, the mobile-to-base links cannot be precisely coordinated, particularly due to the mobility of the handsets, and require a somewhat different approach. Since it is not mathematically possible to create signature sequences that are orthogonal for arbitrarily random starting points, unique "pseudo-random" or "pseudo-noise" (PN) sequences are used in Asynchronous CDMA systems. These PN sequences are statistically uncorrelated, and the sum of a large number of PN sequences results in Multiple Access Interference (MAI) that is approximated by a Gaussian noise process (via the theorem of the "law of large numbers" in statistics). If all of the users are received with the same power level, then the variance (e.g., the noise power) of the MAI increases in direct proportion to the number of users.

All forms of CDMA use spread spectrum process gain to allow receivers to partially discriminate against unwanted signals. Signals with the desired chip code and timing are received, while signals with different chip codes (or the same spreading code but a different timing offset) appear as wideband noise reduced by the process gain.

Since each user generates MAI, controlling the signal strength is an important issue with CDMA transmitters. A CDM (Synchronous CDMA), TDMA or FDMA receiver can in theory completely reject arbitrarily strong signals using different codes, time slots or frequency channels due to the orthogonality of these systems. This is not true for Asynchronous CDMA; rejection of unwanted signals is only partial. If any or all of the unwanted signals are much stronger than the desired signal, they will overwhelm it. This leads to a general requirement in any Asynchronous CDMA system to approximately match the various signal power levels as seen at the receiver. In CDMA cellular, the base station uses a fast closed-loop power control scheme to tightly control each mobile's transmit power.

Advantages of Asynchronous CDMA over other Techniques

Asynchronous CDMA's main advantage over CDM (Synchronous CDMA), TDMA and FDMA is that it can use the spectrum more efficiently in mobile telephony applications. TDMA systems must carefully synchronize the transmission times of all the users to ensure that they are received in the correct timeslot and do not cause interference. Since this cannot be perfectly controlled in a mobile environment, each timeslot must have a guard-time, which reduces the probability that users will interfere, but decreases the spectral efficiency. Similarly, FDMA systems must use a guard-band between adjacent channels, due to the random doppler shift of the signal spectrum which occurs due to the user's mobility. The guard-bands will reduce the probability that adjacent channels will interfere, but decrease the utilization of the spectrum.

Most importantly, Asynchronous CDMA offers a key advantage in the flexible allocation of resources. There are a fixed number of orthogonal codes, timeslots or frequency bands that can be allocated for CDM, TDMA and FDMA systems, which remain underutilized due to the bursty nature of telephony and packetized data transmissions. There is no strict limit to the number of users that can be supported in an Asynchronous CDMA system, only a practical limit governed by the desired bit error probability, since the SIR (Signal to Interference Ratio) varies inversely with the number of users. In a bursty traffic environment like mobile telephony, the advantage afforded by Asynchronous CDMA is that the performance (bit error rate) is allowed to fluctuate randomly, with an average value determined by the number of users times the percentage of utilization. Suppose there are 2N users that only talk half of the time, then 2N users can be accommodated with the same average bit error probability as N users that talk all of the time. The key difference here is that the bit error probability for N users talking all of the time is constant, whereas it is a random quantity (with the same mean) for 2N users talking half of the time.

In other words, Asynchronous CDMA is ideally suited to a mobile network where large numbers of transmitters each generate a relatively small amount of traffic at irregular intervals. CDM (Synchronous CDMA), TDMA and FDMA systems cannot recover the underutilized resources inherent to bursty traffic due to the fixed number of orthogonal codes, time slots or frequency channels that can be assigned to individual transmitters. For instance, if there are N time slots in a TDMA system and 2N users that talk half of the time, then half of the time there will be more than N users needing to use more than N timeslots. Furthermore, it would require significant overhead to continually allocate and deallocate the orthogonal code, time-slot or frequency channel resources. By comparison, Asynchronous CDMA transmitters simply send when they have something to say, and go off the air when they don't, keeping the same PN signature sequence as long as they are connected to the system.

Soft Handoff

Soft handoff (or soft handover) is an innovation in mobility. It refers to the technique of adding additional base stations (in IS-95 as many as 5) to a connection to be certain that the next base is ready as you move through the terrain. However, it can also be used to move a call from one base station that is approaching congestion to another with better capacity. As a result, signal quality and handoff robustness is improved compared to TDMA systems.

In TDMA and analog systems, each cell transmits on its own frequency, different from those of its neighbouring cells. If a mobile device reaches the edge of the cell currently serving its call, it is told to break its radio link and quickly tune to the frequency of one of the neighbouring cells where the call has been moved by the network due to the mobile's movement. If the mobile is unable to tune to the new frequency in time the call is dropped.

In CDMA, a set of neighbouring cells all use the same frequency for transmission and distinguish cells (or base stations) by means of a number called the "PN offset", a time offset from the beginning of the well-known pseudo-random noise sequence that is used to spread the signal from the base station. Because all of the cells are on the same frequency, listening to different base stations is now an exercise in digital signal processing based on offsets from the PN sequence, not RF transmission and reception based on separate frequencies.

As the CDMA phone roams through the network, it detects the PN offsets of the neighbouring cells and reports the strength of each signal back to the reference cell of the call (usually the strongest cell). If the signal from a neighbouring cell is strong enough, the mobile will be directed to "add a leg" to its call and start transmitting and receiving to and from the new cell in addition to the cell (or cells) already hosting the call. Likewise, if a cell's signal becomes too weak the mobile is directed to drop that leg. In this way, the mobile can move from cell to cell and add and drop legs as necessary in order to keep the call up without ever dropping the link.

It should be noted that this "soft handoff" does not happen via CDMA from cell tower to cell tower. A group of cell sites are linked up with wire and the call is synced over wire, over TDM, ATM, or even IP.

When there are frequency boundaries between different carriers or sub-networks, a CDMA phone behaves in the same way as TDMA or analog and performs a hard handoff in which it breaks the existing connection and tries to pick up on the new frequency where it left off.

CDMA features

- Narrowband message signal multiplied by wideband spreading signal or pseudonoise code
- Each user has his own pseudonoise (PN) code
- Soft capacity limit: system performance degrades for all users as number of users increases
- Cell frequency reuse: no frequency planning needed
- Soft handoff increases capacity
- Near-far problem
- Interference limited: power control is required
- Wide bandwidth induces diversity: rake receiver is used

It has been used in military systems for decades because it is secure. Unlike the present analog system and other digital systems, which divide the available spectrum into narrow channels and assign one or more conversations to each channel, CDMA is a wideband spread spectrum technology that spreads multiple conversations across a wide segment of the cellular broadcast spectrum. Each telephone or data calls is assigned a unique code that permits it to be distinguished from the multitude of calls simultaneously transmitted over the same broadcast spectrum.

Note: For analog communications we use technology called FDMA i.e. Frequency division multiple access. In which total bandwidth in divided into several parts and each user get a separate bandwidth.

For digital communication we use technology

– TDMA (Time Division Multiple Access)

– FDMA (Frequency Division Multiple Access)

Time Division Multiple Access

In TDMA, the total frequency is not divided into separate but it combines into one. And in TDMA the one frequency (total frequency) band is given to all user i.e. one band is shared by n no. of user. It is not enough powerful technology, so we next use CDMA. Example: Reliance used CDMA technology. In CDMA, we give each user total bandwidth i.e. Each and every user can able to get all bandwidth. It is based on the coding theory.

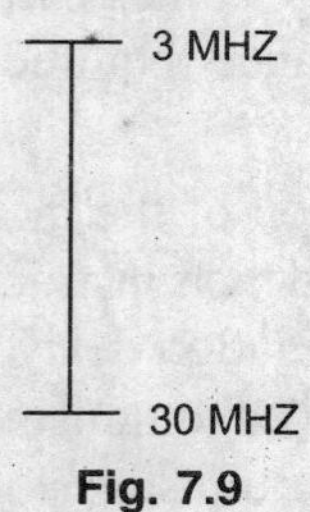

Fig. 7.9

Bandwidth = 30-3 = 27 MHz, i.e. Each user gets 27 MHz bandwidth

TDMA Time Division Multiple Access

Time division multiple access (TDMA) is a technology for shared medium (usually radio) networks. It allows several users to share the same frequency by dividing it into different timeslots. The users transmit in rapid succession, one after the other, each using his own timeslot. This allows multiple users to share the same transmission medium (e.g. radio frequency) while using only the part of its

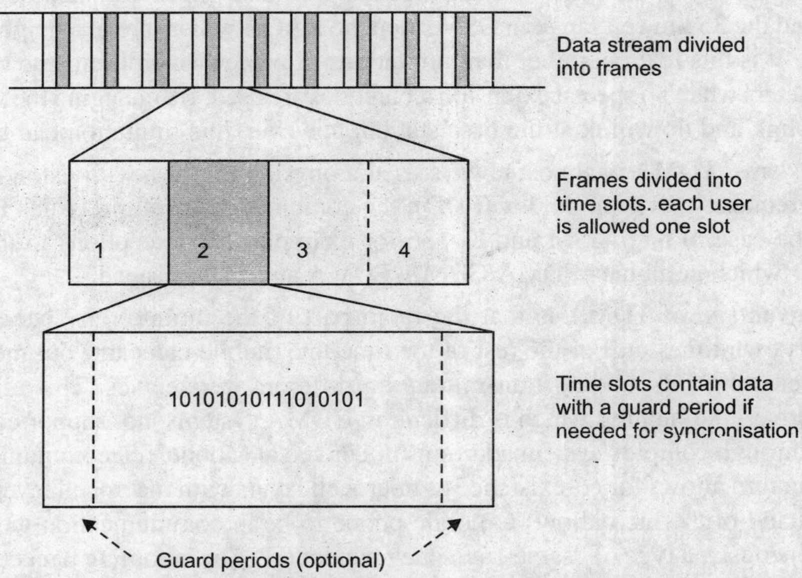

Fig. 7.6: TDMA frame structure showing a data stream divided into frames and those frames divided into timeslots.

bandwidth they require. TDMA is used in the Global System for Mobile Communications (GSM), Personal Digital Cellular (PDC) and iDEN digital cellular standards, among others. It is also used extensively in satellite systems, local area networks, physical security systems, and combat-net radio systems.

TDMA is a type of Time-division multiplexing, with the special point that instead of having one transmitter connected to one receiver, there are multiple transmitters. In the case of the uplink from a mobile phone to a base station this becomes particularly difficult because the mobile phone can move around and vary the timing advance required to make its transmission match the gap in transmission from its peers.

In the GSM system, the synchronization of the mobile phones is achieved by sending timing advance commands from the base station which instructs the mobile phone to transmit earlier and by how much. This compensates for propagation delay as the speed of radio waves is the same as light (finite). The mobile phone is not allowed to transmit for its entire timeslot, but there is a guard interval at the end of each timeslot. As the transmission moves into the guard period, the mobile network adjusts the timing advance to synchronize the transmission.

Initial synchronization of a phone requires even more care. Before a mobile transmits there is no way to actually know the offset required. For this reason, an entire timeslot has to be dedicated to mobiles attempting to contact the network (known as the RACH in GSM). The mobile attempts to broadcast at the beginning of the timeslot, as received from the network. If the mobile is located next to the base station, there will be no time delay and this will succeed. If, however, the mobile phone is at just less than 35km from the base station, the time delay will mean the mobile's broadcast arrives at the very end of the timeslot. In that case, the mobile will be instructed to broadcast its messages starting nearly a whole timeslot earlier than would be expected otherwise. Finally, if the mobile is beyond the 35 km cell range in GSM, then the RACH will arrive in a neighboring timeslot and be ignored. It is this feature, rather than limitations of power which limits the range of a GSM cell to 35 kilometers when no special extension techniques are used. By changing the synchronization between the uplink and downlink at the base station, however, this limitation can be overcome.

In radio systems, TDMA is almost always used alongside Frequency-division multiple access (FDMA) and Frequency division duplex (FDD); the combination is referred to as FDMA/TDMA/FDD. This is the case in both GSM and IS-136 for example. The exceptions to this rule include WCDMA-TDD which combines FDMA/CDMA/TDMA and TDD instead.

A major advantage of TDMA is that the radio part of the mobile only needs to listen and broadcast for its own timeslot. For the rest of the time, the mobile can carry out measurements on the network, detecting surrounding transmitters on different frequencies. This allows safe inter frequency handovers, something which is difficult in CDMA systems, not supported at all in IS-95 and supported through complex system additions in Universal Mobile Telecommunications System (UMTS). This in turn allows for co-existence of microcell layers with macrocell layers. But, CDMA supports "soft hand-off" which allows a mobile phone to be in communication with up to 6 base stations simultaneously, a type of "same-frequency handover". The incoming packets are compared for quality, and the best one is selected. This enables CDMA to perform in areas where TDMA calls would be dropped.

A disadvantage of TDMA systems is that they create interference at a frequency which is directly connected to the timeslot length. This is the irritating buzz which can sometimes be heard if a GSM phone is left next to a radio or speakers. Another disadvantage is that the "dead time" between timeslots limits the potential bandwidth of a TDMA channel. This is why early efforts to incorporate timeslots into UMTS failed, leaving UMTS as a purely CDMA technology. The only country to continue pursuing TD-SCDMA (time division synchronous CDMA) is mainland China, perhaps because the government does not want to pay patent royalties to Qualcomm of the USA or licensing fees to the mainly European UMTS consortium.

TDMA features

- Shares single carrier frequency with multiple users
- Non-continuous transmission makes handoff simpler
- Slots can be assigned on demand
- Less stringent power control due to reduced interuser interference
- Higher synchronization overhead
- Equalization is necessary for high data rates
- Frequency/slot allocation complexity
- Pulsating power envelop: Interference with other devices

Advantages

1. Colliding Frames are not garbed.
2. Multiple signals add linearly.

This technique is also called spread spectrum ie. One user can be able to call down all bandwidth i.e. Spectrum. CDMA can be implemented by various techniques.

Frequency Division Multiple Access

Frequency Division Multiple Access or FDMA is an access technology that is used by radio systems to share the radio spectrum. The terminology "multiple access" implies the sharing of the resource amongst users, and the "frequency division" describes how the sharing is done: by allocating users with different carrier frequencies of the radio spectrum.

In FDMA the given Radio Frequency (RF) bandwidth is divided into smaller frequency bands called subdivisions. Each subdivision has its own carrier frequency. A control mechanism is used to ensure that two or more earth stations do not transmit in the same subdivision at the same time. Essentially, the control mechanism designates a receive station for each of the subdivisions. In demand assignment systems, the control mechanism is also used to establish or terminate the voice-band links between the source and destination stations. Consequently, any of the subdivisions is used by any of the participating earth stations at any given time. If each subdivision carries only one 4-KHz voice-band channel, this is known as a single-channel per carrier (SCPC) system.

When several voice-band channels are frequency-division multiplexed to form a composite baseband signal comprised of groups, supergroups, or even mastergroups, a wider subdivision is assigned. This is referred to as multiple-channel per carrier (MCPC). FDMA also supports demand assignment besides fixed assignment. Demand assignment allows all users continuous an equal access of the entire transponder bandwidth by assigning carrier frequencies on a temporary basis using a statistical assignment process. The first FDMA demand-assignment system for satellite was developed by COMSAT for use on the Intelsat series IVA and V satellites. In contrast to this methodology with Time Division Multiple Access, where users are separated in time, Code Division Multiple Access CDMA where users are separated by codes also exists as well as other multiple access schemes: SDMA – Space division multiple access, CSMA – Carrier sense multiple access, and MF-TDMA - Multi-Frequency TDMA.

7.15.3.4 Mobile Computing Business Application

Today's competitive business climate demands tool that allow users to work and communicate at their own convenience and discretion. It is not enough to have the newest tool. The investment in the new technology should yield an immediate benefit to its buyers without asking them to radically alter the way they live or do their work. This is the vision of mobile computing applications. It is resulting in two chances.

- Remote Communications
- Data Access (Remote Data Access)

Remote Communication: Real time communication has required people to structure their work and personal lives around a predetermined meeting place. The business terminology requires communication hubs (where all activity are centralized, example – College act as communication hub, just to share knowledge).

When you remove constant attachment to a physical space, people are free to be more strategic, creative and flexible about how they make decisions and get things accomplished.

Remote Data Access: An important requirement of the mobile computing is to allow workers to be as effective while at remote locations as they are in their usual offices when fully connected. This implies that traditional applications that assumed continuous connectivity must be redesigned to allow a disconnected mode of operation.

For Example: A sales representative files an order on her Laptop at a customer site. The client software in the Laptop should store the transaction until the user is able to reconnect the Laptop to the network upon re-connection, the transaction is forwarded to the application server in the network.

A growing list of applications are being built on the mobile computing infrastructure they include –

(i) Point of sale system
(ii) Inventory tracking and dispatching
(iii) Sales force automation
(iv) Package tracking and delivery services
(v) Health care
(vi) Online transaction processing (OLTP)

7.16 MOBILE COMPUTING APPLICATION ISSUES

The programs used in mobile devices like mobile phones, laptops, palm computers, etc. for internet connectivity and other computer related activities are called mobile computing applications. The various issues and designs of mobile computing application are discussed under various headings below.

Technical Design

First comes the Technical Design Issues, which consist of network design, capacity planning, response time calculations, data compression considerations, system availability design and security issues. The technical design plays a key role in a mobile computing project and offers unique challenges to the system professionals.

Network Design

Issues regarding Wireless LAN design and Wide Area Radio Network Design which network design comprises are discussed below.

(a) Wireless LAN design issues

- The number of mobile users who will use wireless LAN and the number of them active during the peak period.
- The types of LAN application accessed by them. (Keeping in mind that wireless LANs will not be acceptable for the intended users as they operate at much slower speeds than wired LANs).
- Use of notebook with a wireless NIC as a primary and user device.
- Roaming areas, location & range of needed access point.
- Impact of construction materials in single penetration.
- Preferred technology-spread spectrum or frequency hopping.
- Radio frequency interference from any other devices in office, factory or campus etc.

(b) Wide Area Radio Network Design Issues

- The need of building a private radio network.
- Most appropriate radio network technology for the suite of applications.
- Matching of user application-usage profiles to a given network capacity.
- Integration of RNA technology with a radio network infrastructure.
- Ensuring good coverage & minimum number of dead spots.
- If distributed wireless network design with several MCSSs must be used?
- Managing the way logic networks will be influenced by network design options.

The Capacity Planning & response time Calculations

A mobile computing application transaction has to cover a synchronous set of hardware as well as software components before it reaches the destination server. Diverse physical links, wireless &

wired line in between the end user's client application software and the information server are present in its reverse path too. So scheduling on a network requires complex rules, which makes it difficult to build a mathematical model to estimate response times. Planning reliable capacities in advance is a hard task still. The network providers give an estimate using complex queuing models or rule-of thumb calculation based on the other customer's experience.

Data Compression Considerations

As the bandwidth of wireless network is scarce & inexpensive it is necessary to compress data to get the maximum out of this bandwidth. This is usually done in the modem by going beyond the modem hardware in reducing the quantity of traffic on wireless networks using client application programs.

System Availability Design

Rather than sticking on with the general base station hardware & network controllers, redundancy & message switches are typically built on fault-tolerant platforms. Public shared network providers must be approached for details of their redundancies. MCSS is another vital component that badly needs inbuilt redundancy.

Security Issues

It is tough to track down securing information by unauthorized access. Common security breaches of mobile computing applications include,

- Network by criminal elements.
- Physical breach security at communication centers mainly unmanned base stations.
- Interception of credit card authorization over wireless network.
- Careful security considerations including on-the-air encryption & firewalls must be used.

Other than technical design the next major issue under Mobile computing application is Ergonomics & Logistics Design where the designers evaluates the following.

- Form factor of end user device
- Battery life
- Input method-keyboard, pen, touch or voice
- Ruggedness
- Whether Portable or fixed
- Safety & Health issues.

Mobile computing application deals with the future of computer usage and is therefore of great relevance.

7.17 MOBILE COMPUTING SOLUTIONS BENEFITS

Mobile computing solutions have benefits which come under two headings basically namely tangible benefits and intangible benefits. Tangible benefits include those benefits that are easily quantifiable, while intangible benefits are those that are difficult to quantify.

To be more specific, tangible benefits can be put in quantitative terms, like economic benefits. Mobile computing solutions makes it possible to cut down on the professional's valuable time on administrative work. Boosting industrial productivity and sales per person are few of the tangible benefits.

Tangible benefits also bring along with them some added benefits like the maintenance of high order fulfillment ratio, considerable reduction in real time inventory cost through the timely placement of orders and the smooth flow of information. The mobile computing has also facilitated service vehicles with on-the-spot invoice production which brings in better cash flow with short payment cycle. The citation / ticketing application with credit card payment is a fine way to illustrate the tangible benefits of mobile computing.

Now coming to the intangible benefits which are difficult to be quantified like automating sales, improving customer service or gaining competitive advantage; these must be converted into percentage or should be handled with weights.

The intangible benefits of Mobile computing solutions include a wide range of benefits namely,

- Enhanced business productivity through improving work efficiency by accessing more online resources.
- Quick execution of new procedures, pricing etc.
- Bringing PDA - like resources on line through unlocking value in offline devices.
- Boosts the information sharing between the workers, customers and partners which results in high quality decision making.
- Keeping in touch with customers, which in turn results in fast sensing and responding to their requirements, thus providing better and prompter service.
- Rapid deployment in reaction to an event and fast reaction to adversity through multiple channels facilitates business resilience.
- Lowering the cost of ownership and increased productivity, retention of workers along with cultural improvement, by providing work with customized tools for appropriate information and by giving them flexibility to work.

Knowing the tangible and intangible benefits of Mobile computing solutions will make decision-making a whole lot easier.

7.18 MOBILE APPLICATION DEVELOPMENT PLATFORMS

Mobile application development platforms are aided by various specific as well as generic sets of tools. The following are the various choices in development tools.

- Traditional Microsoft Windows 98 / 2000 / NT / XP tools.
- Palm OS Application Development tools: Java being the standard dominant application development tool for server side programming has made it easier to write safe and reliable

code through features, like automatic memorizing and standard exception-handling. Java interfaces are supported by several application servers.

- Modern Application Server Tools offer application server solutions in a web environment based on conventional application servers and this extension is molded for mobile applications and wireless networks.

7.18.1 Wireless Network specific development

Several mobile gateway vendors like IBM, Broad beam, Oracle, Sybase, and Telecordia technologies offer mobile application development tools kit. Investigating specialized middleware for wireless and mobile applications are conducted to find the vendors who address all these requirements.

Data Synchronization Products

Numerous files & DBMS synchronization products are available to solve the problem of synchronizing information in notebook and PDAs with master information in the desktop or the server. Customization can be done through APIs. The various choices in development tools being furnished for Mobile application development platforms, decision-making regarding use of the same, becomes easy.

7.18.2 Mobile Application Development Strategies & Issues

Care needs to be taken regarding the following mobile application development strategies and issues, while choosing application development tools.

- Application design should be based on the concept of mobile aware nature of users work profile and business process.
- The "client-agent-server" or "thin client-mobile server-enterprise server architectural paradigm should be considered seriously.
- Security matters like leakage, theft and fraud.
- Assess the pros and cons of Java based independent platform development versus platform specific development.
- Mobile applications must be on the foundation of internet development tools and current application servers.

7.18.3 Modern Mobile Application Server Tools

The tools which provide application server solutions in a web environment are based on conventional application servers. Some are extensions, while few others are specifically designed for mobile application and wireless networks.

(i) IBM's AS/400 Mobile Application Development tools have their own development environment, which ensures easier and attractive integration.

(ii) Oracles Mobile Agents and Oracle Lite, which enables enterprises in developing mobile applications that run over a variety of wireless networks and dial-up LAN connections. Its

3-tiered clients / agents / server architecture replaces session-based connection oriented computing with an asynchronous, store and forward messaging system. The Oracle mobile Agents eliminate the need for constant connection.

(iii) Sybase's SQL Anywhere Studio is used for developing mobile applications. This software can reside on multiple server and client platforms.

Mobile Application Development Strategies and Issues and the respective server tools have been discussed briefly above. Being aware of them, makes one to know the various aspects and make decisions accordingly in an intelligent fashion. Count on the services of ITOI and build muscles to your organization.

7.18.4 Mobile Computing Solutions Cost

Mobile computing solutions costs can be quantified only in part. There are several aspects to it which are impossible to quantify..

(A) One-time capital Expenditure

(i) Hardware

- Mobile Workstation Hardware (notebooks, handheld devices, Palm points)
- Wireless Radio Modems-wireless LAN adapters, Access Points
- Mobile Communications Server Switch (MCSS) hardware and software
- Hardware Upgrade Costs

(ii) Software purchase or licensing fee

- Shrink-wrap software license for end user device
- Software for backend switch, network servers, application servers

(iii) Software Development or Customization

- Application development tools unique to mobile computing
- Wireless communication software in the client device and servers
- Software changes and enhancements

(iv) Vertical or Horizontal Application package costs-per user dollar cost multiplied by the number of users

(v) Mobile Application testing costs

(vi) External consulting Services

(vii) End user documentation and Training costs

(viii) Project implementation - Hardware and Systems software Installation cost

(ix) Contingency-No estimate inclusive - allow 10-15% overrun

(B) Ongoing Operations

(i) Telecommunications network services -especially wireless network services

(ii) Computer processing and operation

(iii) Maintenance (hardware/software/equipment)

(iv) Technical Support (internal/external i.e outsourced from external vendors) costs

(C) Other Costs (Intangible)

The risks of Mobile computing project is difficult to quantify. The actual mobile computing solutions cost is the sum of all the above. While developing a business case for a mobile computing project, both the cost and the benefit from undertaking such a project are analysed. Quantitative as well as qualitative analysis has to be done. The costs of hardware and software are much easier to estimate, compared to the application development, application integration and wireless network usage costs, which are difficult to predict.

7.18.5 Defining Mobile Computing Application Server

We would like to define "Mobile Computing Application Server (MCAS or simple MAS)" as a software program which runs in a server and provides the following functionality:

- Application level logic that handles business functions involved in a particular organization (e.g. how to handle information requests from sales personnel in the field) and its integration with backend database or business application systems such as mainframe financial accounting systems, manufacturing systems, inventory, ERP (Enterprise Resource Planning) and emerging CRM (Customer Resource Management) systems
- Presentation services for the Mobile client device (handheld computers, notebook, PDA, etc) i.e. application server takes raw data from database applications/queries and transforms the data on a specific thin client (or a thick client like a PC) considering its presentation space characteristics and limitations. This is also called GUI (Graphical User Interface) in some cases though some handheld are more like older text terminals than PC. It includes breaking the messages into smaller chunks, filtering redundant information, and even logically compressing the data , etc.
- Transaction services, in some cases - including multi-threading for heavy volumes and persistency i.e. recovery across session failures
- Application programming level interfaces (APIs) with specialized communications protocols

An application server may be considered as part of a multi-tier (mostly three tier) architecture. Conventional tiers are:

1. *First tier* – A thin client based on handheld devices or a thick client on a PC - typically a browser-based interface in the Web context
2. *Middle tier consists of business applications on a set of servers* – communications and business applications
3. *Third Tier* – backend legacy data base systems and mission-critical ERP systems on a large server or mainframe

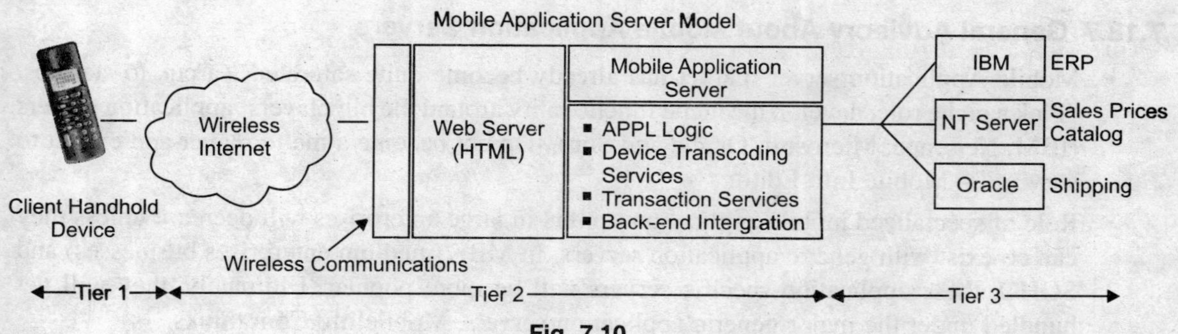

Fig. 7.10

7.18.6 Are All Application Servers Same and Provide the Same Functionality?

Actual implementations of Application Server varies from one vendor to another. Some application servers are generic web servers with an SDK (Systems Development Kit) or API capability to pull data from enterprise database systems and send it to a browser-based client software in a handheld device. Other application servers provide a business application with customization capability in a horizontal application, such as e-mail, sales force automation or field service representative computer-aided dispatch application. Still other mobile application servers are based on WAP protocol. Depending on the heritage of the vendor and their core expertise, you can categorize application servers in the following broad classes:

- Generic application servers with a web-based SDK, e.g. Netscape, Microsoft, Sun, SilverStream, BEA - may have support for handheld devices and wireless networks strapped on (or bolted on) to the basic application server
- Database vendors' Application Servers, e.g. Oracle 9i and Sybase's iAnywhere Application server
- Data synchronization vendors, e.g. Puma, Synchrologic, Extended Systems
- Specialized Mobile or Web Computing Application Servers - IBM's WebSphere
- Mobile Specific Application Servers, e.g. Aligo, Air2Web, Contec Mobile Application Server (aimed at carriers), Aether System (aimed at enterprises)
- WAP-centric Application servers - Nokia's WAP Server - not a true Application server, in IT sense
- E-mail centric Application Servers - Microsoft's Mobile Information server, EdgeMail Application Server

It is important to note that not all application servers are strong in all the functions that you may need in a general-purpose application server. Therefore, you must evaluate the key criteria that your application requires. As an example, application server from Oracle may be strong on integration with databases but not necessarily as strong on interfaces with a variety of handheld devices and wireless networks. It may be the right choice if your environment is primarily Oracle-centric and it supports the particular device and network that you may have chosen.

7.18.7 General Advisory About Mobile Application Servers

- Mobile Application server market has already become quite saturated - a cue to startups. "Pick a niche role, develop the niche functionality around the big players' application servers (IBM, Netscape, Microsoft, Oracle and Sun). Do not become a me-to player and expect to survive" – Mobile Info Editor.
- Role of specialized mobile application servers in large enterprises will decrease unless they can co-exist with generic application servers. In MBE (medium enterprises businesses) and SOHO, these application-specific servers will be more popular. Ultimately, they will get bundled under the major generic application servers, MobileInfo.Com thinks.
- Transaction services are key for future role in pervasive computing model of mobile applications.

7.19 SMART CARD

A Smart Card is a plastic card the size of a credit card with an integrated circuit built into it. This integrated circuit may consist only of EEPROM in the case of a memory card, or it may also contain ROM, RAM and even a CPU. Most smart cards have been designed with the look and feel of a credit or debit card, but can function on at least three levels (credit - debit - personal information). Smart cards include a microchip as the central processing unit, random access memory (RAM) and data storage of around 10MB.

A smart card is a mini-computer without the display screen and keyboard. Smart cards contain a microchip with an integrated circuit capable of processing and storing thousands of bytes of electronic data. Due to the portability and size of smart cards they are seen as the next generation of data exchange. Smart cards contain an operating system just like personal computers. Smart cards can store and process information and are fully interactive. Advanced smart cards also contain a file structure with secret keys and encryption algorithms. Due to the encrypted file system, data can be stored in separated files with full security.

Organizations are steadily migrating toward this technology. The days are numbered for a single mainframe used for computing every directive. Today, the delegation of tasks is being transferred to small, but dedicated smart cards. Their usefulness may soon exceed that of the standard computer for a variety of applications due, in part, to their portability and ease of use.

The smart card is an electronic recording device. Information in the microchip can instantaneously verify the cardholder's identity and any privileges to which the cardholder may be entitled. Information such as withdrawals, sales, and bills can be processed immediately and if/when necessary; those records can be transmitted to a central computer for file updating.

Smart cards are secure, compact and intelligent data carriers. Smart cards should be regarded as specialized computers capable of processing, storing and safeguarding thousands of bytes of data. Smart cards have electrical contacts and a thin metallic plate just above center line on one side of the card. Beneath this dime-sized plate is an integrated circuit (IC) chip containing a central processing unit (CPU), random access memory (RAM) and non-volatile data storage. Data stored in the smart card's microchip can be accessed only through the chip operating system (COS), providing a high level of data security. This security takes the form of passwords allowing a user to access parts of the IC chip's memory or encryption/decryption measures which translate the bytes stored in memory into useful information.

Smart cards typically hold 2,000 to 8,000 electronic bytes of data (the equivalent of several pages of data). Because those bytes can be electronically coded, the effective storage capacity of each card is significantly increased. Magnetic-stripe cards, such as those issued by banks and credit card companies, lack the security of microchips but remain inexpensive due to their status as a single-purpose card. Smart cards can be a carrier of multiple records for multiple purposes. Once those purposes are maximized, the smart card is often viewed as superior and, ultimately, less expensive. The distributed processing possible with smart cards reduces the need for ever-larger mainframe computers and the expense of local and long-distance phone circuits required to maintain an on-line connection to a central computer. Smart cards are defined by the ISO 7816 standards.

7.19.1 Smart Card Usage

The uses of smart cards are as versatile as any mini-computer. At a hospital emergency room, for example, the card could identify the person's health-insurance carrier and transfer all necessary information from the microchip to an admittance sheet. Tests, treatment, billing and prescriptions could be processed more quickly using the card. Major clinical findings could be added to the medical information section within the microchip.

In the U.S., smart cards are utilized in GSM mobile telephones, in DirecTV and EchoStar satellite receivers, and in the American Express Blue card.

7.19.2 Smart Card Operating Systems

Smart cards designed for specific applications may run proprietary operating systems. Smart cards designed with the capability to run multiple applications usually run MULTOS or Java Card.

7.19.3 Smart Cards and Electronic Payment Systems

Smart cards have been in existence since the early 1980 and hold promise for secure transactions using existing infrastructure. Smart cards are credit and debit cards and other cards product enhanced with microprocessors capable of holding more information than the traditional magnetic stripe.

The smart card technology is widely used in countries such as France, Germany, Japan and Singapore to pay for public phone calls, transportation and shopper loyalty programs. Smart cards are basically of two types –

- Relationship based smart credit card
- Electronic purses (which replace money, are also known as debit cards and electronic money)

7.19.3.1 Relationship based smart cards

A relationship-based smart card is an enhancement of existing card services and or the addition of new services that a financial institution delivers to its customers via chip based card or other device.

These new services may include access to multiple financial accounts, value – added marketing programs or other information. Cardholders may want to store on their card.

Enhanced credit cards store card-holders information including name, birth date, personal shopping preference and actual purchase records, relationship based products are expected to offer customers far greater options, including the following –

(i) Access to multiple accounts, such as debit, credit, investments or stored value for e-cash on one card or an electronic device.

(ii) A Variety of functions such as cash access, bill payment, balance inquiry or funds transfer for selected accounts.

(iii) Multiple access options at multiple locations using multiple device types, such as an automated teller machine (ATM), a screen phone, a personal computer, a personal digital assistant or interactive TVs.

Companies are trying to incorporate these services into a personalized banking relationship for each customer. They can package financial and non financial services with value added programs to enhance convenience, build loyalty and retention and attract new customers.

7.19.3.2 Electronic Purses and Debit Cards

Despite their increasing flexibility, relationship based cards are credit based and settlement occurs at the end of the billing cycle. There remains a need for a financial instrument to replace cash.

The electronic purses Wallet – sized smart card embedded with programmable microchips that store sums of money for people to use instead of cash for everything from buying food, to making photocopies, to paying subway fares. The electronic purse works in following manner – After the purse is loaded with money, at an ATM or through the use of an inexpensive special telephone. It can be used to pay for, say candy in a vending machine equipped with a card reader.

The vending machine need only verify that a card is authentic and there is enough money available for a chocolate bar. In one second, the value of the purchase is deducted from the balance on the card added to e-cash box in the vending machine. The remaining balance on the card is displayed by the vending machine or can be checked at an ATM or with a balance reading device.

This allows customers to pay for rides and calls with a prepaid card that remembers each transaction and when the balance on electronic purse is depleted, the purse can be recharged with more money.

7.20 EXPERT SYSTEMS

The main business advantage of using *expert systems* technology is the opportunity to protect business know-how. Many organizations are severely short of experts. With the aging of the work force, and as a large number of experienced workers retire together, this shortage will become worse. Encapsulating the rules that describe an expert's response to a business situation into a stored electronic rules base, provides the substantive opportunity for higher productivity and reduced costs as these stored rules are consistently applied.

In applications using expert systems products, such as those from Trinzic Corp., Nexpert, and others, objects are created that include this expert knowledge. These objects can be reused in applications to support decision-making throughout the entire organization. Figure 7.7 illustrates the benefits organizations can obtain by using expert systems technology.

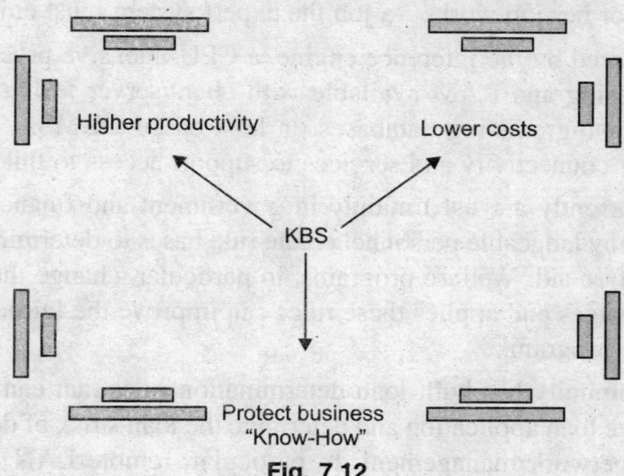

Fig. 7.12

Many expert systems products are merely glitz. They are simplified to enable trivial applications to be developed but are not useful because they do not have the capacity to handle the complexity of real-life business processes. A major flaw in many products is their inability to integrate with a company's information systems and databases. If a product cannot be integrated into the organizational SDE or cannot use the organization's databases directly, it is not useful. It isn't practical to create multiple development environments and copies of data to support real-time decision-making. Some expert systems products are used for after-the-fact analysis, but the best products are integrated into the business. Figure 7.8 illustrates a typical integrated architecture.

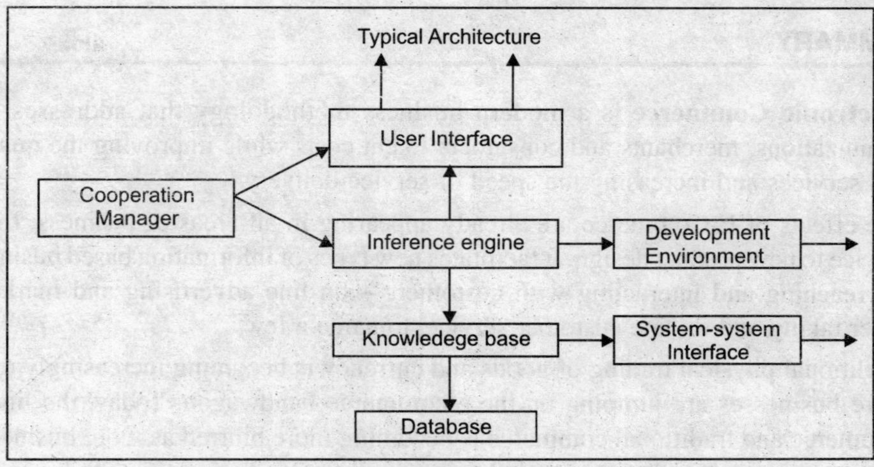

Fig. 7.13

Expert systems applications are well suited to the client/server model. In addition to the advantages offered by the user interface component, the rules base benefits from the processing power and ease of use at the workstation. In most implementations, rules should be managed by a knowledgeable user and not by a professional programmer, because the user is the only one intimately familiar with how his or her job works—a job the expert system must emulate.

The rules are enforced by the inference engine, a CPU-intensive process that takes advantage of the low-cost processing and RAM available with client/server technology. Most applications will be implemented using existing databases on host-based DBMSs. The client/server model provides the necessary connectivity and services to support access to this information.

Expert systems currently are used mainly in government and financial organizations. In the government sphere, knowledgeable personnel create rule bases to determine people's eligibility for programs such as welfare aid. Welfare programs, in particular, change these rules rapidly, and an expert system that manages and applies these rules can improve the fairness and decrease the cost of adjudication for the program.

The financial community has built loan determination rules that can significantly reduce the time required to analyze loan application and determine the loan's risk of default. A new application of expert systems is network management. In particular, remote LAN management is an ideal application for expert systems technology. The network alerts are processed by a rules-based analyzer to help diagnose problems. Historical data is captured and maintained for subsequent comparison. The rules base also can invoke regular preventive maintenance.

The retail sector is beginning to use expert systems for real-time management. In an ideal scenario, a manager uses a rules base to describe the expected results for products as they are introduced or repackaged. The system audits the reality against the expectation in real time. Only when results are different than the defined expectation is the manager notified. This allows unexpected results, good or bad, to be detected early and allows the manager to concentrate on customers or new programs when expectations are being met.

7.21 SUMMARY

- **Electronic Commerce** is a modern business methodology that addresses the needs of organizations, merchants and consumers to cut costs while improving the quality of goods and services and increasing the speed of service delivery.
- The effects of E-Commerce are already appearing in all areas of business, from customer service to new product design. It facilitates new types of information based business processes for reaching and interacting with customers – on line advertising and marketing on line order taking and on line customer service, to name a few.
- Traditional physical trading of goods and currency is becoming increasingly unpopular and more businesses are jumping on the e-commerce bandwagon. Today, the line between e-commerce and traditional commerce is becoming more blurred as more businesses start and continue to integrate the Internet and e-commerce technologies into their business processes.

- Evolution of e-commerce can be attributed to a combination of regulatory reform and technological innovation. Though Internet (which played an important role in evolution) appeared in the late 1960s, e-commerce of today took off with the arrival of World Wide Web and browsers in early 1990s.
- A broad range of financial and information services are performed over the Internet today and sites that offer them are enjoying rapid growth. These sites are popular because they help consumers, businesses of all sizes, and financial institutions distribute some of their most important information over the Internet with greater convenience and richness that is available using other channels.
- Electronic commerce is forcing companies to rethink the existing ways of doing target marketing (isolating and focusing on a segment of the population), relationship marketing (building and sustaining a long-term relationship with existing and potential customers), and even event marketing (setting up a virtual booth where interested people come and visit).
- E – Commerce applications will be built on the existing technology infrastructure – a myriad of computers, communication networks and communication software forming the nascent information superhighway.
- Any successful e-commerce application will require the I-way infrastructure in the same way that regular commerce needs the interstate highway network to carry goods from point to point. You must travel across this highway, whether you are in organization purchasing supplies or a consumer ordering a movie on demand.
- An electronic market is an information system that links together many buyers and sellers to exchange information, products, services and payments. i.e. A market place that is created by computer and communication technologies that links many buyers and sellers.
- The transfer of data between different companies using networks, such as VANs or the Internet. As more and more companies get connected to the Internet, EDI is becoming increasingly important as an easy mechanism for companies to buy, sell, and trade information.
- **Electronic Data Interchange** (**EDI**) is the computer-to-computer exchange of structured information, by agreed message standards, from one computer application to another by electronic means and with a minimum of human intervention.
- In common usage, EDI is understood to mean specific interchange methods agreed upon by national or international standards bodies for the transfer of business transaction data, with one typical application being the automated purchase of goods and services.
- The EDI semantic layer describes the business application that is driving EDI. This laye specific to a company and the software it uses. In other words, the user interface and content visible on the screen are tailored or customized to local environments.
- EDI standards specify business form structure and to some extent influence content seen at the application layer. For instance, a purchase order name field in an X12 standard might be specified to hold a maximum of 50 characters.

- The EDI transport layer corresponds closely with the non-electronic activity of sending a business form from one company A to company B. The business form could be sent via regular postal service, registered mail, certified mail or private carrier such as united parcel service (UPS) or simply faxed between the companies.
- **A Value-Added Network (VAN)** is a private network provider (sometimes called a turnkey communications line) that is hired by a company to facilitate electronic data interchanges (EDI) or provides other network services.
- Financial EDI (FEDI) is the computer-to-computer exchange of payment and payment-related information between companies using a standard format. Financial EDI works much like non-Financial EDI - which involves the electronic exchange of business data such as price quotes, purchase orders, and shipping information - but is also significantly different in that, to move a payment, a bank must be involved. Because of this difference, the buyer and seller must work closely with their respective banks to effect a Financial EDI transaction.

7.22 REVIEW QUESTION

1. Define e-commerce. Name the areas in which companies conduct business online and explain each of them.
2. Discuss the significant issues that are required to implement e-commerce in organization.
3. How do you purchase or sell items or products on Internet?
4. Differentiate between the traditional commerce and e-commerce.
5. What technologies are required for e-commerce?
6. Discuss the economic potential of e-commerce. How does it effect marketing and retail industry?
7. List and explain about the incentives for engaging in e-commerce.
8. What are the various driving forces behind e-commerce?
10. Discuss the advantages of e-commerce in reference to the following:
    (i) Customers
    (ii) Business
    (iii) Society
    (iv) Women
11. Write a short note on disadvantages of e-commerce.
12. Why is the network reliability very important for e-commerce? What factors cause problems for network reliability?
13. What is the effect of cost factors on e-commerce?
14. Discuss the reasons for e-commerce not being very successful.
15. What are the various types of e-commerce? Explain each in short.

16. Write down the differences between B2C and B2B e-commerce.
17. What do you understand by architectural framework for e-commerce? Explain the various services that form the e-commerce architectural framework.
18. Write short notes on the following:
    (a) TCP/IP protocol for network structure
    (b) Impact of e-commerce on business
    (c) Applications of e-commerce
19. Define EDI. Discuss EDI applications in business.
20. Discuss the use of Smart Cards and electronic payment using smart cards.
21. What is role of expert system?

Index

D

M

N

O

W

Y